The Multinational Company in Europe
Some Key Problems

Editors

Michael Z. Brooke
H. Lee Remmers

Authors

Michael Z. Brooke
Lawrence G. Franko
J. David Froggatt
Robert H. Parker
H. Lee Remmers
Barto Roig
John M. Stopford
Theodore D. Weinshall

Ann Arbor
The University of Michigan Press

First published 1972 by Longman Group Limited,
London

First published in the United States of America by
The University of Michigan Press 1974

ISBN 0-472-08182-9

Library of Congress Catalog Card No. 73-93992

Manufactured in the United States of America

THE MULTINATIONAL COMPANY IN EUROPE

Contents

Figures

Tables

The contributors

Editors: Michael Z. Brooke, M.A. (Cambridge and Manchester). Ph.D. (Manchester). Lecturer in Management Sciences and Director of the International Business Unit at the University of Manchester Institute of Science and Technology. Managing Director of FOBAS Limited. Dr Brooke is the author of many papers on the organisation of international companies, and has lectured in numerous countries on this subject.

H. Lee Remmers, B.Sc. (California), Dipl (INSEAD), Ph.D. (Manchester). Associate Professor at the Institut Européen d'Administration des Affaires. Dr Remmers is the author of several papers on investment planning in industry, capital markets in Europe, and financial policy in multinational companies. He has lectured in numerous countries on these subjects.

Chapters 1 and 10 of this book have been written by Dr Brooke and Professor Remmers jointly; **Chapter 2** is by Professor Remmers, and **Chapter 7** by Dr Brooke.

Dr Brooke and Professor Remmers are co-authors of *The Strategy of Multinational Enterprise*, and co-editors of the Longman International Business series of which this book is the first.

Chapter 3 is by Robert H. Parker, B.Sc. (Econ.) (London) F.C.A. Professor of Accountancy, University of Dundee since 1970. Has practised and taught accountancy at Universities in Australia, Britain, France and Nigeria. Author of *Management Accounting: An Historical Perspective* (1969) and *Understanding Company Financial Statements* (1972), joint author of *Topics in Business Finance and Accounting* (1964), co-editor of *Readings in the Concept and Measurement of Income* (1969). Articles in Accounting and financial journals. Member of editorial board of *Abacus* (Sydney University Press). Research interests in the international, comparative and historical aspects of accounting.

Chapter 4 is by Barto Roig, Associate Professor and Director of the International programme at the Instituto de Estudios Superiores de la Empresa (IESE), University of Navarre. An industrial engineer in origin, Dr Roig has held various appointments in Spain and Venezuela. In the latter country he was Industrial Promotions Engineer in the Corporacion Venezolana de Fomento, a technical consultant, and Professor of Economics at the Universidad Central, Caracas. His writings include: *Origenes de la Barcelona Traction*, ed. EUNSA. *La Empresa Multinacional*, Algunos aspectos importantes, EUNSA; 'Unificacion vs. fragmentacion en la Empresa Multinacional', *Nota Tecnica* IESE; 'La Empresa Mediana Espanola ante el cambio de la CEE', *Proceeding* *del VIII Programa Internacional en la IESE*, Publicacion interna IESA; 'Politica de Empresa Internacional como campo de Estudio', *Nota Tecnica* IESE; and more than 100 articles in Spanish and Venezuelan papers and economic reviews.

Chapter 5 is by Lawrence G. Franko, A.B. (Econ.) (Harvard), M.A., M.A.L.D. (Fletcher School of Law and Diplomacy), D.B.A. (Harvard). Faculty member, teaching the Management of International Operations, at the Centre d'Etudes Industrielles (CEI) at Geneva. Director of Research on Multinational Company Organisation related to the Harvard Business School–Ford Foundation Multinational Enterprise project. Consultant to business and governments. Author of the books *Joint Venture Survival in Multinational Corporations* (Praeger, 1971) and *European Business Strategies* in the United States (Business International SA, Geneva 1971).

Chapter 6 is by John R. Stopford, B.A. (Oxford), S.M. (M.I.T.), D.B.A. (Harvard). Reader in Business Policy, London Graduate School of Business Studies. Originally an engineer with Shell Chemicals, has been consultant to several governments and a number of firms in Britain, South America and the United States. Has taught at the Harvard and Manchester Business Schools, is the author of numerous articles, and co-author with L. T. Wells Jnr of *Managing the Multinational Enterprise: Organisation of the Firm and Ownership of the Subsidiaries.*

Chapter 8 is by Theodore D. Weinshall, B.Sc. (Ind. Eng.), B.Sc. (Mech. Eng.) Dipl. Ingen. (Mech. Eng.) (Israel Institute of Technology), D.B.A. (Harvard). Professor at the Graduate School of Business Administration, Tel Aviv. Visiting Professor at INSEAD and at Cranfield Institute of Technology. Managing Director of Weinshall-Raveh Limited, Management Consultants. Dr Weinshall has lectured extensively out of Israel and is the author of numerous papers in academic and management journals. Main research interests: the effects of size on organisation structure, management communications, multinational management education.

Chapter 9 is by J. David Froggatt, B.Sc. (Econ.) (London School of Economics). Deputy Group Economist with Turner and Newall Limited since 1970. He spent five years as a research economist with the Economist Intelligence Unit. During this time he worked on a wide range of international economic, financial and market research projects, and regularly analysed the economies of several countries, including the United States, Canada and the United Kingdom. He then lectured in industrial economics and financial subjects on management courses at the University of Salford, and developed research interests in corporate planning and strategies, and in the management of international business.

1

Growth and change in the international company

The book and its authors

The idea behind this book arose at a meeting held in Brussels under the auspices of the European Association of Management Training Centres. That body, now merged into the European Foundation for Management Development, had invited one of the present editors to chair a small group of scholars interested in the international firm. This group was brought together to examine the problems of research and teaching on the subject, and has produced reports on these and related matters. From the start it was felt that such a group should not only discuss the documents which had been commissioned from them, but should also talk together about the actual content of their research and current findings. This book was planned to make available some of the results of the conversations. It has been organised around the thinking of the authors on critical problem areas which face managers of international companies.

Not all the members of the group have been able to contribute to this book, but all played significant parts in the discussions which produced it. These discussions took place in several European cities, and before a wider audience in Palermo. Some additional contributions have been brought in from other sources. The resulting work is not to be regarded as just a collection of isolated papers. Some key issues in the handling of an international enterprise are isolated and examined, in each case by someone who has done sustained research on his subject and submitted the results for the consideration of the group. The book has been put together as a unity, with the problems examined in a common frame of reference; the chapter headings would not necessarily have changed greatly if it had all been by one author. In effect some extracts from the work of a number of specialists have been picked up and set down again in a new relationship. To ensure the unity of the book considerable editorial work has been carried out on each chapter, and naturally the editors alone accept responsibility for chapters 1 and 10. All the authors have cooperated in this and each chapter has been worked over more than once. It is hoped that the result will provide useful material both for those who manage and for those who teach.

The authors are concerned to bridge the gap between the teacher and the manager. The research has an empirical bias, and has usually been based on interviews. It is hoped that managers will find a relevant analysis of some of their most intractable problems in these pages. Most of the authors are also involved in consultancy, and have looked at the problems in practice as well as in theory. Meanwhile the acknowledged shortage of teaching material has already been mentioned in the Introduction to the series and is in spite of the fact that all the present authors have published extensively already. One aim of this book is to provide a general text for international management courses.

For present purposes a multinational company is understood to be a firm which engages in its principal business activity in more than one country. This includes any foreign investment except that in minor selling subsidiaries. Many experts, including some of the authors of this book, regard this definition as too broad. But at least it allows a wide sample of companies, including some which are just beginning to feel the effects of operating across frontiers. Conversely it allows for the investigation of the effects of foreign investment on company behaviour, as well as on the national and international economies, at every possible stage.[1] Other definitions either imply an economic measure, such as a proportion of fixed investment abroad, or a psychological one like the approach of the company management to the determination of problems. Such definitions are usually connected with arbitrary and imprecise measurements. The significance of the changes defined is in no way comparable to the effect on the whole structure of the company of the first foreign investment leading to manufacture or some other significant foreign investment.

While on the subject of definitions, it should be said that the terms 'home' and 'host' country are used of the nations of origin and of the receiving of any particular investment. This is the normal current meaning of these words. The sense in which other terms are used is explained in the context where any doubt could arise. One word is used in chapters 4 and 9 in this book and not elsewhere, and that is 'synergy'. This word is really a medical analogy, and as such is considered misleading by many authorities. It is used here in its simplest sense of a situation where a number of independent factors which are affecting a situation are seen to be operating in the same direction. Nevertheless, however difficult to define precisely, there are interesting changes taking place in the management process. These changes carry with them a number of choices which may or may not be consciously taken, but which ultimately decide just how international the company becomes. They also decide how it fits into its various markets. One difficulty of studying this process is to distinguish between the truth and the public relations image which the firms try to create. One member of the original group who set out to examine this change was Gabriele Morello.[2] Pressure of other work has prevented him from finishing his chapter.

In the absence of Morello's discussion, this book starts by examining some financial questions. Lee Remmers identifies some of the factors and the criteria used in selecting the various forms of financing foreign subsidiaries. Detailed information on this subject was obtained in the United Kingdom where it is more readily available owing to the laws of disclosure, and has been used to support some of the conclusions drawn in chapter 2. The exact extent to which these can be generalised to foreign investments in other countries must be the subject of future studies. Nevertheless ways that factors found to be important in Britain operate in other countries are shown. It is the details of a different environment that are in doubt, and these may distort methods of financing more than is suspected. With this caution, it can be assumed that the conclusions of this chapter can be generalised. In particular the advantages of what is called a *subsidiary oriented approach* are proposed.

An important insight of the second chapter is the effect of growth on the financial structure of the foreign subsidiary. An attempt is made to show the stages of growth from the initial establishment to a mature and highly developed business entity. This separation into three stages, while sometimes arbitrary and sometimes difficult to make in practice, gives an invaluable means of analysing a changing situation. The emphasis in the third stage on local participation[3] may surprise some readers, but it is a significant theme of this book. Also surprising to some readers will be the author's finding that in many situations transfer pricing has become much less effective in minimising taxes than is commonly believed. It has often been suspected that the expenses of avoiding taxes exceeded the taxes themselves, and evidence is now increasing that this is so as tax regulations become more elaborate and enforcement more thorough. This is not to say that the international group has no means of minimising taxes that are denied to the purely domestic firm, but these are more limited than is sometimes supposed.

One of the most critical variables affecting financial decisions in multinational operations is management's reaction to exchange risks. Multinational firms must deal in many currencies, and simultaneously investing and borrowing in several different ones give rise to risk of loss from devaluations or revaluations. In many respects, these risks are of much less significance than ordinary risks inherent in trading. However, the way accountants commonly report the results of foreign operations tends to exacerbate such losses for they generally appear as a separate item on the financial statements of the parent company. The attempt of financial management to avoid such losses, highlighted by accounting conventions, is one explanation for much of the behaviour noted of companies when they shift large amounts of capital from one country to another where they have operations.

The manner of accounting for foreign operations leads to other problem areas. Measurement of performance, and measurement of indebtedness, are two of them. The third chapter of this book, by Robert Parker, sets out to consider some aspects of this problem in analysing current practices of accounting for foreign operations.

The variations that can occur within one national system are shown to be as confusing as the differences between countries, and group consolidated accounts may contain figures entered at different rates simultaneously. Further, in some countries companies are given the option of consolidating or not their foreign subsidiaries. Experts on international business are well aware of such difficulties; but one wonders what proportion of the many writers, who make generalisations about the extent and rate of return on foreign investment, have really taken account of what Parker is saying. One judges that there is a growing consensus among professional accountants as to how the figures should be presented; it is clear that there is an enormous gap between theory and practice, although there seems to be scope for further improvements in the theory.

The place of the foreign general manager in the international group is the theme of the fourth chapter. This has come from the research of Barto Roig from Spain, a country which is almost entirely on the receiving end of foreign investment. This contribution picks up the point made in the second chapter about the need for a subsidiary oriented approach. The possibility of developing a type of manager who will make a more effective link between the international and the national scenes is a constant aspiration of companies. Roig examines in detail the requirements of the general manager and the pressures that condition his performance. He explains the distinctive characteristics of this job. The general influences are then re-examined in selected industry groups. This method brings out the three aspects of the general manager's task. He needs to be a strategist, a politician and an executive. Systems put together without consideration for the three aspects of the job simply lose for the company many of the opportunities of being international at all. This is in line with studies by the editors which show that firms more easily acquire the problems of going international than the advantages. An additional theme of this chapter looks at some of the different routes abroad which companies have followed.

Many readers of this book will already know the work of Leopold Vansina of Leuven on the development of international managers. Vansina was one of the group which first planned this work but, like Morello, was unable to contribute a chapter himself. His work is complementary to that of Roig in that he looks at the personality required to fit the post, while chapter 4 of this book examines the structural requirements. It does not need an editor to make the obvious comment that the two must be considered together. What is worth considering is the balance between them. The system to which most managers are accustomed is one in which the man is expected to fit the office. The reverse, the fitting of the office to the man, is becoming fashionable in the big international groups. That more sophisticated methods of handling problems of organisation will require improved means of selection and training is clear. An additional and significant point that has come out of Roig's research is the way in which local managers will sacrifice their cultural values for the sake of promotion in an international group.

Improvements in the calibre of management are also likely to influence the determination of other problems, including those of joint ventures described in chapter 5. Lawrence Franko here sets out the advantages and difficulties of the joint venture. This chapter shows how slight are the chances of survival, in spite of the advantages, of partnerships between American and European companies. Greater insistence among American companies on global planning makes them less able to tolerate local autonomy, and significantly it turns out that 'viable' partnerships are those where the jointly owned subsidiary can be fitted into the planning system of the American parent. Joint ventures are seen as a route into a new market that will help to reduce uncertainty, but not as a way to stay in that market. European firms are more likely to wish to continue partnerships in other parts of the world, but it can be expected that they will grow dissatisfied with such arrangements as their planning, information and control systems grow more elaborate. As against this more countries are likely to pass legislation insisting at least on local shareholders if not a full joint venture with a local citizen. Hence formulae for handling the problems of partnerships are likely to emerge.

By a logical progression from the joint venture in the sixth chapter John Stopford looks at the effects of strategic planning on the structure of the group. The lines of reporting, the demands of the reporting system and the assigning of responsibilities are all aspects of the translation of strategy into structure—aspects which incidentally help to make joint ventures unpopular. How conscious the process of 'selection' of different systems is may well be questioned; students of any decision-making process recognise that the passive response to pressure often plays a more significant part than active planning. What is important in this case, however, is the effect of the process, whether understood by those taking part or not. The picture presented is one in which a greater involvement in the foreign operations is required of all managers in the company. Along with this, experience abroad is increasingly a necessary qualification for senior management posts.

In the chapter on structure it is argued that European firms are able to run more informal organisations with greater confidence and with fewer upheavals than American companies. There may well be some 'convergence', another subject discussed in this chapter, as experts on the two continents learn from one another. At least the stereotype of the European manager spending a lifetime with one company is true today of a limited number of firms. Extreme stability, such as that of the group which made all senior executive appointments from among men who had joined as graduate trainees, is rare. American firms, on the other hand, are likely to emphasise the 'need to know your way around the company' these days. The importance of less formal management methods may well be discovered as the company spreads abroad, and lead to a greater emphasis on length of service with the company. This is probably more significant than any attempt to relate structure to an elusive and changeable pattern of cultural differences.[4]

After the structure, some aspects of the decision-making process are examined by Michael Brooke (chapter 7). Here the contrast between the intended and the unintended consequences of various lines of action is examined more closely. An examination of this contrast explains a number of points which often bewilder managers. For instance objectives may be clearly set at the centre, which never seem to become really effective in the foreign subsidiary. This is found even where all the best advice is taken about clarity of goals and efficiency of communications. We are dealing with problems which involve organisation structures, personal ambitions, economic conditions, relationships between different managerial groups and other factors. What is not yet clear is the exact relationship between these various influences. A number of case studies have been assembled which indicate how they operate in particular cases, but generalisation is less easy. This applies equally to the second subject discussed in this chapter, centralisation and local autonomy.

It is recognised that some types of organisation are better at promoting local initiative than others, and that profitable and speedy action on the part of the company depends on an effective decision-making process. But a wide variety of practices result from this recognition, many frustrating their professed objects. Some examples of this are given in chapter 7, but there are distinct limits to our knowledge. For we still do not have adequate tools for monitoring the decision-making.[5] Hence, some generalisations about the relative advantages of more centralised or more decentralised systems are suspect. It is easy, for instance, to find examples of writers who ascribe the success of American subsidiaries abroad to their greater autonomy and to those who give exactly opposite reasons.[6] This chapter looks at some other influences on the decision-making process, such as staffing and planning; but these issues are discussed in more detail in the subsequent chapters.

Staffing problems, in fact, enter into several of the issues discussed in this book, and the eighth chapter looks closely at some evidence on national differences and the effects of one particular experiment in international business education. This chapter brings together the results of some pioneering experiments by Theodore Weinshall. He shows that there are ascertainable cultural differences, and that these are susceptible to the influence of a multinational society. The evidence for this latter point also demonstrates the difficulty of taking account of national differences because they are so unstable. However, there are still some hard facts which must be considered in the establishment of management systems. This chapter demolishes some of the stereotypes of different national attitudes, but reinforces others. The reader can hardly fail to notice the possibility that Weinshall's research has opened up for understanding and therefore handling more effectively the problems of managing an international group, and indeed of promoting collaboration between people of different nationalities in many circumstances.

The internationalisation of management investigated in this chapter is likely to produce problems as well as opportunities. On the one hand, nationals of different countries are learning to work together; the multi-national company is demonstrating considerable ability at organising team-work across frontiers. On the other hand, this very trend is likely to accentuate difficulties between companies and countries. A member of a cadre of inter-national executives is often insensitive to nationalistic reactions. This is likely to be a significant problem in the future.

The ninth chapter examines the strategic planning activities of the inter-national group, one of the most sensitive parts of the management process, and raises significant issues such as planning in the finance, production, marketing, and other specialist functions. Naturally a full discussion of questions of this sort is not possible in the present book. The author, David Froggatt, has worked in both the academic and the business worlds, and draws on both research and experience. He was not a member of the original group and his contribution was commissioned to fill an obvious gap after all the others had been assembled. This chapter includes material from a paper entitled 'The management of the international corporation' read to a seminar at the School of Business Studies at Liverpool University. In laying bare some of the issues involved in planning, this chapter also demolishes some well-established myths. A heavy reduction in the number of international com-panies is not anticipated, nor are the differences between national markets exaggerated. The author does point out the different approaches that are possible to take advantage of the opportunities of the international group. In particular the conditions under which flexibility of operation may be increased or reduced are examined. The complexities of decisions are shown here as they are in chapter 7, but in a different context. Both chapters support what is called a 'bottom up' approach, where planning proposals start from the subsidiary, but with many reservations and qualifications.

The latter part of chapter 9 examines some means of analysing foreign investment decisions. In particular sensitivity analysis is suggested as a sophisticated means of appraising the probable return and critical variables of a particular investment. This enables some order to be brought into proposals made but, as the author emphasises, many unquantifiable factors still have to be considered. In this section, too, there is another close link with chapter 7. The reader is provided with at least some of the contradictory pressures to which the company is subjected. The clarification of where decisions are actually taken has implications for most aspects of the success of the international firm.

The international group

The growth of foreign direct investment has been well documented, but there are still uncertainties both of fact and of interpretation. Figures have been produced to show, for instance, that Western European countries are worrying unduly because in no country is more than 10 per cent of sales in American hands.[7] Figures have also been produced to show that in the fast expanding high technology industries many Western European countries have considerably less than half in their own hands.[8] The same figures are being used to worry and to reassure.

Two facts are not in dispute—that foreign investment is increasing and that this fact is disturbing more people. In a previous study by the editors, it was estimated that the value of all United States foreign direct investment was of the order of £27,000 million in 1968; at the end of 1967, total British direct investment abroad, not counting that in petroleum, was estimated at £4700 million. By the end of 1970, these sums amounted to £32,500 million and £6600 million respectively. Even larger increases were recorded for earnings as well as dividend, interest, royalty and fee income from these investments, reflecting better trading conditions and improved performance. The other major investing countries recorded much smaller figures, but these still represent substantial amounts of business.[9] These figures, however, do not entirely demonstrate the extent of the activities of multinational firms as defined in this chapter. To do this information at present unobtainable is required. The worries are even more difficult to identify and are, in any case, often contradictory.

One example of the contradictions could be entitled 'opportunities for local nationals'. Many countries have increased the obstacles to the appointment of foreign managers. By doing so they have discouraged companies from evolving worldwide promotion schemes and this has proved frustrating to the more ambitious local citizens. So opportunities have been reduced in the long term by short-term measures designed to increase them. But this example contains further suggestive implications, especially in the light of evidence brought together in chapter 8. International management education is there shown to foster outlooks that assist the development of internationalism but which may equally be unsympathetic to national aspirations. Indeed the international manager may be more impatient and insensitive towards his own fellow-countrymen than the foreigner. So, again in the short term, the affront to national sovereignty may be increased by the promotion of local nationals with cosmopolitan outlooks.

The lesson of this example would appear to be that national and company objectives can be better served if government agencies negotiate with companies on specific issues rather than over clearcut regulations whose side effects are not easily foreseen. This proposal raises the question how national or company objectives can be identified for the purposes of negotiation, particularly in view of the different time scales involved. Once again it seems better to examine specific issues. It also seems that some irreconcilable situations have to be faced. A possible example of this is the complex problem of the transfer of technical knowledge.[10] An important company objective must be to get an adequate return on a high research expenditure, and this is a powerful incentive for foreign investment. The results bring advantages to the host countries, but the dominance of international companies in advanced technology can frustrate the development of new skills in the host countries. Only the most optimistic could conclude that problems of this sort can always be resolved in ways that uphold the interests of all parties.

This book does not give all the answers to these problems. Most of the chapters examine the internal problems of the companies and the various methods of resolving them, together with the further consequences of the resolution. But a better understanding of the decision-making process is crucial to policy formation for governments, businesses, trade unions and other interested bodies. In emphasising the delicacy of some of the decisions that have to be made, this introduction has already stressed the undesirable side effects that can accompany legislative action. This point was not intended to preclude the compulsion to reveal more information about business activities; this is undoubtedly needed for intelligent policy making. Such a simple suggestion points to yet another of the ironies in which the subject abounds. For it is the home country of so many of the multinationals, the United States, and not the host countries which enforces the most disclosure. American trade unions are currently pressing for even more laws on this to help mobilise public opinion against the export of jobs.

If there is danger in general legislation, there is certainly also a necessity for governments to enter into some procedure for continuous negotiation with foreign investors. Clearer guidelines need to be laid down for this, as they do for methods of policing agreements reached. No government can afford to allow such powerful independent centres of decision-making to continue unrestricted; but the companies, for their part, are powerful negotiators and well able to represent their own interests. More countries are likely to devise standards of behaviour for foreign firms, designed to encourage their activities while minimising their influence on national economic policies. At the same time governments are also likely to encourage their own national companies to develop internationally. Increasing external investments are likely to affect the way pressures are brought to bear on incoming firms while further influencing the shape of international trade. To control all these tendencies in the national interests is not easy as political advisers have discovered, it is likely to become in some ways harder if a fragmentation of foreign firms develops.[11] If this does happen, individual firms will become less powerful; but the numbers it is necessary to negotiate with will become huge, perhaps unmanageable. Some agreements with a whole industry may be needed, but these will be subject to domestic pressure groups from which other difficulties may follow. Clearly the next few years are going to see a rapid development of international negotiations, and these will alter the business environment considerably.

2

Determinants of financial strategy in foreign operations

A major contribution to the successful growth and development of a multi-national company is the design and implementation of a suitable financial strategy—the framework of policies, planning guidelines, and procedures for managing the finances of the organisation and its diverse parts. For many companies, foreign operations are still relatively new, and financial management is often more dependent on a patchwork of *ad hoc* decisions accumulated over time to guide it, than on any comprehensive strategy. Even in companies with long experience of foreign investment, a systematic approach to financial decisions is often lacking. This is not surprising. Financial decisions are greatly influenced by the various legal and fiscal constraints, business practices and other characteristics of the environment in which the firm operates. And when it develops an international spread of operations, these multiply and the differences that characterise the environment in each country will be likely to have complex and often conflicting effects on the firm's activities. In such circumstances, management response—its attitudes towards new and unfamiliar situations—is liable to different expression.[1]

Some managers at headquarters will see foreign operating problems in terms of their domestic environment; one writer calls this an ethnocentric or home country oriented attitude. Others will look at problems from the point of view of the host country—the polycentric attitude. Perhaps a few managers will attempt to reconcile the two through mutual understanding and collaboration, the so-called geocentric approach to decision-making in a multinational company. But whatever the attitude, the opportunities for conflict between various parts of the company are not lacking. For example those at corporate headquarters are bound to view the withdrawal of funds from a subsidiary in a country with a weak currency in a different way from that of the subsidiary's management. To complicate things further, it is obvious that neither the environment nor management response to it are static. Both evolve over time. Management attitudes change as experience is gained in foreign operations, and as they adapt to new conditions in the environment. As the company or a particular segment of it, a subsidiary for example, grows and develops over time, its relationship to the environment will alter, bringing about a need for further adaptation by management. Too often what comes out of this is a series of decisions made without adequate study of their effects on the whole of the company's activities, or decisions made hastily in an atmosphere of crisis. As a result the company may pay more taxes than it need; assets may be eroded by changes in the value of currencies used in some parts of the company; resources may sit idle in one unit of the company while being desperately needed in another. Much of this can be avoided by implementing a suitable financial strategy which would provide a systematic and analytical approach to these problems.

This chapter examines some of the key variables which, in the way they influence financial decisions in multinational companies, eventually become the determinants of a financial strategy. To take account of the dynamic nature of this process, the way in which a financial strategy might evolve through various stages in the growth and development of a subsidiary is considered. In particular planning guidelines for capital structure and for remittances that would be appropriate at each stage are suggested. While it is recognised that the variables, the problems faced, and their possible solutions are too numerous and complex for them to be condensed into a handful of generalisations, it is hoped that this discussion may lead to a better understanding of the issues involved and provide a conceptual framework for improving decision-making in this area. Before starting, some additional remarks need to be made here. Although we are going to look mainly at subsidiaries, a rational explanation of what is done in practice can only be obtained by taking the view of the parent group. This leads to the suggestion that financial policies of multinational companies have as their objectives the optimisation of group interests rather than those of a particular part of the group. These objectives are translated into policies which, if not always successful, are at least meant to provide the group with the means to obtain capital cheaply when and where it is needed, and to reduce the impact of taxes and some of the uncertainty of foreign operations by shifting profits and funds to areas of low taxation and low risk. If such a group-biased policy is to function properly, it usually means a detailed planning and tight controls over the group's finances. This is a centralising force which tends to push decisions on such matters as the disposition of subsidiary earnings, intersubsidiary financing, hedging against exchange losses, raising outside funds, and management of working capital upwards in the organisation to corporate or international headquarters.[2] The discretion given subsidiary management in these matters is generally less than in other functional areas, and is often negligible. It may give its advice and help prepare the necessary background data, but it would rarely be responsible for taking the final decision.

Sources and methods of financing foreign subsidiaries

The largest single source of finance for foreign subsidiaries is the cash flow from their operations. On average, this has provided subsidiaries based in Europe with somewhere between one-half and three-fourths of their total investment requirements. The amount of the cash flow which will be available for reinvestment is a function of the subsidiary's profitability and of its remittances, both of which can be greatly influenced by management policy. To the extent that intra-company transfers of goods and services are priced at more or less than for value received,[3] the subsidiary's profits and hence its cash flow before appropriation can be increased or decreased. Somewhat similarly, the subsidiary's cash flow is affected by the level of appropriations made, whether in the form of interest, royalties, management fees, or dividends.

The second largest source of finance available to foreign subsidiaries is from what may be termed local external sources. These include funds raised by borrowing from financial institutions in the host country,[4] from sale of securities in the host country, particularly debt, from grants or subsidies made by the government or regional authorities, and from spontaneous sources—mainly trade credit and tax accruals.

The smallest proportion of subsidiary finance comes from foreign sources—outside the host country. Normally these funds are channelled directly through the parent company, but they may arrive via affiliated companies, especially where the group has set up a base company or finance subsidiary as part of its international finance strategy. Essentially of three types, foreign sources of finance appear on the subsidiary's accounts as issued capital, intra-company loans, or intra-company trade credit and accruals. The latter category usually arise as a result of goods received by the subsidiary on credit from the parent or an affiliated company; they may also arise from royalties, fees, interest, or even dividends due to the parent but temporarily deferred. Issued capital and intra-company loans usually arise from a cash transfer to the subsidiary, but may also arise from a transfer of other kinds of assets or services.

It was stated above that cash flow provided the largest single source of finance to foreign subsidiaries followed by local external and foreign sources of finance in that order. This is the general case for established subsidiaries taken over a reasonable period of time. Figure 2.1 illustrates this for certain categories of subsidiaries operating in the United Kingdom. The above order does not necessarily apply, and may even be reversed for subsidiaries that are newly established or operating at or near a loss or undergoing rapid, if temporary, expansion. The discussion which follows focuses on the general case of the established subsidiary undergoing normal development, and is then modified to consider the financing patterns of subsidiaries at various stages of their development.

To analyse what underlies the choice of finance used in foreign subsidiaries, it appears useful to begin by stating the problem in the form of three inter-related questions:

- What determines the amount of cash flow available to the subsidiary?
- What determines the amounts and types of local external finance that will be available to and used by the subsidiary?
- What determines the amount and type of foreign sources of finance that will be made available to and used by the subsidiary?

The hypothesis here is that decisions on financing foreign subsidiaries are made by providing answers to these questions in the above sequence. That is,

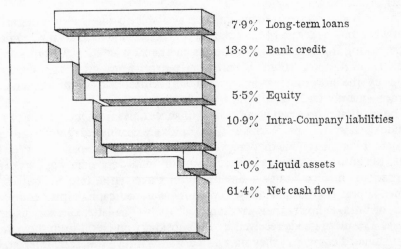

7·9% Long-term loans

13·3% Bank credit

5·5% Equity

10·9% Intra-Company liabilities

1·0% Liquid assets

61·4% Net cash flow

Fig. 2.1 Sources of finance: 119 subsidiaries in the United Kingdom 1959–1968. (Weighted averages)

the starting point will be to decide how much of the subsidiary's cash flow will be reinvested in it, and how much remitted to the parent company or another member of the group or held on deposit abroad. This decision would generally be incorporated in the set of plans and budgets covering the subsidiary's activities over an appropriate time period, typically for the year ahead; modifications would be made as required to adapt to new business conditions or other changes in the environment. Although the company may have general guidelines regarding the form and timing of remittances, these would be spelled out in detail in the routine plans. Following the decision on the disposition of the subsidiary's cash flow, corporate management will decide how the residual financial requirements will be met. Spontaneous sources of finance—trade credits and other accruals—will supply a certain portion of these needs. Investment grants and other forms of subsidies may be available to provide some of the capital. These sources will be available locally more or less automatically merely as a result of the subsidiary's being in business or for undertaking certain projects. For the remaining financial requirements, and these may be very large in the case of a newly established subsidiary or one that is undergoing a period of rapid expansion, the choice lies essentially between borrowing them locally, or having them supplied by the group. Most companies prefer to borrow as much as is possible in the host country itself, and to limit the use of group funds; this was borne out by the data shown in Figure 2.1. Finally, where the circumstances require the use of parent company funds, management must decide on the form in which they will be invested. The possibilities include trade credit, intra-company loans, or issued capital. Let us now turn to look in detail at some of the criteria used by management in making the various decisions outlined above.

How much cash flow will be available?

As suggested earlier, the cash flow that will be available for reinvestment in the subsidiary will be a function of its profitability and of the group's remittance practices. These are examined in the following sections.

PROFITABILITY AND INTRA-COMPANY TRANSACTIONS

Much has been written on the relative performance of foreign subsidiaries, and in particular on the often higher rate of profitability they achieve compared to their local competition. The profitability of any company depends on a number of variables relating to the environment in which it operates on the one hand, and to its relative performance within the environment on the other. Under environmental variables we can include the effective rate of taxation, the existence of controls over prices, wages, and other factors of production, the rate of growth in the economy and its level of sophistication, the size of the market, the climate for foreign investment, and a number of other factors that have an impact on profits. The relative performance of the company within the environment depends on the strength of its market position relative to the competition, and this stems largely from its skill and efficiency in the introduction, production, and marketing of its products. In the case of the foreign subsidiary, profitability is further influenced by the terms of the transactions it has with its parent and affiliated companies. Are the benefits of group research and development, and its skills in production, marketing, finance, and in other areas adequately paid for by the subsidiary? Is too much paid, or too little? Are the goods transferred between the subsidiary and other members of the group priced at an amount higher or lower than what would be asked in a transaction with a non-affiliated company? Is capital provided by the parent charged an economic rate of interest? These can all have an important impact on the profits of the subsidiary. However, an answer to the question how much they are in fact deliberately used as part of a company strategy to shift profits, and hence funds, within the group is elusive.

For some companies, transfer prices on intra-company transactions appear to play an important role in their financial strategy. For example, the Swiss pharmaceutical companies have been alleged to transfer certain intermediates to their United Kingdom subsidiaries at a higher than arm's length price.[5] If true the effect of this has been to reduce the reported profits of these subsidiaries, and hence their cash flow. Presumably the profitability and cash flow of the parent company was increased as a result. The Swiss companies would do this for sound business reasons: taxes on profits are lower in Switzerland than in the United Kingdom and elsewhere; the Swiss franc is among the most stable of currencies; large research and development expenses are borne by the parent company and these must be covered in part by the subsidiary's operations. These companies appear to have chosen to recover the subsidiary's share of these expenses as well as the bulk of the profits they earned through the transfer prices rather than by royalties, fees, or dividends, although these also were used. Probably most multinational companies have used at some time transfer prices to shift profits and funds in pursuit of group objectives; probably most use them still under certain conditions and for specific investments.[6]

Transfer prices are used to shift profits within the multinational group for a number of reasons. Reducing the overall impact of taxation on group profits and accelerating the repatriation of overseas funds and their conversion into hard currency have already been mentioned. The reduction of group taxation offers particular appeal. This operates in two different and generally opposing ways: pricing designed to minimise taxable profits, or prices designed to minimise import duties. Although a low import price may reduce the duties it will, all things being equal, produce a higher taxable profit in the subsidiary and vice versa; hence the overall impact of both types of taxation must be considered if an optimum solution is to be obtained.

Besides being used for tax reasons, transfer prices can often be used as the best and most rapid method of repatriating profits and funds, and thus ensuring their convertibility. Transfer prices may offer the only practical route for the company to realise some return on its investment. This is true especially of operations in countries that impose restrictions on dividend and other remittances, or that are suffering from a high rate of inflation. Different circumstances arise where, for instance, the parent company is faced with restrictions on exporting capital. In this case a subsidiary may still be provided with finance by pricing exports to it at an artificially low price and allowing a greater profit on the eventual sale of the goods. In such situations, the parent company would also be advised to charge the subsidiary little or nothing for the corporate services it received. Such practice might also be used to provide the subsidiary with profits to carry forward against tax losses which would otherwise be irrecoverable. A low price on transfers may also provide the subsidiary with a competitive weapon by allowing it more scope to cut prices in its markets. One could also speculate that in some cases company interests may be well served by causing the subsidiary's profits to be understated. Where a high rate of profitability might risk an investigation (as in the case of detergents or breakfast cereals in England), or demands for wage increases an artificially high transfer price could be used to shift some of the profits to other segments of the group. This scheme could also be used to avoid sharing all the profits of a joint venture, especially if the parent company considered that it contributed more than its fair share to the operation. The list of possibilities offered companies by the manipulation of transfer prices that we have outlined above does not mean they are readily available to be put to use. There are many constraints, some external to the firm, some internal.

The principal external constraints are the tax, customs, and exchange control regulations which have been slowly and continually tightened to eliminate more and more of the most flagrant types of price manipulation. More important has been the increasing skill and sophistication of the various officials who enforce the regulations. It is not an easy task, for pricing internal transfers is at least an imprecise art and poses vexing problems even in domestic situations. For goods with posted prices or which are available outside the firm in question, the problem is relatively simple. Variations from such prices will be generally disallowed unless some special service or conditions are included, such as quantity discounts, after-sales services, and so forth. However, for goods which are only available within the firm, and this represents a large proportion of transfers in the high technology companies, it is much more difficult to judge the validity of a transfer price. Companies usually rely on a pricing formula based on cost; to pass judgment on prices so established implies a high level of technical knowledge on the part of the tax or customs inspector. There are so many possibilities for controversy over what cost is and the reason for a particular formula that many companies, to avoid delays in the transfer of goods, will try to reach agreement on a mutually acceptable pricing scheme. Needless to say, it is with this category of transfer that companies have the most leeway to set arbitrary prices. Controversy seems to arise much more frequently over the customs valuation of transfers than it does with the inland revenue. Perhaps this is because it is much easier to appraise the validity of the transfer price of the goods than their eventual impact on the subsidiary's profits. This closer scrutiny by the customs authorities results in it being much more difficult to import at arbitrarily low prices than at high prices. In some circumstances, it might be in the interest of the host country to permit a low import price if higher tax revenues were obtained from the resulting higher profits earned by the subsidiary. But in general, there appears to be little cooperation of this kind between the two taxing agencies.

The internal constraints on unrestrained manipulation of transfer prices are the potentially damaging effects such practice can have on the management control system of the company. Most subsidiaries operate as profit centres with their performance measured in terms of profitability. The intention is to simulate as closely as possible the operation of an independent company in the belief that this will encourage managers to perform more efficiently and effectively than if they were centrally administered. Ideally, optimum group performance will be obtained if each operating unit optimises its own performance. This implies that the objectives of the individual units should not be in conflict with those of the group. This is hard to attain under any circumstances, but is particularly difficult in the multinational company where, as we have pointed out earlier, the group's overall performance may be improved by shifting profits from one subsidiary to another. Under such conditions the profit centre concept is likely to lead to a conflict of goals and to sub-optimisation of group results. Yet, there is general agreement that the profit centre organisation can provide a powerful stimulus to management; it offers perhaps the most practical way for performance to be measured and appraised. It is our opinion that the advantages gained from the proper functioning of the profit centres are viewed by most companies as outweighing those gained from shifting profits arbitrarily between operating units. As one consequence, arm's length prices on intra-company transfers are more often than not the general rule in the attempt to duplicate as closely as possible the business conditions faced by an independent company. Some companies, however, would like to have the best of both worlds, and try to reconcile the conflict by keeping two sets of accounts. Pricing would be done to optimise group performance in spite of any distortion this may have on individual unit results. One set of accounts would record these results and be used for legal and tax reporting; another set would be for internal control purposes. Here account would be taken of any distortion manipulation of prices would cause, and appropriate adjustments made in the accounts to reallocate profits. These would then be suitable for the appraisal of the performance of the subsidiary as an entity, and of its management. They would be essential for decisions to invest or disinvest in the subsidiary, and for determining sources of supply to certain markets. The disadvantages of this solution are its greater complexity, and the additional administrative expense it involves; however, in a properly designed accounting system, the extra cost may be relatively small. Another method used to reconcile the conflict is to accept any distortion in the budget. Performance would be measured against budgeted goals which may include even a loss. This approach may be acceptable to some managements especially where rules concerning these matters are clearly and consistently applied. The major weakness of this method is that budgeted goals do not appear to have the same impact on management as absolute goals, and most find it hard to agree to arrangements which significantly understate their true perform-ance.

Many of the same points we have been making could also be made concern-ing the pricing of intra-company transfers of services—payment of interest, royalties, management and technical service fees, and head office overheads. Company practice varies from no charge being made to charging subsidiaries as much as the local authorities will allow. Some companies look on these payments as one of the ways to transfer cash and as such a substitute for dividends. Others look on them primarily as a means of spreading the cost of research or headquarters' overheads throughout the group. This is of particular relevance where these costs are not recovered in the price of goods transferred to a subsidiary. Various methods are used to determine the price to put on these services. The most common is to base them on a percentage of total sales made by the subsidiary, or on the amount of a particular product sold. Sometimes charges are related to the cost of providing the services and are periodically allocated on this basis. In other cases, a flat fee for services rendered by the parent is negotiated with the subsidiary. The pricing of services runs up against most of the same external and internal constraints that we suggested affecting the pricing of goods. The tax authorities in both the home and host countries are alert to what they might consider unreason-able charges. American tax authorities, for example, closely watch that United States companies do not subsidise overseas affiliates by providing them with these services free of charge, thus foregoing or postponing foreign income. Host country governments, on the other hand, are interested in preventing the subsidiary from avoiding taxes or exchange controls by paying too much for managerial and technical knowhow. Too high a price paid by the subsi-diary can also have repercussions on its operations: their impact on profits may tend to demoralise its management; there would be an incentive to increase local prices and thus possibly affect its competitiveness.

To conclude this part of the discussion, it is clear that as long as significant tax, currency risk, and cost differentials exist between countries in which a multinational company does business, there will be an incentive for it to try to shift profits to its advantage. However, company discretion in this area is limited by various external and internal constraints; these are narrowing, at the same time tax and cost differentials between countries are becoming less important. This is leading to a tendency for intra-company transfers of goods and services to be made at arm's length prices. The larger the subsidiary, the more likely it is to consider its long-term self-interest is to 'play fair'; the risk of government sanction or adverse publicity is too high to be worthwhile pursuing any other practice. Our view, which is not shared by all observers, is that the days of *broad* discretion in manipulating prices and shifting profits are coming to an end. This is especially true of the industrialised countries. The profits of the majority of foreign subsidiaries are becoming a reasonable reflection of their performance.

REMITTANCE POLICIES

Given the cash flow generated by the subsidiary's operations, what is taken into account in deciding how much will be reinvested and how much remitted to the parent company? The following include most of the variables that are normally relevant.

- The need for funds in the subsidiary
- the effect of taxation on the various payment alternatives, on the route they follow to the parent company, and on their timing
- the attitudes of management in the parent company towards exchange risks and other hazards of foreign business
- the liquidity of the group
- the requirements of minority shareholders in the subsidiary
- exchange control regulations in the host and in the home countries.

THE SUBSIDIARY'S NEED FOR FUNDS

The priority given to the reinvestment of a subsidiary's cash flow can be thought of as a function of its profitability, its rate of growth, and its alternative sources of funds. Put in other terms, the lower the subsidiary's profitability, the higher its rate of growth, and the more limited its alternative sources of finance, the more likely is management to accord a high priority to the reinvestment of its cash flow. This is typically the situation in which the newly established subsidiary is found. In a somewhat similar position is the older subsidiary which is either suffering losses from trading difficulties, or which is undergoing a high rate of expansion. At these stages of development, cash flow generated from operations is small in comparison to investment requirements and often local credit arrangements are inadequate to fill the gap. The only other source of finance available is from the group. In these circumstances the most sensible approach is to make the reinvestment of the cash flow the active policy variable of the decision, and treat any remittances as residuals. Sometimes there may be advantages to remitting the cash flow and then returning it as a loan or as equity to the subsidiary,[7] but this is normally more costly than retention in the first instance.

THE EFFECT OF TAXATION

The impact of taxation on the remittance of earnings from foreign subsidiaries is felt in a number of ways—on the form of payment, on the route the payment takes up the corporate ownership path, and on the timing of the payments. In spite of the progress that has been made towards equalising and harmonising the various systems of taxation, there are still significant differences to be found, even within such trading blocs as the Common Market countries. And as long as these remain, it is in the interest of the companies to consider carefully the effect of taxation on remittances made by their subsidiaries. We have already discussed how taxation may influence the pricing of intra-company transfers of goods and services. There the objective was to reduce taxation by reallocating costs and revenues in such a way that a disproportionate share of the group's earnings arose in a low-tax country. Where intra-company transfers are priced at arm's length, taxes can still be reduced by the careful planning of the most advantageous mix of remittances. Even after payment of withholding taxes, royalties, management fees, and

Table 2.1 Tax advantage in substituting other payments for dividends from foreign subsidiaries*

Subsidiary in	Country A (tax rate = 35%)		Country B (tax rate = 55%)	
	I	II	I	II
1 Trading profit	1000	1000	1000	1000
2 Royalties, fees, etc.	200	nil	200	nil
3 Pretax profits	800	1,000	800	1,000
4 Foreign taxes	280	350	440	550
5 Available for dividends	520	650	360	450
6 Less withholding tax at 15%	78	98	54	68
7 Remittances to parent:				
—dividends	442	552	306	382
—royalties, etc.	200	—	200	—
	642	552	506	382
8 Total tax credits available to parent (lines 4 and 6)	358	448	494	618
9 Parent's taxable income (lines 2, 4 and 5)	1000	1000	1000	1000
10 Parent's tax at 45%	450	450	450	450
11 Less foreign credits (line 8)	358	448	494	618
12 Incremental tax paid by parent	92	2	(44)	(168)
13 Foreign income retained by parent (lines 7 to 12)	550	550	506†	382†

* Assumptions used for example above:
(a) A hypothetical company has two foreign subsidiaries; one is in country A where the tax rate on earnings is 35 per cent, and the other is in country B where the tax rate on earnings is 55 per cent. Dividends paid by both subsidiaries to the parent company are subject to an additional 15 per cent withholding tax. The parent company's earnings from domestic and foreign sources are taxed at 45 per cent.
(b) The parent company has the option to remit up to 20 per cent of trading profit as royalties, fees, or contribution to corporate overheads. These are allowable as business expenses, and additionally are not subject to withholding taxes. All after-tax earnings will be remitted.
† Excess foreign tax credits assumed to be lost.

interest payments on intra-company debt are often a cheaper form of remittance than dividends; the former are normally allowable as a business expense against taxes whereas dividends must be paid out of earnings after tax. The example shown in Table 2.1 illustrates the advantage under some circumstances of substituting other payments for dividends. The repayment of an intra-company liability would provide an even greater advantage since in most cases this will be considered a return of capital and completely exempt from tax. However, it will be recognised that this particular form of remittance requires the creation of the liability in the first place—a loan or an accrual—and is therefore quite different from the other remittances which are appropriations of earnings or charges against income and, as such, of a continuous nature. Table 2.1 also shows clearly that the analysis needs to go beyond the subsidiary and consider the incremental tax which the parent company must eventually pay upon receipt of the foreign income. Some tax systems, including the United States and the United Kingdom, levy all foreign income at the domestic rate even though the subsidiary may have already paid tax on it to the host country. However, the foreign tax paid is allowed as a credit against the parent's tax liability. Under this type of tax system, where the subsidiary's tax rate is *less* than that of the parent company (country A in Table 2.1), there is generally no advantage in substituting other payments for dividends because the parent company eventually pays the difference (line 12 on Table 2.1). Where the subsidiary is taxed at a *higher* rate than the parent company (country B in Table 2.1), the parent company will have an excess of credits. Here the advantage in substituting other forms of remittance for dividends depends on whether or not the excess credits can be applied to other foreign income. In the United Kingdom they cannot be used under present tax law (the per country, per item limitation); United States companies, on the other hand, can calculate credits on a combined basis for all foreign income, although in some cases they still may not be able to use all of the excess credits.

A decision rule to apply in such problems is that there is a tax advantage in substituting other payment alternatives *only* when (*a*) the parent company is taxed at a lower rate than the subsidiary, and (*b*) excess credits on foreign taxes cannot be used. This, however, ignores the possible effect of inserting a holding company situated in a low tax country between the subsidiary and the parent company.[8] In this case, the holding company becomes the 'parent' company in the context of the example shown in Table 2.1. Although the income would be eventually taxed when received by the ultimate parent company, this additional tax would be deferred and provide the group with correspondingly larger foreign financial resources in the meantime. Put in other terms, the discounted cost of this alternative would be lower. Because of differences in bilateral tax treaties between countries, there may also be advantages in routing payments between the operating subsidiaries and the parent company via a holding company. An optimum solution to problems of minimising taxes may be obtainable; at least they lend themselves relatively easily to rational analysis by mathematical models. Some of the other determinants of remittance policy do not.

THE ATTITUDE OF MANAGEMENT TOWARDS RISK

In addition to the usual commercial and financial risks that are expected in an entirely domestic business, the management of a multinational company must also face the possibility of loss from fluctuations in the value of foreign currencies, from restrictions on repatriation of earnings and capital and, in extreme cases, from expropriation. Events have shown that fear of such losses is well founded: the rash of devaluations and revaluations that occurred in the latter 1960s in Western Europe, and since the summer of 1971 throughout the world, showed that changes in exchange rates are a frequent and almost commonplace hazard even in the highly industrialised countries. Management attitudes towards such risk vary, of course, from company to company; and within a company they can change quickly in response to changes in the operating environment. Without pursuing the question in detail, suffice it to say that fear of loss from changes in exchange rates is a major influence on companies' remittance practices. Most management, *given a choice*, will favour a policy which promises to get home—or perhaps to a low-risk country—the most hard currency in the shortest time.

How is this attitude reflected in remittance policies? First of all, some companies make it a practice to repatriate systematically all or nearly all of the subsidiary's earnings. Managers in these companies feel more comfortable if surplus cash, even if only temporarily not required in the subsidiary, is in a bank at home. Besides reducing the amount of liquid assets exposed to potential loss, such practice also permits the parent company, by holding the purse strings, to exercise more control over the subsidiaries. Secondly, companies react to the threat of devaluation by changing the timing and amount of dividends from the subsidiaries concerned. Frequently, dividends are paid out of retained earnings in such cases.

Finally, in circumstances where it is feared that the host country might impose exchange controls, some companies believe that it is important to maintain a record of consistent and continuous payments from the subsidiary, even if this means that the parent company must return the funds. The rationale is that the acceptance of such a policy by the host country is good assurance that it will be allowed to continue in the future. Each of these policies have their impact on the amount of the subsidiary's cash flow that is available for reinvestment and, in general, tend to reduce it.

GROUP LIQUIDITY

The ability to get liquidity to the various units of the corporate group when they need it is an important factor in determining the pattern of some companies' remittances. In most companies, detailed forecasts and projections of their expected operations are prepared for a period from one to five years ahead. From these the net amount of funds available from, or required by, each unit of the group can be estimated. Normally, the various parts of the group will not be at the same stage of development and the financial requirements of any one subsidiary will be subject to periodic fluctuations. Thus, plans will call for dividends and repayments of intra-company liabilities to be increased from those subsidiaries which are forecast to have surplus cash for the period under consideration; conversely, payments will be reduced during periods when the subsidiary is expanding rapidly and in need of funds. In some companies, one of the most important demands on corporate liquidity is to meet the parent company's payments of dividends, interest, and other fixed obligations. For example, the proportion of earnings that are distributed as dividends by some parent companies tends to be reflected in the amount appropriated of their subsidiaries' earnings. Where a parent company pays out a high percentage of earnings as dividends, it has been found that the subsidiary will be likely to be directed to do the same. And where the parent pays little or no dividends, frequently the subsidiary follows suit. Similarly, the servicing of loans raised by the parent or by a finance affiliate on behalf of a particular subsidiary is very likely to be supported by its remittances—especially when it is a question of matching up foreign currencies. Such a policy of requiring subsidiaries to contribute *pro rata* to the capital costs of the group appears both sensible and equitable; it is but another aspect of the more general policy of considering foreign investments as profit centres and requiring them to 'stand on their own feet' as it is often expressed.

MINORITY SHAREHOLDERS

Where a subsidiary has local shareholders in the host country, and occasionally even where it is 100 per cent owned but enjoys a highly autonomous relationship with the parent company, local factors will provide a major influence on remittance policy. In such circumstances royalty and fee payments are likely to be less than from a wholly owned subsidiary. The minority group can be expected to oppose any arrangement which they suspect diverts an excessive share of the profits to the parent company. If the minority shareholders are few, for example, another company or small group of local investors, agreement on dividends can generally be reached by all concerned. However, a firmly accepted piece of folklore surrounding foreign investment has it that local investors are typically less willing to reinvest earnings than the parent company whose financial resources are larger and whose time horizon for realising a return on investment is longer. Though there seems to be no special reason that this must necessarily be so, disparate goals between partners in a joint venture can and do exist, and require careful consideration.

If the subsidiary is quoted on the local stock exchange, it is likely that dividend payments will have to conform to local market expectations. This normally means that they must be stable in terms of what was paid in the past, and will be adjusted in relation to expected long term profits. Within these constraints, where the dividend is the active variable and the reinvestment of earnings is treated as a residual, the tax, risk, or other considerations of the parent company are of secondary importance to the decision, if not irrelevant altogether. Hence the dividend policies of such subsidiaries would be less extreme than is often found in those that are wholly owned; payments would tend to fluctuate very little and would generally amount to between 40 and 60 per cent of earnings, which appears to be typical for companies quoted on a stock exchange. This is one of the few examples of decisions of this kind that would be made at local level. Some of the advantages which have been outlined earlier that result from the fact of being multinational are lost when there are minority shareholders present. It is not difficult to see why sharing ownership in subsidiaries is often unpopular with those determining policy in multinational companies.

LEGAL REQUIREMENTS

Up to now we have been discussing the internal factors that influence remittance policies of foreign subsidiaries. These in turn are influenced to a more or less significant extent by certain external factors—primarily the legal regulations covering repatriation of earnings and capital that are applied by both host and home countries. The general aim of such regulations as they affect remittances is to improve the balance of payments position and protect the monetary reserves of each country. As was implied earlier, they may also be designed to assure each country its fair share of the tax revenues from the company's operations. It is not difficult to see the inherent conflict between the host and home countries that can arise as each pursues its objectives—the host country restricting the amount of remittances from the subsidiaries, and the home country trying to increase them. It is not the intention here to follow the matter out in more detail; we can only reiterate that they represent a sort of legal Scylla and Charybdis through which financial managers must chart a course.

Sources of finance

The various factors that influence decisions on the disposition of a subsidiary's cash flow have been outlined. It is evident that the investment needs of the subsidiary which are not covered by the funds it generates internally will have to come from external sources of finance—local or foreign, or a combination of both. How is this choice made?

HOW MUCH LOCAL FINANCE?

Considerations in answering this question include: availability of local finance, its relative cost, attitudes of parent company management towards exchange risks, and other factors such as an attempt to gear up the earnings on the parent's own investment, the effect of local debt on the company's consolidated financial position, and an aversion to debt for policy reasons.

Many host countries have explicit policies on lending to foreign controlled companies by the local banks and other financial institutions. A few of these are designed to attract and encourage certain categories of investment and to welcome foreigners; however, most are intended to place limits on local borrowing by foreign subsidiaries—especially where capital is scarce, or where foreign exchange is needed. Government control over foreign investment is a vast subject, and it is beyond the scope of this paper to look at it in detail. This being said, a few characteristics of controls on lending to foreign subsidiaries in some countries in Western Europe are worth noting.

In general, a distinction must be made between long-term and short-term loans. A rule of thumb applied by many host countries is that permanent capital should be brought into the country by the parent company, and local sources of finance be used only to meet the subsidiary's working capital requirements. In this sense, foreign subsidiaries suffer from discriminatory treatment compared to local companies. In practice, however, long-term loans are available to foreign subsidiaries, often under very favourable terms, if they are to be used to finance projects considered to be in the national interest of the host country. These include investments in regional development areas such as Scotland in the United Kingdom, the Mezzogiorno in southern Italy, former coal-mining regions in Belgium, the Vosges in France, and elsewhere. In addition, subsidies and outright grants may be offered. Subsidiaries which export a substantial proportion of their output, and those which are large, long established and well integrated into the local economy, are also generally granted permission to borrow long-term capital in the host country. Within the framework of these constraints, the local financial institutions will appraise the loan request according to their own criteria. Here foreign subsidiaries may have an advantage over a local company. With the backing of the parent company, the risk of default on the loan is usually minimal, and the bank may also have the possibility of acquiring other business from the international group; consequently, lending to foreign subsidiaries is often more attractive to the banks than to local companies, and the terms that they offer are better.

Any given availability of local credit still requires that its cost be compared to the costs of raising capital elsewhere in the group and getting it to the subsidiary, assuming that this will be possible. Conceptual problems arise here over defining the costs that are to be compared. From the point of view of the subsidiary, the appropriate measure is obviously the explicit cost of the specific debt that is being considered; that is, a local overdraft would be compared to an overdraft elsewhere. For the company, however, the appropriate measure is the explicit cost of a similar type of debt, or its average cost of capital, or an opportunity rate of return after taxes and costs of transfer have been taken into account. Does the extent to which the subsidiary is integrated into the group make any difference? Though it would be interesting to examine this further, for present purposes let us settle for the appropriate measure to be the cost of a similar type of debt raised outside the host country. Acceptance of this measure will normally make capital supplied by the company relatively more attractive (that is, cheaper) than if its average cost of capital, or its opportunity rate were used as the yardstick.

The explicit cost of debt consists of a number of elements. First of all is the effective rate of interest that must be paid; this includes the nominal interest, any discounts from par at issue, redemption premiums, issue expenses, standby fees, commissions, taxes, and so forth. Secondly, the expected rates of inflation should be brought into the calculation. Thirdly, account should be taken of any expected movements between the exchange rates of the currencies being compared, although forecasting these is at best sophisticated guesswork. Taking all these elements into account in the cost calculation, the rational decision would be to raise the funds where they were cheapest. If, for instance, the terms of the loan could be negotiated to include accelerated repayment, discounting techniques should be used to test the effect on cost from differences in the timing of certain events—the repayment of principal as well as possible changes in the rate of inflation and in the value of the currencies. We suggested above the difficulty in measuring the cost of potential changes in the exchange rates. To cope with this, a common rule of thumb used by many companies is to try to match the financial assets of their subsidiaries—accounts receivable, cash, and near-cash assets—with an equal or greater amount of liabilities denominated in the local currency. Such a policy may result in the company not using its apparently cheapest source of finance, where local are more expensive than foreign funds. But any additional cost in such cases is considered to be a sort of premium for insuring against an even greater cost of devaluation, the timing and extent of which may be impractical to measure in the terms we outlined above.[9]

Among the other considerations that were mentioned at the beginning of this section as influencing the use of local debt, its effect on the group's consolidated financial position bears comment. The indebtedness of one unit in the group theoretically should affect the capital structure of the entire group and, therefore, its implicit cost of capital where consolidated accounts are produced. It is not clear how far lenders and investors in fact do take account of the foreign obligations of a multinational company. Do they view each unit of the group as a separate entity for borrowing purposes; or does a loan to a subsidiary in one country affect what can be borrowed by an affiliated company in another? Although there is ample scope for future research here a partial, if only tentative, answer is that debt capacity is closely linked to the security that can be offered. It is common to find subsidiaries that are not credit-worthy in their own right. Local financial institutions will generally ask for explicit guarantees from the parent company, or its bank, as security for loans in such cases. Even where the subsidiary can provide security, a guarantee may be necessary for the loan or may improve the terms significantly. Companies are notably reluctant to provide guarantees and some will go to considerable lengths to avoid giving them. By doing so they at least imply that the contingent liability, if not the loan itself, has an effect on the corporate debt capacity. In some cases, this reluctance may prove a deterrent to borrowing locally. The effect of foreign obligations on the value investors put on the company is even more obscure, as is how they value foreign earnings that are held abroad. One suspects, however, that the fact of their being foreign tends to reduce their significance, though solid evidence is lacking on this point.

In practice, companies overwhelmingly prefer to finance as much as possible of the subsidiary's needs from local sources of debt. A rational explanation would require that this was the cheapest course of action. Although a straight comparison of similar types of debt may show this not to be the case, when account is taken of the potential loss from fluctuations in the exchange rates, local debt may turn out to be cheaper. If the parent company's average or opportunity cost of capital were used as the standard for comparison, this would tend to reinforce the cost advantage of local debt.

HOW MUCH FINANCE FROM THE PARENT COMPANY AND IN WHAT FORM?

The residual financial requirements of the subsidiary, those not met from its cash flow or local sources of finance, must be provided by the parent or an affiliated company. We have already discussed how the cash flow of the subsidiary can be increased by the discretionary pricing of intra-company transfers which is one means of supplying the funds it needs. Most intra-company finance, however, is provided in the form of trade credit (current accounts) or loans, and relatively little as equity. What are the considerations for choosing among these different methods of channelling foreign sources of finance to the subsidiary?

First of all, there are inevitably certain minimum amounts of equity capital required by company law in each country. Beyond this, permission from the local authorities to invest as well as to obtain credit from local financial institutions may be made contingent on a minimum ratio of total capital being put up by the parent company. For this purpose, the form in which the capital is supplied may not matter; however, intra-company loans would generally have to be subordinated to local liabilities. There may also be certain restrictions put on the repatriation of capital and earnings to prevent remission of the loan proceeds. Within this framework the length of time the capital is expected to be required by the subsidiary appears to be important in deciding between an intra-company loan or trade credit, and issued capital. If the need is expected to be temporary, then a loan will often be provided. Sometimes this is effected by adjusting the payment terms on intra-company trade; sometimes a formal loan will be made for a specific period often less than one year, but renewed if needed. If the need is expected to be permanent, then equity will often be the form in which the capital is transferred. Where there is more doubt, intra-company debt may be used for the initial transfer and, should the need become permanent, the liability would be capitalised.

The advantages of loans are several. There may be tax savings because of more favourable treatment of interest than dividend payments. This appears to be one explanation of the extensive use of intra-company loans by Swiss companies to finance certain subsidiaries. Apart from this, the eventual repayment of the loan is generally considered a return of capital and is not taxed by either the host or the home countries. At least twice as much pretax profit normally would be needed to give the parent company an equivalent amount of dividends which is how the capital would have to be recovered if the investment were financed by equity.[10] As a variant, a few companies have used redeemable preference shares to accomplish similar ends. In this way, use of the intra-company loan may permit the company to speed up its recovery of the initial investment. It may also be easier to obtain permission and the necessary foreign exchange to repatriate interest and loan repayments than dividends from certain countries where exchange controls are in effect. One of the most useful features of loans is the flexibility they provide the group to transfer funds from one unit to another. If one subsidiary temporarily has excess funds, or if it can borrow at especially attractive terms from local banks, an intra-company loan provides one of the best, often perhaps the cheapest, means to transfer it to a subsidiary needing cash. Though an outright loan may be used and is likely to be preferred by the management of the lending subsidiary, extended credit terms or delayed invoicing is frequently more convenient a vehicle to accomplish this. Flexibility is also increased by not capitalising retained earnings of the subsidiary; this allows it the option to pay an occasional extraordinary dividend out of reserves—providing it has or can find the necessary liquidity. This very possibility sometimes leads the banks to insist on the subsidiary capitalising a portion of its retained earnings as a condition to the loan being granted. This is to prevent it from using the loan proceeds to remit additional dividends. As a result of these practices foreign subsidiaries often have a substantial percentage of intra-company liabilities in their financial structure, although this tends to be a relatively volatile part and fluctuates widely as the subsidiary's needs for finance change. Many subsidiaries also can be found to have a relatively small ratio of issued capital in their balance sheets.

Effect of growth on the financial structure of foreign subsidiaries

Up to now we have aimed at describing the principal methods used to finance foreign subsidiaries, at identifying and analysing a number of variables that influence management's choice among these methods, and have suggested a general frame of reference in which these decisions are customarily made. In the discussion that follows, we want to introduce the time variable and show how the 'mix' of various methods of finance may evolve over time as the subsidiary itself develops, as changes occur in the environment, and as those responsible in the company for financial decisions gain experience and sophistication in adapting to these new conditions. We will try to do this by tracing the evolution of a financial strategy for a hypothetical foreign subsidiary through three stages of its development: initial establishment, growth and consolidation, and maturity. Our approach will be normative; that is, we will suggest what in our opinion is a logical set of guidelines for planning capital structure and remittances. It is assumed that the objectives of the investing company are long-term growth and profitability, that the subsidiary will market, assemble, and eventually manufacture a range of the company's products, and will be located in a country with an economic and political climate similar to what existed in Western Europe and North America during the 1960s.

STAGE ONE: INITIAL ESTABLISHMENT

For purposes of this discussion, we will arbitrarily consider that this stage of the subsidiary's development lasts until it begins to earn a profit. This might be for a period of from one to three years, possibly more in some circumstances. It will be marked by rapid growth and, consequently, a high rate of investment and a large need for finance. Little or none of this need will be furnished by its cash flow which may well be negative during the early part of this first stage. On the other hand, cash flow may be augmented by allowing favourable prices on intra-company transfers. The subsidiary will not be credit-worthy in its own right, and any local external finance will require guarantees from the parent company or otherwise be secured. The bulk of the finance will be provided by the parent company. It is assumed that the subsidiary will be wholly owned; hence local equity will not be available as a source of finance. Given these operating conditions, the following planning guidelines would appear to be appropriate.

Capital structure

Owners' equity will be small since profits are low or nil. Issued capital should be held to the minimum allowable under local regulations and bank lending practices. Local trade credit, bank loans, and government loans and subsidies will vary depending on the willingness or the success of the parent company in arranging the necessary security, and on whether or not the investment is in a development area. Intra-company liabilities will comprise a moderate to high percentage of total capital. Inventory will be supplied by the parent or an affiliated company on current account with extended credit terms as needed. Remaining working capital needs and fixed assets will be financed by intra-company loans and renewed if necessary.

Remittances

Royalties, fees, allocations of corporate overheads, and interest on intra-company loans will be paid if the liquidity of the subsidiary permits. If it is temporarily illiquid, all or part of such payments would be allowed to accrue, subject to any constraints due to tax or exchange control regulations.

STAGE TWO: GROWTH AND CONSOLIDATION

This stage of development is considered to begin when the subsidiary starts earning profits, and to last until such time that it has firmly established its market position and the parent company has recovered its own investment stake with interest. It is recognised that neither the events which we use to delimit this stage, nor the period of time that it might span are or can be very precise; indeed, they will vary considerably according to the type of industry the subsidiary was in, the characteristics of its market, its success, the availability of local finance, and various other factors. In terms of these specifications, it is unlikely that this stage of development would end before the seventh or eighth year following the initial investment and could last as long as, say, the twelfth.[11] This will be a period of rapid growth, though it may tend to slow towards the end if markets for the company's products become saturated and more competition is faced. It should also be a period of unusually high, perhaps monopolistic, profits; as with the rate of growth, these may decrease somewhat towards the end of the period. In the meantime, the rate of investment and need for finance will continue to be high. However, the subsidiary's cash flow should be able to supply an important part of these needs. This, supplemented by an increased capacity to borrow from local financial institutions, should provide most of the funds required. The credit standing of the subsidiary would improve in line with its development, and permit it to obtain loans from the local banks to finance normal working capital needs without the guarantee of the parent group. Additional loans may be locally obtainable, but would require guarantees. Beyond the credit given on normal intra-company trade, funds would only be supplied by the parent group if a large project, special opportunity, or a temporary crisis required more finance than was available locally. As much as possible, intra-company indebtedness would be reduced during this period by sub-stituting retained earnings and locally borrowed funds. The subsidiary would continue to be wholly owned, thus ruling out the possibility of finance from local shareholders. Although the options are very broad, the following guidelines list those most likely to be used in establishing financial policies for the subsidiary during this stage of its development.

Capital structure

Owner's equity will increase substantially during this stage as growing profits are at least partially reinvested or used to repay intra-company indebtedness. However, this equity will still comprise a smaller proportion of the financial structure than would be likely for a similar local company because of a relatively high level of remittances in the form of royalties, management fees, interest, and dividends. Issued capital would not be increased unless the local authorities or banks required a portion of intra-company indebtedness or retained earnings to be capitalised as a precondition for a loan. Local trade credit and other current liabilities, excluding bank credit, will be normal for the industry. Because of the better security which can be offered where there are parent company guarantees and a policy of trying to match financial assets with locally denominated liabilities, bank loans will be relatively larger than normal for the local industry. Long-term debt will be relatively smaller, primarily because of discrimination by the local finance authorities and the relative weakness of the subsidiary's credit standing. Intra-company liabili-ties will make up a moderate to small proportion of the financial structure. They might be very small if devaluation by the host country were anticipated. Exceptions would be in situations where: there would be an advantage in remitting interest rather than dividends, or where local sources of finance were temporarily insufficient and the parent group had to fill the gap. In both events, intra-company liabilities would be relatively large; in the first permanently, and in the second only temporarily until they could be replaced by local finance.

Remittances

Royalties, fees and the allocation of corporate overheads will be used to supply a steady flow of income and tend to be as large as can be negotiated since the parent company will aim at recovering as much as possible of the cost of technology and skills supplied to the subsidiary. There may be also tax and other advantages in such a policy. Interest payments on intra-company loans will probably have to be made at prevailing market rates. Formal terms may be required on such loans to avoid payments of interest from being taxed as 'constructive dividends'. Intra-company loans would be used to provide flexibility in transferring funds to and from the subsidiary for various group purposes and hence will fluctuate within broad limits. Dividend payments will be adjusted to current investment needs of the subsidiary as a general rule; they may be increased in amount and accelerated if the local currency was threatened by devaluation.

STAGE THREE: MATURITY

The final stage of development begins after the subsidiary has firmly established its market position, and the parent company has recovered its investment with interest. Increasing competition would reduce its rates of growth and profitability from the average achieved during Stage Two of its development; but we shall assume that, by benefiting from its affiliation with the multinational group, it will still turn in an above average performance compared to the local industry. Cash flow and locally obtainable funds would be sufficient to meet investment needs and to support a reasonable level of remittances. The subsidiary may be a largely if not a totally self-sufficient operation —in product design and development, in production, in marketing, in management development, and in finance—and in such cases therefore will be forced to rely relatively little on the support of the multinational group.

But even in spite of this assumption, it may be increasingly difficult to reconcile the fact of their foreign ownership and control. One can expect pressures to build up in the host country for greater participation in their success and greater control over their activities; and with the parent company having recovered its investment with interest, local interests may feel a certain righteousness in their demands. In defence, one can argue that there are benefits to be derived from an affiliation with a multinational group that would not be realised by an independent company. These would include certain economies of scale, greater access to markets as well as to ideas and skills, the sharing of costs of certain activities such as research and development, planning and finance. The trick will be to demonstrate to the host country that these benefits exceed the costs of the affiliation—a loss of control over its internal affairs, an eventual drain on its capital, manpower, and other resources, and possibly a loss of prestige that comes from being the 'colonised' rather than the 'coloniser'. One solution to this problem would be to plan for a strategy which would in effect say, to alter slightly an old maxim, 'don't let 'em lick us, let 'em join us'. In other words, participation in the subsidiaries would be invited. The parent company would give up a share of the future earnings of the subsidiary and incur possibly greater administrative costs and inconvenience in exchange for, hopefully, the investment's long-term acceptance by the host country and a capital sum received from the sale of the minority shareholding.

In some of the groups that have been built up, there are complications. Some subsidiaries are not self-sufficient and are likely never to be so. In some industries it is not economically feasible to have a completely integrated operation in any but the largest country. Important economies of scale can be obtained by specialising production in one plant for serving a number of national markets. In such a group, the individual subsidiary does not represent a viable economic entity by itself, but only when linked with other similarly specialised subsidiaries in an expanded market area. However, it is unlikely that the pressures for greater local participation that we suggested above will be any less with regard to this type of organisation. A possible way to reconcile this problem would be to create a regional holding company where regional interests and identities coincide closely with local national ones. The regional holding company—IBM Europe or SKF Europe might be examples—would own the various operating subsidiaries in the region, and would invite a minority shareholding in itself. This would take place at a time after the regional grouping of subsidiaries, *taken on a consolidated basis*, has reached Stage Three of development. The financial policies of the *individual subsidiaries* could conform at least partially to those we suggested as planning guidelines for Stage Two, which would permit them to retain some of the benefits of integration, although this would not extend beyond regional level. Planning guidelines for Stage Three of development, whether a national subsidiary or a regional holding company, would have the following characteristics.

Capital structure

The capital structure of the subsidiary will approach what would be considered to be the local acceptable standard for the industry. Issued capital would make up a larger percentage of owner's equity compared to the previous stage of development; to accomplish this, retained earnings would be capitalised. Local loans will normally no longer be guaranteed by the parent company, and will hence have to remain within the standards acceptable to local lenders on the same basis as loans to independent companies. Intra-company liabilities will be small and only consist of the normal trade credit arising from purchase of goods from the parent or affiliated companies, or from accruals of unpaid dividends, royalties, or fees. Intra-company loans would not normally be made, although in some circumstances this may present advantages when compared to an increase in equity if funds in excess to those locally available were needed temporarily.

Remittances

Dividend payments will be kept stable in terms of what was paid before. This means they will be held to some ratio of current profits which can be maintained in the event of short-run fluctuations in earnings; changes in the amount paid will be geared to the long-term trend expected in profits. Royalties and fees will be negotiated at arm's length prices (the difficulties in determing such amounts was pointed out earlier). Proceeds from the sale of the minority shareholding in the subsidiary will provide a one-time return of capital.

Conclusions

From our discussion at least two basically opposed strategies for financing foreign subsidiaries can be identified. One of them, a subsidiary oriented approach, would consider each subsidiary at Stage Three of development, as a semi-autonomous member of a federation of related companies. Finance would be available mainly from its own cash flow and locally raised funds; the group would provide additional funds if a gap remained, but the general rule would be to have it 'stand on its own feet'. Dividends would be determined by the subsidiary in the light of its own requirements; transfer prices, royalties, and fees would be negotiated on arm's length terms with the parent group. The main advantage of this approach is that it will probably be more acceptable to the host country, and hence help to ensure the long-term viability of the subsidiary; besides, by enjoying relative autonomy, the performance of local management is likely to benefit. By optimising the performance of each subsidiary, this approach implies that the long-run performance of the group will in turn be optimised. As we have pointed out earlier, differences in taxes, risks, and costs among countries may result in this approach becoming suboptimal for the group.

At the other end of the spectrum, a group-oriented approach attempts to look at each subsidiary's stock of funds as belonging to a common pool of capital. Funds would be raised and transferred within the group as needed in order to minimise its taxes, risks, interest, and other costs. In this way, an optimal performance by the group may require something less than the optimal performance of each subsidiary. The trouble with this approach is that it is likely to lead to trouble with the host countries where they suspect the loss of tax revenues or damage to their balance of payments. And in spite of the possibility of mutual understandings among managers at different levels of the multinational group, the closer control from headquarters required to make this approach operative may also damage the morale of the subsidiary management and lower its performance.

In practice the problem is too complex, the variables too numerous, and the opportunities for conflict too great, for either approach to be optimal as they are outlined above. A partial solution might be obtained by applying operations research techniques as a first step in strategic planning. One start in this direction that offers promise treats planning the finance of foreign subsidiaries as a linear programming problem.[12] Such an analysis can deal reasonably well with many of the variables discussed above and can even take account of them over time by applying discounting techniques. It does not handle so well the risk and the behavioural costs, and adequate formal planning techniques to cope with these variables remain to be developed.

In the meantime, a strategy for financing foreign subsidiaries will tend towards one or the other of the two approaches we have outlined above. Whereas there are easily measured advantages in the group-oriented approach, these are likely to be rather short lived. In its long run self-interest, the multi-national company will find, in our opinion, a subsidiary oriented approach to be more advantageous if not necessary.

Accounting practices:
translation and consolidation

The purpose of this chapter is to discuss the translation of foreign currencies in financial statements. Like many other areas of accounting, this is one where practice is diverse and principle somewhat confused. It is also an area which is steadily gaining in practical importance as companies spread more and more across national boundaries. The major Anglo-Saxon professional accounting bodies are already interesting themselves in the consequences to them of such a movement. The Accounting Research Division of the American Institute of Certified Public Accountants has in progress a study entitled 'Reporting of foreign operations of US companies in US dollars'; Sir Ronald Leach, a Past President of the Institute of Chartered Accountants in England and Wales, has stressed depreciating currencies, foreign exchange and consolidated accounts as important unsolved accounting problems.[1]

The chapter is divided into three parts:

* a survey of current practices in Western Europe and the United States;
* an analysis of various 'authoritative' statements justifying the practices;
* suggestions, based on the above, as to what the principle and practice ought to be.

Current practices

The main source of current practices has been a study of the annual reports to shareholders published by major European and American companies.[2] These, as we shall see, differ in the amount of information they provide. Indeed, for many continental European companies one can gain no information about translation practices from this source. Current practice in Western Europe and the United States is outlined below.

BRITAIN

The reasons for beginning with this country are that, unlike all the other countries considered here, the publication of consolidated financial statements is normal, and the exclusion of foreign subsidiaries is unusual.

There are basically two methods of foreign currency translation in use, the 'closing rate' method and the 'historic rate' method, although the detailed application varies from company to company (especially in relation to stock-in-trade). The two methods are easily described. The closing rate method is the simpler: all amounts in foreign currencies except actual remittances are translated at the exchange rate ruling at the date of the balance sheet. The historic rate is the method still described in most textbooks. It is based on the conventional accounting distinction between fixed assets (for instance land, buildings, plant and machinery) and current assets (such as stock-in-trade, debtors and cash). Only current assets and current liabilities are translated at closing rates. All other items in the balance sheet are translated at the rates ruling at the date of acquisition. Revenues and expenses are translated at the average rate during the accounting period, with the exception of depreciation which is translated at the acquisition rate of the fixed asset concerned.

Both methods are widely used; sometimes simultaneously by the same group. For example, British Petroleum in general favours the closing rate method, but uses acquisition rates for some fixed assets, mainly in production areas. British-American Tobacco formerly used the historic rate method, is now a convert to closing rates, but still translates its leaf tobacco inventories at acquisition rates. On the other hand, the Imperial Tobacco Group still, with minor exceptions, translates fixed assets at acquisition rates, and current assets and liabilities at closing rates. Imperial Chemical Industries prefers closing rates, with special rates for its South American subsidiaries. Unilever uses closing rates, but translates its overseas sales according to the rates ruling at the end of each quarter. GEC and British Leyland Motors use closing rates. Shell translates property, plant, equipment and related provisions at acquisition rates; Courtaulds translates fixed assets and investments at the rates ruling at the dates of acquisition or revaluation and current assets and liabilities at closing selling rates.

FRANCE

We find a completely different situation here. Unlike the British Companies Act, the law no. 66–537 of 24 July 1966 which governs business organisations makes no reference at all to consolidated financial statements. Decree no. 67–236 of 23 March 1967, however, includes the following (my italics):

The company *can* annex to its balance sheet, profit and loss account and trading account, a consolidated balance sheet and accounts taking account of the asset and liability position and the results of its subsidiary companies and of the companies in which it holds shares, directly or indirectly.

The way in which the consolidated balance sheet and accounts are drawn up must be indicated in an attached note (Article 248).

Consolidation, including that of foreign subsidiaries, is also being encouraged by fiscal legislation, the rules of the Paris stock exchange, the activities of the Conseil National de la Comptabilité (the body charged with the management of the national accounting plan) and by the professional accounting body (Ordre des Experts Comptables et des Comptables agréés).

As an encouragement to French companies operating overseas, such companies may now elect to be taxed on their *bénéfice consolidé*, that is after allowance has been made for the profits or losses of their domestic or overseas subsidiaries.[3] This was not previously possible: a French company could not set off losses suffered overseas against its domestic profits. By a decision of the Commission des Opérations de Bourse companies making a public issue of shares must, as from 1 July 1971, include consolidated statements in their prospectuses.[4] In 1968 the Conseil National de la Comptabilité issued a comprehensive study[5] of consolidation which was approved by a decree of 20 March of that year by the Ministry of Economics and Finance. This document is now the most authoritative statement on the subject in France.

In spite of all this, consolidated financial statements are still relatively rare in that country. The progress of consolidation in France can be judged from the fact that consolidated financial statements were not included in the annual report of the Compagnie Française des Pétroles (Total Oil) until 1969. The 1968 report contained summaries of the 1965, 1966 and 1967 consolidated statements but not those of 1968, whereas the 1967 report did not include any consolidated statements at all.

On the other hand, foreign subsidiaries are not usually excluded from consolidation in France. It is the view of the Conseil National de la Comptabilité that such subsidiaries should be consolidated in the same way as domestic ones, unless there are exceptional circumstances such as war or seizure of the company's assets by the foreign government, or if the practical difficulties are too great because, for example, of important differences in accounting plans. It is expressly stated that monetary instability and blockage of funds by a foreign government do *not* necessarily constitute reasons for not consolidating a subsidiary; nor does the impossibility of repatriating funds, although these facts should be stated in the consolidated report.[6]

Of the companies publishing suitable annual reports, the closing rate method is used by Total Oil and Roussel-Uclaf, and also by Rhône–Poulenc (except for its Argentinian and Brazilian subsidiaries).

GERMAN FEDERAL REPUBLIC

In the German Federal Republic, the situation is again completely different. It is true that the West German Companies Act (*Aktiengesetz*) of 1965 pays considerable attention to company groups (*Konzern*) and makes it compulsory for all public companies (*Aktiengesellschaften*) to publish consolidated financial statements; but only domestic subsidiaries *have* to be consolidated. The inclusion of foreign subsidiaries is optional. The result is that very few German companies indeed consolidate foreign subsidiaries. These few include Vereinigte Elektrizitäts-und Bergwerks-Aktiengesellschaft (VEBA), Hibernia AG, Hugo Stinnes AG and Vereinigte Industrie-Unternehmungen AG (VIAG). The first three of these companies all belong to the same group, the largest shareholder of which is the Federal Republic itself. VEBA and Hugo Stinnes both use the closing rate method.

OTHER COUNTRIES IN WESTERN EUROPE

So far as other European countries are concerned, consolidated financial statements are usually published in the Netherlands and Sweden, but not in Belgium, Denmark, Italy, Spain or Switzerland. In the Netherlands, Philips apply the closing rate method to financial statements prepared on replacement value rather than historical cost principles. Both Sandoz of Switzerland and SKF of Sweden use acquisition rates to translate fixed assets and depreciation. CIBA (Switzerland) uses acquisition rates for fixed assets and the average rate of the year for inventories. Nestlé translates at closing rates except in certain cases where a lower rate is adopted on grounds of prudence.

UNITED STATES

Out of 600 companies whose 1969 annual reports were surveyed by the American Institute of Certified Public Accountants, 376 (63 per cent) indicated that all domestic and Canadian subsidiaries had been consolidated, 201 (33 per cent) that some domestic and Canadian subsidiaries had *not* been consolidated and only 23 (4 per cent) gave no indication of domestic or Canadian subsidiaries. The picture is different, however, for subsidiaries outside North America. Only 177 companies (30 per cent) consolidated all foreign subsidiaries; 143 companies (24 per cent) consolidated *some* foreign subsidiaries; 47 (8 per cent) consolidated *no* foreign subsidiaries; 213 (35 per cent) gave no indication of foreign subsidiaries; and the consolidation policy of 20 (3 per cent) could not be determined.[7]

Although it is the American Institute's view that there is 'a presumption that consolidated statements are more meaningful than separate statements and that they are usually necessary for a fair presentation when one of the companies in the group directly or indirectly has a controlling financial interest in the other companies',[8] its recommendation on foreign operations and foreign exchange still states that:

in view of the uncertain values and availability of the assets and net income of foreign subsidiaries subject to controls and exchange restrictions and the consequent unrealistic statements of income that may result from

the translation of many foreign currencies into dollars, careful consideration should be given to the fundamental question of whether it is proper
to consolidate the statements of foreign subsidiaries with the statements
of United States companies.[9]

It is only fair to add that these views were first published in December 1939,
reaffirmed in 1953, and are now widely regarded as out of date and in need of
revision.

Many United States companies, the Goodyear Tire and Rubber Corporation is an example, merely state that foreign currencies have been translated
'at appropriate exchange rates'. This is hardly a useful piece of information.
It is obvious even to the non-expert that exchange rates of some kind must
have been used and unlikely that the company would have used 'inappropriate' ones. The reader is left in some doubt whether the American Institute's
recommendations have been followed and if so to what extent.

Of those companies that are more explicit, some variant of the historical
rate method is usually followed. General Motors, for example, uses acquisition
rates for real estate, plant and equipment and accumulated depreciation and
obsolescence; and, in general, current rates for the remaining assets and for
liabilities and reserves. IBM translates plant, rental machines and other
property, and long-term indebtedness at approximate acquisition rates, and
income and expense items except depreciation at average rates. Corning Glass
uses acquisition rates only for fixed assets and depreciation.

Analysis of 'authoritative statements'

Practice in many countries is strongly influenced, though not necessarily
determined, by statements published by professional bodies or semigovern-
mental organisations. In this section four such authoritative statements are
analysed: the English Institute of Chartered Accountants, 'Accounting treatment of major changes in the sterling parity of overseas currencies' issued in
February 1968, a few months after the devaluation of sterling; the American
Institute of Certified Public Accountants (AICPA), 'Foreign operations and
foreign exchange', *Accounting Research Bulletin* no. 43, 1953, chapter 12, as
amended by *Opinion* no. 6 of the Accounting Principles Board; the Conseil
National de la Comptabilité, 'Consolidation des bilans et des comptes', Paris
1968; and the Research and Publications Committee of the Institute of
Chartered Accountants of Scotland, 'The treatment in company accounts of
changes in the exchange rates of international currencies', 1970.

Different though they are in many ways, the four statements have certain
characteristics in common. First, their authority is merely persuasive; none
of them has the force of law. The most authoritative is that of the American
Institute: departures from principles set out in a *Research Bulletin* are possible,

but must be disclosed in footnotes to the financial statements or in independent auditors' reports when the effect is material.[10] The recommendations of the English Institute, the French Conseil National and the Scottish Research and Publications Committee carry less authority. No company is forced to follow them, nor to state whether or not it has done so.[11]

In any case, and this is the second common characteristic, all three statements fail to come to any firm conclusions. The American Institute, for example, stated in 1965 that the translation of long-term receivables and long-term liabilities at current exchange rates was 'appropriate in many circumstances', but neither specified what these circumstances were nor disapproved of the continued use of historical rates to translate these items.

The French Conseil National appears to favour the historic rate method, but then leans to closing rates because it thinks that it may be too difficult for many companies to find out what the exchange rates were at the dates of acquisition of fixed assets. The Scots recommend the use of the closing rate method on the grounds of simplicity and lack of bias towards the view that the domestic currency is necessarily the stable one. They recognise, however, that modifications may be necessary for subsidiaries suffering chronic inflation. They describe two methods for achieving this but make no choice between them.

Thirdly, all four statements fail to provide a satisfactory theoretical framework for their practical recommendations. Indeed, the intention of the Scottish statement is specifically said to be 'to recommend a set of accounting conventions, selected from those at present in general use, which are considered to be the most satisfactory for dealing with the more common problems, and the emphasis throughout . . . is more on a practical solution than on a theoretical ideal'.

The American statement appears to be based on a combination of respect for the traditional distinction between current and fixed items in balance sheets and extreme pessimism about other countries and other currencies, for example: 'Most foreign assets stand in some degree of jeopardy, so far as ultimate realization by United States owners is concerned'. No specific reasons are given for the procedures recommended; the possibility of exceptions to general rules is explicitly recognised. Since the original statement was issued, both practice[12] and theory[13] in the United States have moved away from the current and fixed classification to the distinction, which is more useful in this context, between monetary assets and non-monetary assets. It is to be hoped that the accounting research study in course will lead eventually to an opinion more in accord with current practice and based on a defensible theoretical foundation.

The English statement is unconvincing from a theoretical point of view. It claims that the historic and closing rate methods are equally acceptable in practice, and that the selection of the method to be used is 'a matter for judgment in the light of the facts of individual cases'. This surely requires that the criteria of choice should be made clear, which is not done. The arguments put forward for the closing rate method are weak. First, it is said to express overseas operations in 'current and realistic sterling amounts'. Since the Institute describes an historic rate method based on the distinction between current and fixed assets and not between monetary and non-monetary it is true that the closing rate method will translate long-term receivables and liabilities realistically; but the statement is untrue for fixed assets in most South American countries. The Institute states only that the historic rate method may 'sometimes be preferred' where an overseas currency has a history of instability in relation to sterling. Why 'sometimes'? Secondly, it is stated that the closing rate method had the practical advantage of simplicity of operation. This is true but of greater relevance, one would have thought, to nineteenth-century book-keepers than to twentieth-century accountants.

Nowhere in its recommendation does the English Institute stress the important distinction between monetary and non-monetary assets and liabilities. It is disappointing that, instead of accepting the diversity of current practices, it did not select a suitable method on the basis of accounting theory. It could then have discussed to what extent the exigencies of practice might legitimately allow for slight deviations from the theoretical ideal.

The discussion of the problem by the French Conseil National also suffers from some theoretical confusions. Whereas in one paragraph the important distinction is said to be that between non-monetary assets, including inventories, and monetary assets, in the next it appears to be between fixed assets and current assets, with inventories included in the latter category. Finally, as we have already noted, although the unmodified historical rate method is preferred in principle, the closing rate method is chosen as the only currently practicable method for most French companies.

Suggestions for improvement

The opening statement of this chapter that, in the area of foreign currency translation, practice is diverse and principle somewhat confused, should have been adequately illustrated by now. The diversity and confusion are not confined to any one country. The problem is, in fact, just one illustration of the truth of a statement recently made by the English Institute in the course of commenting on the proposed Uniform Code for Contents, Form and Audit of Financial Statements within the European Community.

Article 2 (1) requires accounts to conform to 'normal accounting procedures', but the term is not defined. To achieve uniformity and consistency in practice it will undoubtedly prove necessary to make available authoritative statements in clarification of what may be regarded as normally accepted procedures. At present, these may differ not only between states but even within national boundaries. We believe it should be the task of the Community's recognised accountancy organisations to cooperate with the object of progressively narrowing such differences, in the same way as it is the policy of this Institute to do so in the United Kingdom.

In this section it is suggested that the historic and closing rate methods as generally practised are unsatisfactory, and what might be considered a more theoretically sound approach is put forward. The main reason for the confusion about translation lies, we believe, in the failure to consider explicitly the relationship between the internal price level and the exchange rate.

Consider the case of an American subsidiary of a British company whose balance sheet before the 1967 devaluation, when the exchange rate was £1 = $2.80, could be summarised as follows:

	$
Non-monetary assets (net)	336
Monetary assets (net)	168
Stockholder's equity	504

All the assets and liabilities were acquired when the exchange rate was £1 = $2.80. The net worth of the subsidiary in sterling is obviously £(504/2.80) = £180. Overnight, sterling is devalued so that £1 = $2.40. Assuming that this has no effect on the *dollar* values of the assets, then the group has clearly made a gain on devaluation of:

$$£\frac{504}{2.40} - £\frac{504}{2.80} = £30$$

It is better off in sterling terms because dollars have become more valuable. Both the non-monetary and the monetary assets should appear in the consolidated balance sheet at increased sterling amounts, the former rising from £120 to £140, the latter from £60 to £70. This implies the use of the closing rate method, since the historic rate method would keep the *sterling* as well as the dollar amount of the non-monetary assets constant.

Suppose, however, that the change in the exchange rate had been an exact reflection of a change in internal United States price levels, that is, assume that the replacement cost of the non-monetary assets fell from $336 to:

$$\$\frac{336 \times 2.40}{2.80} = \$288$$

What is their sterling value now? A number of figures are possible:

- historical cost ($336) divided by the post-devaluation rate (2.40), £140;
- historical cost ($336) divided by the pre-devaluation rate (2.80, which is the same as the acquisition rate), £120;
- current replacement cost ($288) divided by the post-devaluation rate (2.40), £120;
- current replacement cost ($288) divided by the pre-devaluation rate (2.80), approximately £103.

Thus we have a choice between £140, £120 and £103. Recall that before the changes in price levels and exchange rates the sterling value was £120. Given the facts of the case—the equal and opposite effects of price-level and exchange rate changes—it is difficult to argue that the subsidiary has suffered either gain or loss on its non-monetary assets. This suggests the use of either the historical cost divided by the *pre*-devaluation (acquisition) rate or the current replacement cost divided by the *post*-devaluation (closing) rate. There will of course be a gain on the monetary assets of:

$$\pounds\frac{168}{2.40} - \pounds\frac{168}{2.80} = \pounds 10$$

If one is unwilling to abandon the historical cost approach to accounting —and this appears to be the case with most accountants in most countries not afflicted with galloping inflation—then the second possibility above (historical cost divided by the pre-devaluation rate), which is of course the historic rate method, is appropriate. It is suggested that the historic rate method was in fact developed as a rather crude way of adjusting for both changes in overseas price levels and exchange rates. If one accepts the implied assumptions of exchange rates based on purchasing power parities and of historical cost accounting, the only illogicality in the unmodified method is the confusion of the current and fixed classification with the monetary and non-monetary. By the late 1950s, American practice was, as we have seen, recognising this.[14]

By the time *Accounting Research Study* no. 7 ('Inventory of generally accepted accounting principles for business enterprises') was published in 1965, the official view of the American Institute of Certified Public Accountants was clearly recognised as being out of date. The rather belated rectification came in *Opinion* no. 6 of the Accounting Principles Board of the same year. The English Institute and the French Conseil National de la Comptabilité have, however, still failed to recognise clearly this important point.

The weaknesses of both the historic rate method and the closing rate method should now be clear. The former is only satisfactory for major devaluations at infrequent intervals if we make rather heroic assumptions about changes in local replacement costs. This is, I think, the reason for the current move away from this method in British practice and literature, especially as the foreign assets of British-based companies are increasingly held in North America and Western Europe. On the other hand, the closing rate method works very badly where the home country is one like the United States and the foreign country one in which inflation and devaluation are continual, as in much of Latin America. It is not surprising that American practice and theory shows almost no interest in the closing rate method. There is, I suggest, a more universal approach to this problem, namely combining the use of current replacement costs with closing rates. This is the approach adopted by Philips[15] in the Netherlands and also, one suspects, by some British companies using the closing rate method. The suggested approach works satisfactorily in both the situations considered so far. If dollar values are *not* affected by the devaluation then the gain is £30 as suggested at the beginning of this section. If the dollar value of the non-monetary assets falls *pari passu* then there is a gain (£10) on the monetary assets only.

The conclusion, therefore, is that the currency translation problem is just one aspect of the much wider problem of choice between using historical costs and replacement costs. The present author has set out elsewhere[16] his position in this controversy.

A different approach has recently been suggested in a statement issued by the American Institute of Certified Public Accountants: 'Financial statements of foreign branches or subsidiaries to be combined or consolidated with the financial statements of their United States parent company should first be translated into U.S. dollars using presently accepted methods and then restated for changes in the general purchasing power of the U.S. dollar.'[17] This sentence is embedded in a statement which is concerned to encourage adjustment of financial statements for general but *not* specific price changes, and to do so with the explicit intention of extending the use of historical costs, not of adopting current replacement costs.

Summary

Current practice in Western Europe and the United States regarding the consolidation of foreign subsidiaries and the translation of foreign currencies shows considerable variations. In no country can one find a uniform practice based on a strong theoretical foundation. In general, however, one can distinguish the historic rate method, based on either a monetary and non-monetary or a current and fixed classification of assets, and the current rate method. It is suggested that a more universally valid approach is the use of current replacement costs combined with closing rates.[18]

The role of the national manager in a multinational company

A key position

Too little attention has been paid to analysing the managerial situation of the managing director of the national subsidiary of a multinational company. Most work has concentrated on factors external to the local company, such as the strategy and structure of the group as a whole and its impact on established national economic policies. The purpose of this chapter is to work out a framework for a study of the role of national management in the multinational firm.

The great amount of anonymous power involved and the apparent lack of individual responsibility seem to have deflected attention from the subsidiary's situation as such. Among the many elements which affect this situation are some personal ones, including individual characteristics and human relationships. A complete analysis must take these into account. The pressures which condition the policy situation include attitudes, aspirations, ideas, patterns of thinking, intentions, interactions, achievements, decisions, actions, appraisals as well as a number of other processes both recognised and unrecognised. Naturally the outside observer cannot grapple with all these, but much fascinating information is already being assembled.

Similarities between the companies involved can be discovered, and much work has already been done on their identification. Investigation in depth of significant differences between firms apparently similar is more difficult. Valuable raw material is available in the form of annual reports, business magazines and press cuttings to assist as a first approach. Nevertheless there are problems in undertaking a thorough study of this aspect of the subject. There is, for example, the need somehow to get inside the thinking and feelings of the top executive team of the local company, and to be able to ask questions about the diversity of courses of action being undertaken, and the choices that existed. How coherent are these, and what are the reasons or lack of reasons which make up the particular pattern discovered in each case?

The scope of such an analysis should cover all major points involved in any business situation. These include opportunities, classified by products, processes and markets as well as actual innovations. Also included are the capabilities and the resources available to cope with the selected opportunities. The picture would not be complete without a serious consideration of the attitudes, preferences and aspirations of the management team, as well as the social responsibilities that they believe ought to be taken into account. All these factors, closely examined in a multinational setting, constitute the frame of reference of this chapter. Conclusions are drawn, partly from interviews and experience and partly from existing literature, about the role of the national manager as a key element in a multinational company.

His position becomes more crucial, it can be said, as the group becomes more internationally oriented. Further, by the way the system works at national management level, we can determine the efficiency of the organisation. The power of the manager is naturally limited by that of the owners. Ownership may only act as a sort of silent supreme court with the ultimate right to steer the final decision towards the will of the owner or majority shareholder. Yet, however autonomous it may appear, the role of the national manager is ultimately a subordinate one. Even where his autonomy rests more solidly on a joint ownership, the majority holder can withdraw or buy out the minority if there is a deadlock. If the national manager is backed by a local majority, he must respect the foreign minority partner for obvious reasons.

The foreign national manager is in a different position from his domestic equivalent. The contrary is often suggested, namely that the operating unit in the home country is in the same relationship with the centre as the operating unit abroad. This does not happen in practice for the head office has evolved out of the domestic operating management to which it is still strongly linked. In other words, the foreign manager does not have a historically confirmed relationship with the head office as such, although this may develop in the course of time. Nevertheless the performance of the national management is the real measure of whether the strategy adopted suits the economic and political environment of the company. The more the local subsidiary responds to the needs and characteristics of its local environment, and brings to them the resources and facilities of the group, the more will the opportunities of the multinational firm be realised. For this to happen, the national manager must have been allowed to translate into local terms a global strategy which he had helped to formulate. This does not normally occur at present. What does happen is related to the way the framework of the organisation is designed.

The connection between this framework and the strategies of the company has been developed elsewhere.[1] The current study relates such findings to the role of the national manager. Many firms start abroad through licensing agreements and foreign agents. At this stage, the local management is not directly controlled by head office. The nature of the commitment does not permit such direct control. There is an economic and contractual arrangement, not a joint strategy. However this is not sufficient for firms exploiting new technologies. They must at least have some of their own personnel seconded to the agent. When these personnel are controlled by an international division at head office, there will develop pressures towards greater control over what is happening locally as far as it is required by the needs of the market. Hence the fully fledged subsidiary comes into existence.

In some cases this happens through the takeover of a family firm in which the existing management retains a measure of control. But this and other pressures towards autonomy usually break down eventually and greater integration is established. However the exact relationship established clearly varies considerably from company to company. The nature of the variation, as between complete autonomy and complete integration, affects the type of demand made on the national manager. But his main preoccupation is likely to be the representation of local interests as against central ones and vice versa. Management development programmes, where they exist at all, have not taken sufficient account of this.

It has been shown that feedback valuable to policy formation from local operations is rare, even in the case of joint ventures.[2] This is to be expected when a fast-growing international firm, using modern management techniques and with an advanced research department, is the senior partner. The drive for profits and the intensity of competition often leaves very little scope for developing peculiarly local opportunities. Furthermore, the parent company can be insensitive to local needs. What is clear is that both centralisation and decentralisation can be consistent with a high standard of local management. The actual authority and responsibility of a national manager will depend on several contradictory pressures which together make up an unstable and changing balance, which is not shown by the apparent organisation pattern. It has been suggested that the business world is entering a new phase of entrepreneurship.[3] The suggestion is that this new phase will see people with the characteristics of the old entrepreneur working within the large organisation. If this is happening, a new role for the national manager is indicated. He will need qualities which have previously been a hindrance rather than a help.

Such a change in the role of the subsidiary executive is made more likely by the continuing rapid expansion of multinational business. If he cannot maintain and promote vigorous growth in his foreign units, their activities are bound to slow down. Some of the risks of fragmentation would seem to be unavoidable if business risk-taking is to be promoted. It is possible, however, that more decentralised decision-making will involve more centralised planning of management development. The right sort of manager will have to be carefully trained. These considerations set the scene for a detailed examination of the national manager's position and opportunities.

The job of the national manager

What does the word 'job' mean in this connection? As in any business situation, we can approach this question from two sides. On one side of the coin we see the individual personality of the manager with his attitudes, motivations, capabilities, and any other characteristics which affect his handling of the business. On the other side are the business opportunities external to the individual. These include the resources allocated, the market situation, the local services available, together with the political and the cultural environment.

Four major factors must be considered in an exploration into the nature of the local manager's job. Of these, three are subsidiary and the fourth is primary.

- Cross-cultural interaction.
- Authority relationship with head office.
- Local business environment.
- Multinational business situation.

The way the national manager fits his individual job, the subjective aspect, is not examined in this discussion. Here the objective external elements will be investigated.

One of these is *cultural interaction*. Much has been written about the cultural problems which hinder the efficient working of international management. Less has been said about the beneficial consequences of the cross-fertilisation of ideas, supported by cultures, from which can emerge relevant and suitably fragmented strategies. There is a potential here which has been little exploited. Head office managers seem seldom aware of the possibilities perhaps because they have so far had too little experience with which to acquire confidence.

Cultural interaction within the multinational group is produced and fertilised in a number of ways. These include, clearly enough, the necessary communication between the local managers and head office. There is also the impact of the local branches of the firm in coping with the local market, and the feedback which results. Another form of interaction occurs either within a head office or a local unit where there are individuals or groups with attitudes drawn from different cultural backgrounds. There may also be actual mergers across frontiers. Europe has seen Agfa–Gevaert, Fiat–Citroën, Laporte–Solvay and Dunlop–Pirelli. More such international amalgamations can be expected, and will lead to multicultural head offices.

To understand cross-cultural interaction an unbiased approach is required. This is often more difficult than is imagined and special training may well be required. The point has been made strongly,[4] that the development of empathy for foreign personal characteristics, as well as methods of organisation and social patterns, is vital. The alien business situation has to be viewed as a personal challenge. One technique for the necessary training in a more cosmopolitan outlook is by using what has been called a *self-reference criteria correction routine*. This routine can be practised in evaluating an international exercise, when a judgment is being made of one business situation[5] within a culture from the background of another culture. It has been suggested that the same framework should be used both for the evaluation and for the correction. Hence a careful analysis of the evaluation process is the first step in the correction routine. This includes identification of, and differentiation between, the facts and the assessments, as well as the outlooks which produce these assessments. The next step is to pinpoint those outlooks which are not based on universally accepted principles, and therefore spring from individual cultural conditioning. These then need to be restated in a manner which fits the different cultural environment under consideration.

This routine applies whenever global strategies are being formulated, and can be accompanied by attempts to produce some synergistic process of cultural interaction. This does not mean just an acceptance of the new environment, nor a simple adaptation of customary routines to suit new purposes. On the contrary, a scientific study of the real nature of the differences is involved. Out of this can be expected to come unprecedented business opportunities, together with corporate structures which produce more efficient decisions and actions.

One example of cultural interaction that has been well documented in recent years is that between European and United States styles of management.[6] The American style can be described as more formal and more carefully defined than the European. United States companies are concerned to develop and implement a clearcut structure as far as the distribution of authority and responsibility are concerned. Europeans are accustomed to a less closely defined arrangement. Between the two cultures there remains the possibility of establishing a clearly detailed structure which also has a built-in flexibility. If this can retain ease of communication and an atmosphere of confidence it is likely to evoke a positive response from the individual manager. It remains to be said that there is yet little evidence of such a result, and there seem to be factors actually preventing the development of synergistic programmes. Resources are unused because of existing socio-economic patterns.

However some notable appointments have thrown together individuals in key decision-making positions from different sides of the Atlantic. One is the appointment of an American to the previously all European board of Shell. Another is that of a French president to the foreign operations division of IBM. A close examination of the effects of these two appointments on their organisations might well tell us something about likely and fruitful developments in the future.

Naturally it is possible to investigate the effects of cultural integration on the individual performance of managers, and on the whole decision-making process. Many opportunities for such investigations exist in multinational companies at present, and especially with regard to the position of the national manager. The results are so far inconclusive, but tend to suggest certain broad conclusions.

The first of these is that any cultural group within a business context contains some genuine traits which can be distinguished from the characteristics which are common to the human race in general or to businessmen in particular. Identification of these particular features can lead to the drawing up of cultural profiles to aid in the formulation of staffing policies. In particular cross-fertilisation can take place at national manager level. For in this position are men who must inevitably work between cultures, interpreting each to the other. The potential resources have often not been realised because one culture (usually the 'Anglo-Saxon' one) has tended to absorb, and not merge with, the other.

Because of this failure to merge, a number of things tend to be happening at the moment, all unhelpful to the multinational corporation. One is that local nationals may sacrifice their own cultural values for the sake of promotion in the foreign firm. In Europe lack of cultural integration often means also a breakdown of corporate policies, which the local subsidiary finds effective ways to sabotage. This also causes problems in joint ventures. Where the cultural differences include ethnic and religious factors, radically different attitudes to work and leisure may be involved. In some cases the more ruthless aspects of Western business outlooks are transferred without the restraining philosophies which have grown up beside them.

Currently the American business style is dominant because it appears to produce the efficiency required. Commenting on this, a European executive of a United States company has emphasised five major traits in the American managerial philosophy which have produced a successful penetration into other cultures. One is the belief in growth as a vital need in its own right. Another is the belief in profit as a mark of efficiency and good performance, and as a producer of social benefits. The third is a belief in free initiative and private enterprise as a system which, in spite of its imperfections, has hitherto performed more effectively than any other. The fourth element in this philosophy is that hard decisions must be accepted for the sake of the well being of the whole organisation. Such decisions include the elimination of inefficient businesses, the dismissal of weak executives, and the downgrading of conventional status symbols. The final feature is that change must be accepted in every aspect of the working existence.

Other cultures have yet to formulate their distinctive contributions. But these will come as a fruit of greater self-awareness among businessmen. In particular Europeans may well develop a new confidence that can produce a greater efficiency at a smaller cost in wasted human potential. Evidence is contained in another paper in this series[7] that substantial feedback has occurred in both American and European multinational firms to reshape conventional managerial patterns. Thus the Americans have tended to assimilate traditional European backgrounds with their greater emphasis on individual human needs and more intangible types of motivation, even when these militate against pure efficiency. The Europeans, for their part, are evolving towards a more professional approach to management techniques.

The authority relationship with head office and the communication pattern

The authority relationship is the accepted 'statement', which may be written or unwritten, defining the allocation of authority and responsibility as between the head office and the national management. Normally written policies cover far fewer decisions than those unwritten, and these latter are individual to particular subsidiaries. One well-known authority[8] has identified the factors which condition the actual authority relationship. These include the current business situation, the condition of the environment, past experience, and the capabilities of the national management. Normally, it would appear, there are well-understood means of resolving outstanding problems. These means are part of the basic understanding of the national manager's job, and current practices can be summarised as follows.

The relationship cannot be completely defined, but there is usually a framework which defines the bounds of normal activity. This is intended to be designed so as not to inhibit the initiative of the national management. Moreover local conditions, including special access to profitable opportunities, may provide grounds for special privileges; other local features, on the other hand, may produce restrictions and limitations. From these arise antagonisms between the head office and the subsidiary. These will be accentuated if the management takes a narrow, nationalistic view, and similarly modified if there is a degree of cultural integration. It is probable that some degree of antagonism is necessary. Policies evolve through arguments between the central and the local managers.

Within the relationship, there is some method of measuring the performance of the national manager, and some understanding about the assistance available from headquarters. The appraisal is usually based on quantitative indicators, notably profit and market share. Experimental attempts are being made to introduce qualitative concepts as well. These experiments include efforts to measure attitudinal factors and creative contributions, such as those which help in strategic planning. Nevertheless some of the most crucial elements in the national manager's effectiveness cannot be measured at all. These factors include his local knowledge and his ability to see and take advantage of a changing situation. Indeed the more changeable and sophisticated the local position, the less easy is it to operate some standard method of appraisal. The risk-taking, entrepreneurial national manager cannot easily be evaluated by bureaucratic criteria. The terms of the relationship should include the supportive function of head office.

Problems of communication are accentuated by the inevitable lags. Issues that arise cannot be discussed face to face, and hence the nature of the problem and the proposed solutions are often differently understood by managers at head office and those in the subsidiaries. Typical complaints from subsidiary managers about head office attitudes include: desire to retain all control, failure to accept local knowledge, slow consideration of problems, incorrect assessment and prejudgment of the local situation, attempts at impossible levels of standardisation, carelessness at disseminating information, lack of direct access to the top, and the wide gap between the thinking at the centre and the realities of the local situation. Other problems include the lack of information available to national managers about changes of policy at the centre and the lack of support when quick decisions must be taken.

Certain factors appear to influence the volume of the complaints if not of the underlying problems. One of these factors is the level of sophistication in the outlooks of the managers concerned at both ends. Another is the quality of the national management. If it is of high quality the difficulties may disappear; on the other hand, if it is of particularly low quality they may also be removed by a thoroughgoing measure of centralisation. So the problems are most real with an 'average' manager, but there are certain areas of special interest.

One such is research and development. It has been suggested[9] that a degree of unification in strategies for distributing research and development is desirable, although, this 'does not necessarily mean centralization in one country'. The allocation of research and development work to local subsidiaries is indeed consistent with central determination of policies and procedures. The centralised initiation of research and development activity, through a consistent corporate strategy, is a fundamental fact of the power situation in a multinational company. But this does not have to be so. It is the ability to plan and to undertake on a global scale a wide range of discovery and invention that is a crucial business asset of the multinational firm. It follows from this that overcentralisation may be losing for the firm a part of its potential—the creative ability of the local national manager.

Current local business environment

From the authority and communications patterns which affect the local subsidiary, we turn to the environment in which it works. This can be viewed from three angles. The first is the total business activity of the group, including the mixture of products and markets throughout the world. The second is the local business situation, the influence of the subsidiary's own market. The third is from the point of view of the national manager's own position in the firm, taking account of the more intangible political and personal factors.

A preliminary examination of the first of these angles, the total business activity, can begin by setting out the product groups which are most frequently found among multinational firms. There are several of these, and the more important are briefly examined.

PETROLEUM

The petroleum companies are multinational because of the nature of their business. Usually the most profitable resources are not found within the main consumer areas; further, the manufacturing units may serve more than a national market, especially in the less developed countries. Moreover, the different qualities of petroleum and of its derivatives make logistic considerations between producer and consumer units of great significance. So that an international network of commitments and interests involving companies and governments has always existed.

The fact that oil is an important source of energy, and therefore a basic and crucial resource for a country, inevitably brings politics into the negotiation of international agreements. In many instances the local companies, although private or mainly in the hands of a foreign parent company, accept a close relationship with the local government involving considerable intervention of a political nature. Rarely does local capital have a minority holding, but there are some examples of joint ventures between the local and the multinational company.

The oil companies have great experience in managing sophisticated operations on an international scale. Since the major interest, from the marketing side, has been focused on the industrialised areas of the world, these firms have given less attention to opportunities in the developing countries. The policies for these countries are more concerned with political negotiations than marketing considerations.

The organisation of the oil firm is usually elaborate. This arises partly from the use of specific management techniques, and partly from the variety of activities involved in the business. The products are in increasing demand, and it seems that this trend will continue for at least another decade. Present indications are that, from the point of view of market demand, the industry does not suffer from long-range uncertainties. For this reason, product diversification policies have not had a major impact on the business. Indeed some of these policies appear to be mainly aimed at improving the company image. The promotion of scientific research in advanced countries is one example of this; the development of products which contribute to the improvement of economic and social conditions in developing areas is another. So profits are assisted indirectly by fostering the reputation of the business in parts of the world where goodwill is needed for the extracting of raw material.

The limits of diversification are shown by the fact that in 1969 the chemical revenues of Standard Oil of New Jersey were only 6 per cent of the group's total income. The figure for Royal Dutch–Shell was higher, but still only 12·7 per cent. For these companies, the most important chemical products were basic materials and intermediates, plastics, elastomers, fertilisers and other agricultural chemicals. Depressed prices and overcapacity in the agricultural sector have been one consequence of the diversification strategies, making further appraisal likely. Esso has more recently introduced new developments in the manufacture of plastics, a new synthetic rubber for the electrical and automotive industries, a new refined ingredient for cosmetics, new computer techniques for offshore exploration, and a new control for automotive emission.

Another company—Standard Oil of Indiana—has a joint venture in Europe with the Dutch textile and chemical group, AKZO, and is starting to manufacture chemicals used in polyester fibres and film processing. Phillips is manufacturing basic plastics, chemicals and carbon black. British Petroleum, on the other hand, is moving mainly into basic industrial chemicals; its engineering developments are also well known.

The primary authority in the petroleum companies rests usually with the geographical managers, but there are substantial functional responsibilities. As major organisational units, for example, Shell is divided into about twenty principal functions, ten regional areas and three main product groups. There are numerous other ways of operating in the industry, although most companies have some variety of activities. It is hard nowadays to sustain an oil business solely on exploration and production. In politically stable countries, for example Venezuela and Saudi Arabia, there have been successful agreements with governments in recent years without threats of nationalisation; in others it seems that some equilibrium of mutual understanding has been reached. Nevertheless future negotiations between companies and countries can be expected that will produce agreements in which governments play a larger part.

It appears that the national manager's own position in the firms in this industry is much influenced by national political issues. No such manager is supported by his own personal shareholding, nor are shares sold on local markets to any great extent. Two major political forces balance one another to sustain his authority and in part his autonomy. One is the need to achieve a satisfactory relationship with the local government, and the other the necessity of being integrated in a large multinational enterprise. A third force might be added in industrialised countries. That is to maintain or increase market share where strong competition for customers occurs in an apparently oligopolistic situation. Despite the stated philosophy of the major oil companies which is 'local nationals in all managerial posts as far as possible', this is only achieved completely where there is close integration with a highly developed Western culture. Thus in European countries, although not in

Spain, the national managers are mainly locals. This is not so in nations that are rich in oil, like Venezuela and many countries of the Middle East. In these countries the problem of teaching local nationals to assimilate modern managerial techniques still exists. There is also the political problem of bridging the gap between governments and oligopolistic companies which foreigners are often better equipped to handle.

The multinational oil company is an organisation which has emerged from the Western world and which is beginning to overcome what have been narrow and isolated national political systems. It can be anticipated that issues involving nationalism within the multinational firm will be less significant as more understandings and commitments develop among the nations involved. Meanwhile the oil companies cannot escape the peculiar link between their product and political and national power.

CHEMICALS, PAPER AND RUBBER

The principal chemical concerns are widely diversified within their own industry. Natural molecular linkages among compounds as well as production similarities mean that a chemical plant can manufacture efficiently a wide range of products, although their end uses are totally different. Industry leaders like BASF, Dow, ICI, Union Carbide, American Cyanamid, Solvay, Bayer, Hoechst and others are large and long-established firms dating back to the origins of modern basic chemical processing. Some of them are still organised round their original products; others have achieved substantial diversification. As a broad generalisation, the European companies are less diversified, and more involved with basic chemicals; the United States firms are more widely diversified, and are reaching through vertical integration more closely towards the consumer market. The longer established and more complex the basic chemical process, the more closely has the company kept to the main product line. In some cases the firm has become multinational, as have the oil companies, because of the location of resources. Diversification and overlapping among chemical, textile and rubber concerns often occurs.

The largest German and Swiss firms have for many years concentrated on dyestuffs and pharmaceuticals. The need, intensified by modern competition, for expensive research and development has limited the amount of diversification. Thus Hoechst A.G. is at present in the following main product groups: plastics and paints and allied products (22 per cent), fibres and films (17 per cent), dyestuffs (15 per cent), pharmaceuticals (15 per cent), fertilisers and crop protection chemicals (8 per cent), plant construction and welding technology and industrial gases (9 per cent), inorganic chemicals and miscellaneous (14 per cent). Other European firms follow a similar pattern. A large foreign sales volume and a number of joint ventures make these firms established multinationals.

A typical United States product mix is that of Allied Chemicals. This consists of fibres and plastics (19 per cent), synthetic organic chemicals (18 per cent), alkalies and allied substances (12 per cent), acids and heavy industrial chemicals (10 per cent), roadmaking material (9 per cent), gas and petroleum products (7 per cent), coke and byproducts (6 per cent), ammonia (5 per cent), insecticides (4 per cent), natural gas and oil and concentrates (3 per cent), miscellaneous (7 per cent). Another example of the United States style of diversification is American Cyanamid. This company used to be mainly in agricultural products, but has now diversified into such industries as building materials and cosmetics.

The British ICI follows more the United States pattern than most European companies. Like du Pont this firm produces a wide range of products, and is especially strong in textile fibres. Other firms which are strong in textiles, like AKZO and Courtaulds, are not so widely diversified. Indeed, besides its other chemical activities, the latter company has gone in for a more integrated textile operation.

We continue with our programme of integrating forwards into textiles. This programme of ours has been set out in detail for some years past, and I will not go into it again. Suffice it to say that in our view the criticisms our policy has received from various quarters have been so much humbug. The special price deals, and virtually tied relationships, which exist between the chemical fibre producers operating in the UK market and their various customers are well known to all the trade. . . . The plain fact is that the chemical fibre industry in which we were late entrants is now acutely competitive both in the UK market and in all other countries too. . . .

The capital intensity of chemical fibre production, and the fragmentation and lack of capital resources of the traditional UK textile areas, has made integration forwards inevitable. We simply saw this a little sooner than our competitors.[10]

The multinational paper firms are less diversified. Some of them, like Svenska Cellulose, are located near raw material supplies and are basically single product companies. However there has been some movement towards products like building materials, packaging, and consumer goods.

The other industry using mainly chemical processes is rubber. Their principal activity is in tyre manufacture, but they also produce other basic rubber goods and plastics. Dunlop and Goodyear, with about sixteen main product groups each, have taken similar diversification routes. Firestone is, if anything, even more diversified; many of its products are for the automotive industry. On the whole the large multinational firm dominates in the rubber industry even more than in chemicals or paper. All three industries are normally financed with private capital and nationalism is a less significant factor than for the oil companies. On the other hand, the chemical industry employs more local nationals in senior executive posts, especially in the developing countries.

FOOD AND HOUSEHOLD CONSUMER PRODUCTS

Firms in this industry group have tended to become multinational as the tastes of industrialised societies grow more alike. This is characteristic of companies in soft drinks, breakfast cereals, soups, convenience foods, and other such products. Research and development is concentrated on finding new universal needs and desires and better ways of satisfying existing ones. The potential market is everywhere in the world where personal incomes are high enough. However a careful study of demand in local situations is required. The use of the self-reference criteria correction routine mentioned earlier (p. 51) is especially relevant to the introduction of domestic products in new areas. Selling and new product promotion used to be left to the local management; but nowadays global marketing techniques, as well as finance for introducing new products, are handled by central staffs.

Some companies in this industry started business basically in an early stage of industrialisation, exploiting a particular process in connection with a specific raw material. Unilever, Nestlé, and Corn Products are examples of this. Product and geographical diversification have been carried out, according to apparently logical strategies in at least the three companies named. Some of the local national subsidiaries have been small or medium-sized local firms operating conventional and often rudimentary processes. These have been bought out by multinational firms, or become licensees to them. The national manager has a varying amount of autonomy, but usually more than in other lines of business. Sensitiveness to the local market is important.

THE MOTOR CAR INDUSTRY

The paradox of the motor car has often been pointed out. It 'represents a major value choice of modern man. It is also one of the energisers of modern society and in itself a propellant towards economic growth and development. It knits together a nation.'[11] The same author goes on to point out how the car is also on the defensive. The attack comes on account of its contribution to congestion, to atmospheric pollution, and to inflation. The world market is shared for the most part by a very few giant companies, which are hardly diversified at all. General Motors has only 7 per cent of its turnover outside the main product group. Although a small proportion this is still a substantial amount of business consisting of refrigeration, air-conditioning, and earth-moving equipment, as well as specialist contributions to defence and space programmes. Research and development is mainly devoted to improving existing products and processes, in the case of this company notably emission control systems. Ford is also conducting research on this subject, as well as safety measures.

Chrysler and Fiat have both undertaken some diversification, notably in heavy duty and defence equipment. Fiat and Ford have extended their geographical diversification by successful negotiations with Eastern Europe. In smaller countries the scope for factories of more than one large firm is obviously limited. Sometimes there are local shareholders, including governments. The potential for growth makes it likely that the multinational car firms will establish more plants in developing countries in the future, and under a variety of different terms and conditions. It is also likely that there will be a limited extension of product diversification as well.

The organisation of service facilities is a significant strategic point for the motor car industry, being the first step in the penetration of a new market. In the establishment of workshops, the importer may become the local partner. However, frequently the parent company will buy up this minority interest before beginning manufacture. In this situation the national manager needs to be production oriented, understanding fully the significance of quality and productivity. For he has to establish efficient mass production in an intricate process to back the sales effort that has already been undertaken. The emphasis will need to change to marketing as competition, or market saturation, or both become significant problems.

COMPUTERS AND OFFICE MACHINERY

This has been one of the most rapidly growing industries in recent years, and with enormous potential for the future. Research is vital and continuing, but it is research which has a high pay off since new commercial developments are constantly occurring. In spite of current success, diversification strategies are beginning to appear. IBM has moved into copiers, and Xerox into computers. Future profits are being underpinned by moving into new products as well as, in the case of the large firms, by a geographical spread of operations. This latter development is now being extended to Eastern Europe, pioneered by ICL in Russia and now followed by European, Japanese and United States companies.

The national manager relies largely on his knowledge of managerial techniques, for he has to respond quickly to technical change, and do this in the face of intense competition. He does not have the problems with governments that some other businesses suffer; but the political aspect cannot be ignored altogether as the Machines Bull case showed in France.[12] As far as internal policies are concerned the computer companies are building up corporate systems which can avoid many of the usual nationalistic constraints, mainly because of the attractiveness of the technology. Logistic advantages contribute to this effect.

HEAVY EQUIPMENT

This heading covers a wide range of firms manufacturing industrial apparatus. Companies in this group need well-developed techniques, a substantial organisation, and also considerable attention to the developing of new methods. For many of them international operations are necessary to earn a sufficient return on the research effort. The companies include General Electric, Westinghouse, Siemens, AEG, Matsushita, Caterpillar, International Harvester, Foster Wheeler, Otis Elevator, and many others. There are certain characteristics which many of them have in common, in particular the route by which they spread abroad.

Foreign markets are usually developed by exports, using local agents who are carefully trained and controlled. Thus efficient services, both technical and marketing, are built up. If a particular agent shows some managerial flair, his organisation may be absorbed into the company. In some developing countries, high customs duties make local investment essential if the market is to be developed at all. In Western countries, and notably the European Economic Community area, the economies of scale make an international strategy desirable. Such a strategy for heavy industrial equipment is often coordinated so carefully that the individual national manager has little part in it. His role becomes limited to operating marketing and servicing policies which are largely determined for him. He will provide some feedback to the coordinating aspects of the organisation. This feedback often seems to be minimal, and it would appear that there is scope for greater responsiveness in the group to local opportunities in some circumstances.

There seem to be several constraints on expansion in this industry. One is that the established firms are themselves heavily protectionist, and put up obstacles against newcomers. Another is that the problems of keeping pace with new developments in their established fields seem to have discouraged diversification. Some of the companies are still virtually single-product, but with a product that is so much in demand as to leave room for considerable expansion. Nevertheless there are clear signs that strategic considerations turn them towards greater variety. General Electric, with about a quarter of its sales in each of its four main product groups for the last ten years, is producing an average of three new patents a day. Whether this is to be regarded as intensification or diversification, it is certainly a symptom of change. There is likely to be increasing pressure for new products as growing competition forces down profit margins.

LIGHT EQUIPMENT, DOMESTIC APPLIANCES, AND MISCELLANEOUS

Some of the largest firms in the heavy equipment group are in domestic appliances as well. These include General Electric, Westinghouse, Phillips and Matsushita. Being closer to the consumer increases pressures for local policies, and a higher degree of autonomy for the national manager. It is usually necessary to be quickly responsive not only to the local consumer but also to the local competition. A different product range is possible in each different country. This applies also to a number of companies which are difficult to classify owing to the range of their activities. An example is ITT which derives half its income from manufacturing, mainly electrical and electronic equipment, and the other half from a variety of consumer and business services, and utilities. Another such firm is W. R. Grace which in 1969 had one-third of its sales, and in that year two-thirds of its income, from non-agricultural chemicals. Other activities include agriculture, food processing, paper, petroleum and shipping. There are a number of other large multi-national firms which have activities with no close links at either the production or marketing end.

These companies may operate in as many as six or seven main fields, but draw most of their profits from one or two of them. In spite of the diversity of their activities, some of these companies are integrated and centralised as far as their foreign activities are concerned. Profitable opportunities are among the major criteria for acquisitions, and the patterns of business activity within these firms can change annually. But in spite of the centralised decision-making, with its great concentration on global policies, an able national manager can find considerable scope in these companies. Here is the sort of situation in which the new type of entrepreneur already mentioned may well come into existence.

SUMMARY

Before examining the linkage between the business activities of a multinational company and the distinctive task of the national manager, let us summarise:

- The special characteristics of the industries in which the multinational firms are involved will influence the options available to the national manager and his authority.
- Diversification seems to be a favourable factor. The more diversified is the firm the more opportunities there are for developing local strategies.
- Other factors which determine the local opportunities for the national manager include the sophistication and autonomy demanded by the job itself. Opposite pressures are the degree of coordination required with the other local or central parts of the corporation, as well as the political issues at stake where a high degree of negotiation with governmental and other local institutions is required.

The distinctive task

One analysis of the task of the national manager starts from the need to make a contribution to the corporate planning of the group, which makes the best possible use of local opportunities and takes account of rapid social and technical change. He must be able to frame local policies in line with corporate plans once decided; and finally he must guide his organisation in accordance with the decisions.[13] To do this, certain traits need to be developed, including the mental ability and training to take part in the formulation of plans. This ability needs to be matched by motivation and personality.

Effectively there are three types of personality among national managers: the *strategist*, the person who is best able to grasp the issues and put together a coherent planning proposal; the *politician*, with emphasis on the ability to influence other people; and the *executive*, the highly motivated decision-taker. An analysis of the role of the national manager based on this scheme is required. This would make possible the designing of a suitable profile and would assist the selection process.

Many executive posts do not require the three personality types, and it may well be asked how many national managers have any chance of being strategists. The immediate answer, in line with the main theme of this discussion, is that many openings are undoubtedly being missed for the lack of well formulated local contributions to the planning system. The lack of feedback to the centre is a significant problem area in many multinational firms. The national manager is discouraged from developing the necessary abilities because of centralised decision-making, reinforced by the policy of wholly owned subsidiaries which persists in so many companies. Further he is likely to be understaffed, and perhaps lacking in talented subordinates, and hence to be overburdened by routine problems. In spite of these difficulties, it is clear from the evidence collected that the national manager can play a more positive role than at present, and that his distinctive contribution varies with the different industry groups.

For instance, in the petroleum industry, government–company relations are all-important in the extracting countries. This gives a special position to the national manager in these countries, and a special need to be alert to likely changes in the relationship. In all businesses, he is in a position to give advance warning of changes in the local market. But generally the possibilities of his role expand as the market becomes more sophisticated. This is where so often the current situation does not match the opportunity. There is room for more strategists in the highly industrialised countries, but at present the local manager is not given enough scope by most companies. Whereas in the developing country he may have, theoretically at least, more power than he can use given the limited business opportunities. The opposite can also occur. Other special activities include being the architect and executive of the launching of a new product. If his position is not too circumscribed, he can gain greater autonomy by working out new and more subtle strategies which will increase the company's profitability in his own market. One opportunity would seem to be working out new relations with national customers whose special characteristics may be unsuspected by the planners at group headquarters.

At the same time, local managers are likely to have to integrate themselves more and more with regional groupings in the company. This need to think regionally rather than nationally, if carried to its logical conclusion, will produce a new type altogether. The local multinational manager of the future may find himself responsible for a group of countries rather than one, with fragmented policies that yet operate across frontiers.

Among the issues that are likely to become important, whatever the framework that develops, are increasing competition and the increasing drawbacks of the overlarge organisation. These two are likely to go together because the large multinational firm may become unresponsive to change and not conducive to an entrepreneurial spirit. Efforts to cope with these problems may well bring a greater significance to the role of the national manager. Another addition to his responsibilities is that political problems are almost certain to increase, although against a background of decreasing differences in culture and management style. The kind of difficulty which the national manager will have to resolve is illustrated by the way in which modern methods of communication, along with other technical innovations, are making national frontiers less significant to companies; but the same developments do not make them less significant to governments, who can equally devise more sophisticated policies but find the firms effectively blocking them.

As the companies are forced to recognise that global policies conflict with local aspirations, and perhaps harm their own markets, the role of the national manager becomes more significant. Some of the ways in which this significance is growing have been outlined in this chapter.

5

The art of choosing an American joint venture partner[1]

European manufacturing companies have, over the years, entered over 700 joint ventures with the largest, most international American companies. Most of these European–American joint ventures resulted from startups or acquisitions on the European side of the Atlantic, but thirty or so have been joint ventures between large European and American companies in the United States.[2]

It is only a slight oversimplification to say that most European–American joint ventures in Europe occurred when United States companies had technological innovations that were in demand in Europe, but only European companies had the channels of distribution and market knowledge that could allow these innovations to be successfully exploited. Much the same sort of process seems to have led to the fewer joint ventures entered by European companies in the United States market. Joint ventures have been a means of entry into the United States market for European innovations when European parent firms lacked knowledge of the United States way of marketing. The example of the Swedish company ASEA's recent entry into a fifty-fifty transformer venture in the United States to which it 'brings technical know-how and product expertise ... while its United States partner (RTE Co) brings a marketing force' is but one of many that could be cited.[3]

The simple but powerful fact of the complementary nature of one partner's technology and the other's market knowledge has been the primary reason why the 170 United States' companies with the widest international spread chose the joint venture form for nearly one-third of their 3400 entries into foreign manufacturing between 1900 and 1967. If we look at these 170 companies' entries in developed European countries alone, the proportion of 'managerial' joint ventures with private or corporate European partners has also been about one-third. This one to three ratio of entries into managerial joint ventures to all entries into manufacturing subsidiaries and affiliates has been relatively constant irrespective of European country entered, even in countries like Britain and Germany where few legal or other pressures to take on local partners have been brought to bear on American companies.

Turning to entry by European companies into the United States, we find that thirty out of the ninety-four manufacturing subsidiaries of the forty-five largest European companies with American operations were also entered as 'managerial' joint ventures. Thus, the proportion of European entries into joint ventures in the United States seems to be remarkably similar to the proportion of United States companies who have entered Europe by joint ventures.

Benefits of American–European joint ventures

The vast majority of these entries into joint ventures have occurred on companies' own volition, without encouragement or pressure from governmental or other outsiders. Joint ventures were entered because partners made substantial contributions to such operations.

Managers of eighty of the 170 American companies studied indicated that the three most important contributions made by their overseas joint venture partners were:

- General knowledge about the local environment,
- Local general managers, and
- Marketing personnel.

Other contributions reported were, of course, local capital, access to local raw materials and local production, technical or research and development skills. However (on a scale ranging from 0 to 6), the weightings of these contributions were each less than half the average score of 3·4 or greater for the contributions mentioned above. The major benefits European companies get from entering joint ventures in the United States appear to be very similar. In the ASEA–RTE joint venture cited above, for example, 'the four-man board of directors is shared equally by both partners. However, the personnel managing the joint venture on a day to day basis—from the president on down—is exclusively drawn from RTE since the purpose of the joint venture is to sell in the United States market.'[4] These benefits can be summed up in the statement of one manager who explained that his company had entered several joint ventures in the United States because 'we were scared stiff of marketing in that highly competitive environment, but we did have some awfully good products'.

What are the major benefits to the firm in the host region? *The Economist's* description of the benefits Olivetti obtained from a now defunct European joint venture (presently 100 per cent owned by Olivetti) appears to be representative: 'Olivetti cannily bought a third share in S.G.S. Fairchild, an Italian company specialising in the production of vital electronic components. Through this arrangement Olivetti gets access to advanced American know-how (Fairchilds in the United States is one of the world leaders in microcircuit production).'[5]

The problem of viability

Satisfaction at entry, however, is no guarantee of the medium or long term viability of a joint venture. Nearly 35 per cent of all the joint ventures that American companies have entered into with European companies in Europe have ended either in divorce, usually with the American company taking over, or in a significant shift of power, to a majority holding in favour of the American partner.

On the other side of the Atlantic, ten out of the thirty 'managerial' joint ventures entered into in the United States by the forty-five European companies we examined are now no longer joint ventures. They are now fully-owned European subsidiaries.

A proportion of these joint venture divorces consisted of amicable separations. Yet a large number, indeed we suspect the majority, had unpleasant consequences for those concerned. A number of United States multinational company managers have hinted publicly at the high cost of joint venture divorce in both financial and less tangible terms such as relationships with local managers, competitors, and governments. Dr Antonie Knoppers, international division Vice-President of Merck, Sharp and Dohme, a major American pharmaceutical firm, related his experience with joint venture divorce as follows: 'Divorces can be miserable. The one I had for Merck in a joint venture in Europe is still a traumatic memory.'[6] Looking at the problem of joint venture divorce from the European partner's point of view, *Business Week* probably summed up the issue well when they said that 'many a European company has taken in American partners only to regret it after the warm Yankee embrace became a crushing bear hug'. The article describes a particularly nasty divorce. The ten joint venture divorces of European companies in the United States referred to above have not yet caused anyone in American industry to complain of a crushing European bear hug. Yet the financial, human and goodwill costs of these joint venture break-ups appear to have been of nearly equal importance to those incurred by divorces on European territory.

Just which partner might bear a disproportionate financial cost from a break-up of a joint venture would seem impossible to determine in advance. The division of whatever would be left after an unhappy business marriage would depend on bargaining and negotiating skills at the moment of the divorce and on the expected value of the trade-off between post-divorce returns and the cost of continued conflict. But clearly, when conflict becomes so irreconcilable that divorce is the only solution, both partners lose in terms of managerial time and disappointment. The partner that has put the greatest managerial commitment into the joint venture probably stands to lose the most, particularly if he finds his managerial role diminished by the change from a joint venture to a wholly owned, centrally directed corporate subsidiary. And if, as many suspect, managers and management time are the scarcest resources in international business operations, this human cost alone should induce managers to devote considerable thought to the viability of their joint ventures.

ASSESSING THE VIABILITY OF AN AMERICAN–EUROPEAN JOINT VENTURE

If joint venture viability is an important issue for company managers (and occasionally governments, unions, competitors, suppliers, and perhaps customers), what, then, makes some joint ventures survive better than others?

Our research has examined a number of variables for their usefulness in predicting the long-term viability of joint ventures between corporate partners. The variables we found to be useful for the prediction of viability are these:

- The strategy of the enterprises concerned, particularly with respect to the degree that their product line is diversified or not.
- The organisation structure of the companies involved, and particularly the organisation structure of the company from the investing country (as opposed to the host country).
- The degree to which the investing company feels that its headquarters can predict—and therefore plan and control—the outcome of the marketing and production activities of the joint venture subsidiary.

Some variables which did *not* appear to have much to do with the medium- or long-term viability of joint international business ventures were:

- 'The cultural distance' between the United States and the country of its European partners.
- The industry of either parent or foreign joint venture subsidiary.
- The degree to which conflicts or problems existed in joint ventures over such points of contention as the slowness of decision-making on the side of one (usually the bigger) partner, or the desire of one or the other of the partners to integrate the joint venture subsidiary into its accounting system or dividend policy.

Since much of the literature on joint international business ventures is concerned with the cultural or administrative conflicts that can occur in joint ventures, perhaps a word is in order about why these variables did not turn out to be useful in predicting joint venture viability and why, indeed, *no* statistical relationship was found between such conflicts and the occurrence of a joint venture divorce. The fact of the matter seems to be that conflicts of this sort occur regularly even in the most 'successful' joint ventures. This may be why most managers when pressed will say that they 'don't like' joint ventures. Managers interviewed said that neither increased precision of the legal joint venture contract, nor any procedure they knew of could eliminate the bargaining and negotiating that goes on continually in joint ventures. The comments of a manager of a Scandinavian firm with a joint venture with a large American company are typical:

> Concern with the joint venture is at the fourth or fifth level of their [the partner's] organisation. In ours, it is at the first level. We do not take very much time to come to decisions concerning the joint venture, but our American partner seems to take forever. In addition, we are continually having problems over re-investment of earnings. But neither one of us wants to break up the joint venture because our skills complement each other too nicely.

From comments such as these one suspects that the 'bargaining-learning process' of negotiation and the 'quasi-resolution of conflicting goals', said to be typical of any business organisation, are merely more active in joint ventures. The true reasons for their demise lie elsewhere.[7]

What sorts of conflicts, then, cause joint ventures to cease to be viable? It is not conflict over short-term tactical issues. Rather, viability is called into question when basic strategies clash. And the timing of joint venture divorce follows as the organisational structure of the *multinational* partner evolves in a way that is consistent with its original strategy choice.

Strategy, structure and joint venture survival

Authors who have developed the concept of corporate strategy have defined this as a set of 'decision rules' for future growth which specify 'course of action and the allocation of resources necessary for carrying out the goal of growth'.[8] One investigator,[9] studying the evolution of organisational forms in domestic United States companies, found that the structure, or the pattern of allocation of decision-making authority and responsibility, followed strategy.

Large corporations tended to make a distinct strategy choice of either concentrating on one particular product line or 'end-use market', or of continually diversifying into new and different product lines sold to non-traditional customers.[10] A further finding was that the strategic choice between product concentration and diversification implied very different consequences for organisational structure within companies. Firms which were not diversified, while frequently going through stages in which operations were decentralised by geographical area, typically ended up having highly centralised 'functional' organisational structures. In these, general management decisions across frontiers were made only at the top level of the firm. However, firms actively diversifying their product lines were found to adopt a decentralised 'divisional' structure with one or more levels of general management responsibility from below the corporate office. It is this same relationship between strategic choice and eventual centralisation or decentralisation of authority, responsibility, and decision-making found in the domestic United States arena that explains much of the survival potential of international joint ventures.

Joint venture viability in Europe

The ways in which centralisation and decentralisation of decision-making in foreign subsidiaries of the 170 largest American multinational companies were related to the original strategic choice of their American parents are described in an earlier study.[11] The results of this research showed that when American firms first went overseas their ventures into new markets typically were accompanied both by considerable entries into joint ventures and by organisation structures that left a great deal of autonomy to foreign subsidiary general managers. Relative autonomy was usually given whether or not the American firm had a high degree of product diversification at home. In this early stage of overseas involvement, marketing, product mix, and output decisions were typically taken at the local subsidiary (including joint venture subsidiary) level of the corporate system. The reporting lines between parent and subsidiary in these early days of United States foreign manufacturing involvement were typically of the 'mother-daughter' type in which the president of the subsidiary reported—in so far as he did so—to the president of the home corporation.[12]

If American companies eventually appoint a director of an international division, not a great deal seems to change in terms of the relative autonomy of the foreign subsidiaries, or of entry into joint ventures. The role of the international division director seemed more typically to be one of facilitating the transfer of new products and processes out to the subsidiaries from the domestic product divisions rather than one of 'controlling' foreign operations.

In American companies that went to a so-called 'worldwide product division' organisation structure, the domestic product divisions of United States companies were typically more interested in, or more able to run, their domestic operations than control closely the overseas subsidiaries that reported to them. This form of organisation, which has been shown to follow a high level of overseas product diversification,[13] appears to have gone hand in hand with decentralisation of decision-making to foreign subsidiaries in a fashion quite parallel to the decentralisation found typical of domestic United States companies with considerable product diversification.[14]

It is when undiversified American companies form regional or area headquarters that a high degree of central control over foreign country subsidiary operations begins to exert itself. Numerous managers with whom we spoke corroborated the view first expressed some years ago that area or regional forms of organisation seemed to be a response to a corporate need for cross-country 'rationalisation of production and marketing'.[15] Such cross-country rationalisation decisions tend to become desirable when the products of the individual subsidiaries in a region reach the mature stage of the product life cycle.[16] The kind of marketing rationalisation decisions that usually accompany the implantation of a regional headquarters in an American company have been described as follows:

> One large food processing company has been distributing a successful, highly profitable prepared soup brand in practically all the European national markets for several years. At present, however, the product is being sold in eleven different packages. The company believes it could achieve a significant savings in cost and at the same time reduce consumer confusion by standardising the packaging. This will require very careful analysis of each national market, followed by a firmly implemented decision.

It is such 'firmly implemented' decisions emanating from regional headquarters that have been the single greatest cause of joint venture divorce in European–American ventures in Europe.[17] The adoption by American multinational corporations of regional headquarters associated with rationalisation decisions of this sort is very clearly accompanied by a reduction in the decision-making power of local subsidiary chief executives. These are often either the joint venture partner or are 'contributed to' the venture by local partners. In an interview, the head of the international division of a prominent American company with regional headquarters reporting to him noted that his firm's local chief executive 'had full responsibility for setting salaries and benefits, creating management development programs, training personnel, and ensuring customer satisfaction and follow-up servicing'. However, he also noted that subsidiary managers had little to say about what products would be produced, what volume of product would be produced, or at what price goods would sell. He added that, as a consequence, his firm 'has had difficulty in persuading its country managers that they are not just glorified salesmen'. It is hardly surprising that this company bought out the only European joint venture partner it ever had.

Let us put what has happened in statistical terms. Over the history of American investment in Europe from 1900 to 1967, and elsewhere where companies were free to choose 100 per cent ownership if they so desired, the odds that a joint venture with an American multinational company would survive in any given year were as follows:

1. Joint ventures with American companies that had a 'president to president' kind of relationship characteristic of early international involvement of United States companies had something like a 30 : 1 chance of surviving in any given year while the American firm retained this organisation structure.

2. Joint ventures with American companies that had international division headquarters but had not interposed any regional layer of decision-making between the subsidiary and the United States partner's headquarters have historically had a 25 : 1 chance of surviving in any given year during the time the United States partner had such an organisational structure.
3. Interestingly enough, joint ventures with widely diversified American companies that had the so-called 'worldwide product division' organisational structure also had a 25 : 1 chance of surviving in years in which the American partner had this type of structure.
4. Joint ventures with American partners who have organisational structures that include regional headquarters, however, have odds in favour of their survival in any given year of only 2·5 : 1. These vastly lowered odds in favour of joint venture survival are hardly surprising in the light of the marketing and production rationalisation decisions undiversified American companies typically wish to take when they impose a regional headquarters on various national subsidiaries.[18]

Uncertainty and joint venture survival

The causes of the viability or lack of viability, of joint ventures between European companies and large international United States firms in Europe contain one final element in addition to those of strategy and organisation structure. This final element is the degree to which the headquarters of a multinational company feels it can plan for the operation at the level of the European joint venture. If headquarters can predict the market for the output of joint manufacture, it can plan for the venture. And if it can plan, the desire to control by 100 per cent ownership is not far behind. Naturally, if the local joint venture opposes any attempt with the American partner to acquire full control, the latter may break up the joint venture by selling out and then going into direct competition.

Since formal organisation structure is directly related to the degree of centralisation of planning and control, it is hardly surprising that the ability of headquarters to predict European subsidiary operations varies with the different stages of international organisational development described above. Predictability by headquarters for foreign subsidiaries is difficult when markets are new. We find that of eight United States companies which were in the 'early' stages of international involvement in Europe and whose European managers responded to a questionnaire on this issue, seven said that their parent headquarters could not predict cost and demand in European operations within a 10 per cent margin of error for more than two years in advance. Similarly, in widely diversified companies, predictability is difficult in Europe when the parent company is continually introducing new products from United States to European manufacture. Thus, of seven worldwide product and diversified international firms responding to a questionnaire on the predictability of European operations, six said that their parent corporate or divisional headquarters could not predict unit demand or costs for European operations within a 10 per cent margin of error for two years or more.

Predictability seems much easier in undiversified international corporate systems that have reached the stage of having regional headquarters. Six out of ten European-based managers in regionally organised United States companies stated that their parent headquarters could predict unit demand and costs within a 10 per cent margin of error for *more* than two years. The desire of the parent company to predict, plan and control centrally appears to become particularly marked in undiversified companies that have no, or very few, new product introductions into Europe.

A number of managers' comments were consistent with these more general findings. One multinational corporate manager noted that:

> Our staff is always trying to reduce or eliminate the uncertainty they face in planning. This puts continual pressure on line managers to integrate joint venture operations into our overall management information, planning, and control system. If markets are not new, if products are not new and uncertain, we can control the operations centrally and a joint venture partner becomes pretty superfluous.

A high level manager of a continental European chemical company with numerous joint ventures with American multinational firms in Europe stated that he saw the risk of joint venture divorce to be greatest in the older activities where the American company 'will eventually try to impose its ways of doing things on the joint venture'. He saw considerably less risk of such an irreconcilable conflict and eventual divorce in joint ventures in new activities undertaken as a part of product diversification moves on the part of the United States firm.

In sum, the most important factors determining the viability of European–American joint ventures in Europe appear to be the strategy and organisational structure of the *American* partner and its ability to predict, plan and centrally control. At first glance this dominance of the American multinational partner's strategy may seem perplexing. One might have expected the relationship to have been more symmetrical. However, there are at least two reasons why the viability of a joint venture in Europe depends more on the American partner's strategy than on that of the European. The first of these, the most obvious and perhaps the least important, is that American multinational firms typically have a number of subsidiaries in Europe, whereas the European partners tend to be a single national firm. Thus the American partner is more likely to have something to rationalise and to centralise, on a supranational basis, unless he has highly diverse operations.

Secondly, and more important, it is the American joint venture partner that typically already has, and has exploited in the United States, the new products or processes that make the joint venture interesting at the date of entry. The American partner probably has both a disproportionate bargaining advantage and a disproportionate psychological commitment to these products and processes. The advantage and the commitment stem from the fact that a way of doing things with a particular product evolved first in the United States before the move to Europe. The fact of having done well in the United States market with this product undoubtedly gives the American joint venture partner a psychological certainty, or a strong feeling of 'distinctive competence' that may sweep aside the European partners' objections based on the relevance of their experience with the British, French, German or any other market, when a product-committed United States firm begins to think it can plan and control on a central level.

Joint venture viability in the United States market

For slightly different reasons European companies' strategies for operations in the United States appear to have been the dominant determinants of the viability of joint European–American ventures in that market. In our research we did not find that cultural, attitudinal, and ordinary business conflicts were absent in parent–subsidiary relationships across the Atlantic when the parent is a European firm. But such conflicts are neither specific to joint ventures nor do they seem, once again, to constitute the major reasons why joint ventures lose their viability.

On account of the very small number of 'managerial' joint ventures entered by European companies in the United States, patterns emerge with much less clarity. However, a number of the ten cases of joint venture divorce that we discovered were quite consistent with the notion that a foreign investment strategy of concentrating on one limited product line is inconsistent with long-term joint venture viability. At least five of the cases of joint venture divorce observed seem to fit the pattern of initial entry due to an uncertain new market, followed by apparent learning of the market, followed by transatlantic co-ordination inconsistent with a large amount of power left to a local partner. Regrettably, because of lack of information, it is difficult to say in any of these five cases if similar changes in organisation structure occurred within the European multinational parent corporate system as occurred more or less concurrently with the joint venture divorces in Europe precipitated by organisational changes in undiversified American multinational corporations.

A unique reason for the break-up of European–American joint ventures in the United States market also emerged from our research. The American competitive environment appears to have exerted a special pull away from the 'managerial' joint venture form of operation for European companies manufacturing there. Contrary to the viewpoint of some authors, the direct influence of antitrust as a 'special factor' in United States operations has been quite a negligible factor in precipitating divorce in joint ventures in that country. It has been argued, for instance, that the Mobay case in which the Justice Department 'forced' Monsanto, an American firm, to sell out its 50 per cent interest in a joint venture with the German firm Bayer, has in some sense deterred European firms from entering joint ventures.[18] One could employ that argument to say that this has been one reason for the high incidence of joint venture divorce, invariably ending up with 100 per cent European ownership, in the United States. Despite this contention, our interviews with managers of most of the large European companies with 'managerial' joint ventures across the Atlantic indicated that antitrust really has no effect on entry or continuation decisions.

The special factor about the United States market that seems to bring to an end European–American joint ventures, even in European corporate systems pursuing a strategy of product diversification, results from the very rapid pace of product development and change. This pace of competition, development, and innovation[19] appears occasionally to make the complicated 'bargaining-learning process' of life in joint ventures much more of a luxury than it is in less competitive markets. When the markets alone are uncertain, the joint venture seems to be a useful way of operating. When products as well as markets become uncertain because of the extreme rates of obsolescence prevailing in the United States, the need for close coordination between functions apparently can drive European companies to buy out American partners. Such partners typically handled marketing for a product introduced at one time for which the demand at another time had either changed or was no longer there. A new product response was called for and the separation of marketing from research and development in United States joint ventures got in the way of this response. At least this is the way that two managers in European companies that had bought out joint venture partners in the United States saw the situation. In the final analysis, of course, one could argue that this particular turn of events is merely a special case of a more general proposition: that strong commitment to a particular product line, to a particular 'business that we are in' on the part of the firm that is transferring technology across the Atlantic, is the true seed of destruction that eventually causes joint ventures to break up.

Summary

In the past prospective joint venture partners, students of international business and economics, and government officials have paid little attention to the problem of viability in joint ventures. What attention has been paid to the problem has been given to it by lawyers drawing up appropriate contracts. But even a specific legal contract cannot prevent basic conflicts over company strategy from destroying even the most secure corporate marriage. Most managers as well as government officials drawn into corporate divorces would, one suspects, agree with this verdict.

The research on which this chapter is based attempted to examine the problem from a new perspective and relate the survival potential of joint ventures to work already done on the implications of corporate strategic choices for decentralisation and centralisation of decision-making in various types of corporate hierarchies.

To recapitulate briefly, international firms find decentralised, semi-autonomous joint ventures a useful response to the uncertainty of new markets when they first go overseas. If they pursue a strategy of continual product diversification, the introduction of new products to new markets creates additional uncertainty to which joint ventures can be a useful organisational response. The company that concentrates on a particular product line, however, eventually attempts to impose its way of doing things on a joint venture and a typical result of this attempt to centralise and control is the break-up of the venture. Of course, when joint ventures are broken up depends not only on company strategy, but on the degree to which the company perceives its centre as being able to predict, plan and control for foreign operations. The sequence of strategy choice leading to decentralised or centralised structures closely parallels the organisational development found typical of United States firms in their domestic market. Joint venture survival then follows organisational needs.

6

Organising the multinational firm
Can the Americans learn from
the Europeans?

The continued rapid growth of foreign direct investment has been accompanied by an increasing awareness among businessmen of the vital role that the organisation structure can play in the successful conduct of their international operations. This awareness has stemmed in part from the fact that there has been a succession of well-publicised structural changes among firms already heavily committed on a global scale. The organisational practices of these leaders in the international business area can set precedents that others follow eagerly and sometimes blindly in the effort of promoting their own version of the fashionable image of 'multinationality'. For many firms foreign ventures are a relatively new form of activity. As they grapple with the problems of developing organisations, skills and control systems appropriate to their new and unfamiliar environments managers tend to find that the structures previously built up on the domestic front are not entirely appropriate abroad, so they look outside their own firms for guidance from their more internationally experienced competitors.

Any given strategy of growth demands an ordering of priorities among the various management tasks if the strategy is to be effectively implemented. These priorities tend to become established by the form of the management structure that is developed in the firm. Unless the characteristics of the structure match the needs of the strategy inefficiencies are likely to occur.[1] Hence decisions made to change the strategy of growth are likely to be accompanied by changes in the structure. Each of the possible strategies of achieving the international growth and development of a firm leads to a particular structure. The form of the structure is closely associated with the firm's style of management, so that different firms may develop different strategies to implement similar structures.

Management style is greatly influenced by the attitudes and assumptions of the senior executives in the firm. These attitudes and assumptions vary enormously among individuals, but there are certain common denominators among United States executives that differentiate them from their European colleagues. These differences reflect the divergent cultural and social philosophies on either side of the Atlantic. The management style and organisation structure that is appropriate for implementing one strategy in the United States may not, therefore, be appropriate for the implementation of a similar strategy in a European firm.

The growth of international operations as an integral and increasingly important component of a firm's total business has made the export of one managerial style from one country to a large number of foreign countries increasingly difficult. The foreign activities are more and more being managed by foreign nationals who do not share the attitudes and assumptions of the senior executives in the parent company. Adaptations of the organisation structures to allow these differences in style to be managed effectively and to reduce the possible conflicts are beginning to appear. These adaptations are occurring on a two-way basis across the Atlantic as Americans learn about the distinctive skills of the Europeans and vice versa.

The purpose of this chapter is to describe and contrast some of the American and European practices in managing foreign operations and to speculate about the changes that are beginning to appear. Naturally the descriptions contain a high degree of generalisation about factors that are subject to widely differing interpretation and to the criticism that no generalisations in this complex field are possible. The analysis therefore should be considered as an attempt to map the gross dimensions of change in international organisational practice and not as an attempt to define the full spectrum of management practices in different cultures.

The American experience

The development of organisation structures for administering the foreign activities of United States manufacturing firms has followed three distinct stages, with a fourth stage possibly in the process of emerging. The first three stages are similar to the phases of development that have been identified for the domestic activities of American manufacturing enterprises.[2] First, there is the initial expansion and accumulation of manufacturing resources abroad; second, the foreign activities are centralised under the responsibility of a single executive; and third, further expansion into new products and new markets abroad is accompanied by the development of new organisational arrangements to ensure the continued effective administration on a global scale of the resources of the firm. A discussion of the fourth emerging stage is delayed until the end of this section.

The evidence on which these generalisations are based is described in detail elsewhere.[3] The sample used for this study comprised 170 United States manufacturing firms that were in the 1964 or the 1965 *Fortune* 500 classifications and that had manufacturing subsidiaries in six or more foreign countries at the end of 1963, and where the parent company owned 25 per cent or more of each subsidiary. These firms represent over three-quarters of all American-controlled manufacturing activity abroad. By using interviews, annual reports, and secondary sources,[4] histories of each firm were developed to describe the organisational and strategic changes involved in the process of expansion outside the United States.

The initial foreign expansion of firms has been well described by others.[5] The early penetration of foreign markets through exports generally precedes the investment in manufacturing facilities within the export markets. The initial manufacturing investments typically do not have a great deal of management input from the corporate headquarters, since there are few, if any, executives in the firm with experience in managing foreign business. The fledgling operations may have only a dividend reporting responsibility to the corporate controller, or they may have a reporting relationship with the president of the firm if he happens to have a personal interest in the international scene. Control procedures are largely non-existent, and the men running the foreign subsidiaries are left virtually on their own.

The uncertainties that surround the initial foreign investments are so great that many firms regard them as portfolio gambles, not subject to the usual investment criteria for domestic expenditures. So long as they continue to be treated in this way the lack of direct management may continue. However few United States firms are prepared to gamble large sums of money for very long without introducing a control mechanism. The first stage of foreign expansion, therefore, is likely soon to give way to the second stage when controls and organisation are introduced.

The typical organisational response to the perceived need for control is to place all the foreign subsidiaries in a single division, normally called the international division. The single executive who has the profit responsibility for this division is charged with the additional responsibility of developing the appropriate control system. The early timing of this organisation change in the growth of a firm's international commitments is indicated by the fact that fifty-seven of the 106 firms for which data were available established an international division when they had four or fewer foreign subsidiaries. A few firms even missed out the first stage of uncoordinated expansion altogether and charged one man with full responsibility for spearheading the move abroad. Such men were normally recruited after they had acquired international experience in other firms.

The international division is at the same organisation level as the domestic divisions, but does not have their autonomy. It is dependent on the cooperation and assistance of the product divisions and is therefore in a position that can readily generate conflicts and organisational stresses. The product division managers, who are evaluated on their own domestic profit performance, tend not to provide the services that are in the interests of the firm as a whole, leaving the international manager to fend for himself. While the international division accounts for only a small proportion of the business, the costs of these natural responses are usually outweighed by the benefits that accrue from having a centre of international expertise to provide the foreign subsidiaries with the necessary inputs that would not otherwise be available.

If the foreign markets are growing faster than domestic markets, which has often been the case during the last twenty years, the international division starts to account for an increasing share of the firm's operations. Problems of capital allocation and transfer pricing become relatively more important. Consistent and rational resolution of these problems requires better communication across the domestic–international fault in the organisation. Top management has responded to this need for better communication by giving domestic product and functional managers international experience by means of short-term assignments abroad. Such action, however, has proved in many firms to be only a limited palliative for the more fundamental need to establish practices and procedures capable of bringing a global perspective to the management responsibilities of the firm.

Reorganisation by replacing the international division with new structure has been a second and important response. By the end of 1968, fifty-four of the firms studied had introduced alternative structures. In twenty-four other firms, where growth abroad had been primarily through merger with other firms whose foreign activities were in different industries, the problems of the international division had been bypassed altogether.

Three alternative structures have been used to replace the international division. Firms choose one of these structures in accordance with their strategies of growth abroad.

In cases where the principal international growth vehicle has been the transferring of diversified product lines sequentially from the United States to the foreign subsidiaries, the international division has been divided into its product components regardless of location. These components are attached directly to the erstwhile domestic product divisions. This change contains many of the potential conflict areas within a single division, and in addition reduces the problems associated with containing product diversity within a single division. Such problems are similar to those experienced by firms that attempted to diversify by-product in the United States whilst maintaining a centralised structure of functional departments.[6] Most of the thirty firms adopting worldwide product divisions were heavily engaged in research and development activities. They were transferring abroad relatively new products for which the technology is still developing, requiring close control and rapid communication among the manufacturing units and the laboratories. The new structure facilitates such communication.

A second strategy of growth abroad is to expand a limited product line into an increasing number of foreign markets. Products for which manufacturing in a large number of markets is justified tend to be mature and technologically stable;[7] marketing being the crucial management ingredient. Since marketing requires a detailed knowledge of local conditions, directives from the head office to the subsidiaries are often inappropriate. The communication requirements in implementing this strategy are, therefore, less than they are for the previous one. The typical structural adjustment to the successful implementation of this strategy is the formation of regional divisions partitioning the world. Product diversity, if it is present in the firm, is largely confined to the United States division and managed by its separate subdivisions. Firms generally make this structural change when the foreign activities are a very large and important part of the overall firm. In fifteen firms choosing this combination of strategy and structure, the international component of each accounted for at least 30 per cent of the total activity, and in some cases more than 50 per cent.

A third possibility is a combination of product and area diversification. One mature product line is extended by manufacturing in many foreign countries, and at the same time newer products are introduced in a limited number of foreign markets. For example, several international food companies that have diversified into chemicals in the United States have chosen to manufacture some chemicals abroad. The typical organisational response to this strategy is to separate the product lines by retaining the international division for the food lines and establishing a chemical division with worldwide responsibilities. Twenty-six firms had chosen this 'mixed' structure by 1968. They adapted the organisation to the needs of the subsidiaries on a product basis with little or no attempt to integrate the diversified product lines on an area basis.

These three structures are used to replace the international division and all have various characteristics in common. They all require more than a single international general manager. Indeed the shortage of such men may often delay the reorganisation until well after the need to cope with the organisational stresses has been clearly recognised. The organisation has to be divided into clearly separated units for which responsibility is assigned on the basis of establishing product differences or area differences as the variable of prime importance. Such organisational choices provide a clear focus for identifying where the conflicts and stresses are to be managed and how performance is to be measured. Each operating division has the minimum possible overlap in responsibility with other groups. Divisional autonomy, however, is often provided at the cost of duplication of effort. For example, a firm with worldwide product divisions can have many subsidiaries in one foreign country, each subsidiary having its own facilities for functions such as law, government and industrial relations that might be shared among all of them. Other costs of these choices have been described in some detail elsewhere and need not be elaborated here.[8] In general, though, firms attempt to develop a form of structure that minimises these costs.

A significant feature of the development of the firms studied is the consistent direction of organisational change. Only a few instances were observed where firms abandoned their international divisions and later reformed them.

These few firms had all had severe problems of profitability abroad; a situation where recentralisation of management attention is a natural response under conditions of severe 'threat'. The implication of this consistency in the direction of chance is that the eighty-two firms that retained an international division in 1968 may be expected to adopt one of the other structures in the future when their foreign operations reach the levels of foreign diversity by product or area that characterise the operations of the firms in stage three.

The three stages in international development correspond closely to the organisational practices that are central to the conduct of these firms' domestic activities. They are based on a number of management principles that are exported with little or no modification. These principles appear in turn to be closely related to the American culture and philosopy of personal behaviour in a managerial context. If comparisons are to be made with European organisation practices these principles and cultural attributes need to be explored, since the procedures by which a given strategy is implemented in an organisation are inevitably influenced by behavioural characteristics of the men concerned.

One author[9] summarised a number of these underlying American management characteristics and discussed reasons for the differences between them and the characteristics of management in other cultures. This agrees with much of the work of others[10] and provides a convenient framework for analysis. The American manager is seen as a man who believes strongly in his ability to determine to a large degree the future fruits of his own labours, who is committed to forward planning both personally and for his firm and who values facts more highly than intuitive judgments. His primary commitment is to the success and growth of the enterprise. He expects promotion on the basis of ability rather than social status, and shares the belief that frequent changes from one assignment to another are stimulating for the individual and productive in terms of training for future increased responsibilities. He considers interfirm mobility to be consistent with his attitude that executives perform a 'professional' service. These management concepts allow United States enterprises to develop into networks of coordinated action and to assume a vitality of their own divorced from the individuals who manage the various intersections of the network. Consistency of behaviour in all parts of the network is vital.

> Enthusiasm for decentralisation rests on assumptions that men down the line share similar *mores* regarding self-determination, hard work, morality of commitments, and the significance of time. If such *mores* prevail then supervision can be general and consultative, instead of close and disciplinarian. The nature of control can become constructive feedback rather than suspicious verification. (Haire, Ghiselli and Porter, 1966, p. 9)

If the *mores* are changed, the shape of the resulting network must necessarily be changed. Transferring the American style of management to other cultures cannot, therefore, be accomplished without major and painful modifications.

These characteristics and *mores* of the United States are usually expressed in familiar operating practices that may be summarised as:

- Unity of command.
- Clear definitions of responsibility, especially between line and staff functions.
- Clear definitions of reporting relationships.
- The setting of detailed budget targets.
- Evaluation of performance by profit performance against budget.
- Rapid promotion patterns.
- The development of large staff groups to process information.

The first three stages of the international expansion are managed largely according to these principles. Firms that have not adapted their basic procedures to the needs of the foreign environment have paid some penalties. For example, American personnel and labour relations policies are a common and expensive source of friction in the foreign subsidiaries. Furthermore in spite of the extreme difficulties of forecasting accurately even twelve months ahead in countries subject to rapid political, social, or economic change, detailed budgets are prepared and executive effort directed towards achieving the set goals. Often in such environments the critical function is not so much the setting of targets but the speed with which the appropriate responses to changed market circumstances are made. An elaborate reporting system may act to delay a rapid re-direction of effort.

Offsetting this penalty is the advantage that, under conditions of rapid executive turnover in the international activities, an elaborate reporting system allows newcomers to become effective in a short time by providing a rule-book of behaviour. Perhaps it was the function of the system rather than inexperience internationally that prompted Max Gloor of Nestlé to observe:

Many American companies seem (here as in other things) to have a tendency to establish and follow gospels, either those of centralised or decentralised management or management by exception or so forth. Being mostly new-comers to international management I guess they have to be more dogmatic and start with certain policies, learn from mistakes and re-adapt them. They have had no time to follow a pragmatic approach.[11]

Such rigidities in the organisation may not be a serious problem when the foreign environments are favourable to American firms, as was generally the case during the 1950s and early 1960s. With an enormous initial advantage over local competition in terms of technology, products and money, the highest degrees of managerial effectiveness were not required in order to generate rates of growth and profitability far in excess of those recorded by the domestic side of the firm. Decentralised operations, often administered by second rate managers[12] working with procedures designed in the head office, were adequate.

In the last few years the international competitive situation has become much less favourable to United States firms. These are now competing fiercely among themselves for the same foreign markets, and competition from local firms has increased. An indication of the degree of this competition is the rapid decline in the profitability of all United States direct investments in Europe from 14 per cent in 1960 to 8 per cent in 1968.[13]

Abandoning the international division and introducing a global perspective to the management task is only one part of the response to these changed conditions. Other responses are common. In more and more firms foreign assignments are now becoming accepted as prerequisites for promotion to the highest executive levels and first-class men are taking over the foreign subsidiaries. These changes in top management attitude have stimulated a far greater effort to streamline the control of the international commitments. Duplication of staff groups that could previously be rationalised by the performance of the subsidiaries is now being carefully examined to find cheaper and better ways of performing the same functions. New procedures are being tried out, often at the prompting of foreign nationals who have risen far on the executive ladder.

In a few firms these new efforts have resulted in further major reorganisations, heralding the emergence of a fourth stage in international development. They responded to the international organisational dilemma that has been expressed as: 'How to provide for functional and geographic specialisation, and for corporate guidance and coordination on a company-wide basis, without blurring lines of accountability and authority, and without impairing the freedom of action and the drive of the executives in charge of the major operating divisions.'[14] These firms were all highly diversified by product abroad and the foreign operations accounted for a very large proportion of total business, usually more than 40 per cent. None of the alternative structures previously described had proved to be a satisfactory solution to the dilemma; each provided clarity of responsibility and authority on one of the dimensions, product or area, at the expense of coordination and clear responsibility on the other equally important dimension.

The reorganisation has taken the form of abandoning the principle of unity of command and establishing a grid structure, in which worldwide product divisions and area divisions are profit centres of equal status and share spheres of responsibility. Functional departments perform a worldwide staff function. This three-dimensional structure reflects the three-dimensional nature of the dilemma. One large chemical firm has even introduced a fourth dimension, that of time, in the attempt to resolve the conflicts of overlapping responsibility. In this firm, the product divisions take prime responsibility for all investment projects with a time horizon of more than eighteen months, and the area divisions have prime responsibility for all operations with a time horizon of less than eighteen months.

The final forms that these grid structures will eventually adopt cannot be predicted yet with any degree of certainty, as they are still in a formative and turbulent stage. New ways of budgeting and controlling, and perhaps even new ways of thinking about the problems, need to be worked out and proven by experience. Furthermore, managers will have to adjust their assumptions about what constitutes the 'American' way of doing business. Yet the fact that these very large firms consider the expense and disruption of further reorganisation to be worth while suggests that others will soon follow suit as they also become highly diversified by area and by product around the world.

One possible alternative to the problems of establishing this multidimensional structure is to choose not to attempt to achieve a full reconciliation of the dilemma. Some firms may value the benefits of executive autonomy more highly than those of full coordination and accept the possible consequences of imbalance among the three dimensions of the enterprise; others may start to divest those parts of the enterprise that are not readily susceptible to integrative treatment. There are, as yet, few examples of this latter course. The Olin (a large international chemical, plastics, metals and paper enterprise) divestiture of its worldwide pharmaceutical business is one of the rare examples. The current difficulties of the American conglomerates may, however, help to reinforce the attractiveness of this alternative.

The European experience

European manufacturing firms have long been actively engaged in foreign operations. Indeed if the proportion of the total assets held abroad is an indication of international commitment, many European firms are far more international than their American competitors. Yet organisation developments that have accompanied their expansion abroad have not followed the American pattern. This is perhaps not surprising, because the management practices and styles used abroad almost of necessity reflect domestic practices; European practices differ in many important respects from American. A brief description of some aspects of European management in its home environment is needed before the international extensions of those practices may usefully be examined.

The wide differences in cultural and social assumptions between the various nations in Europe make single generalisations about aspects of European management behaviour necessarily controversial. Quite possibly no general truths exist. The discussion that follows is intended to provide no more than an identification of aspects that appear to be different on either side of the Atlantic. No attempt to delineate them precisely is made. To make such an attempt would be foolhardy, as some of the available evidence appears to be contradictory.[15] Besides European business practice is in a state of such rapid change that judgments based on data collected even five years ago are suspect in terms of their current and future validity. For example, the changes in attitude in Britain's British Leyland Motor Corporation have been described as follows:

> Until four or five years ago we were a highly authoritarian company. The hallmark of the company style was action; thinking was something you did in your spare time. And as all the important decisions were made by the men at the top there really did not seem to be much point in setting up a management development programme. . . . Over the next five to ten years a steady improvement in the quality of management is going to be of crucial importance in a business which in the past has given the emphasis to engineering excellence. Clearly management training must be given a high priority and we have a great deal of leeway to make up.[16]

The European executive in the middle-1960s was perceived by one writer[17] to have certain distinctive traits. He was more concerned with the past than with the future; he valued wisdom more highly than vitality and preferred values to facts; he preferred experience to training in management; he tended to spend his career within a single company and did not accept that the American concept of job rotation had great value; he disliked egalitarianism among his colleagues; and he preferred thrift and secrecy in his organisational practices. To these traits others may be added. The European manager did not accept the American gospel that all men are created with equal managerial aptitude; social status and, increasingly, education were important prerequisites for promotion to some jobs. There was an acceptance of impersonal regimentation at lower levels of management, and what has been described as 'a fear of the face-to-face situation'.[18] An easy interchange of ideas and plans among men at different levels in the hierarchy was difficult to establish. Furthermore, many Europeans were reluctant to accept business success as their prime goal in life, preferring to retain other cultural ideals of the individual in society.

This perception of the European manager is essentially a caricature. Caricatures are useful nevertheless for highlighting important influences of characteristics that can become obscured in more detailed and comprehensive portraits. Each of the traits above has a bearing on the organisation structures and procedures that are of interest here.

Until recently cartels and a seller's market were pronounced characteristics of the European scene. In such circumstances a historical perspective among managers is hardly surprising as there was little need for investment in expensive forward-planning procedures. Planning where it existed tended to be intuitive, short term in focus and largely production-oriented.[19] The established markets yielded high profit margins and were capable of continued growth; firms could be successful without having to use a complex array of control techniques. In the absence of pressures for planning and control, targets and budgets, the European manager could perform perfectly adequately without the necessity of giving his prime loyalty to the firm.

The most prevalent European organisation structure, the centralised assembly of functional departments, reflects these factors. Such a structure has many bureaucratic features that are congruent with the attitudes of many of the managers. The interdependence of the departments means that it is virtually impossible to assign autonomous responsibility to one man and to measure his performance by results. Promotion tends to be slow and to be contained within a single functional activity.[20] As a result, the senior management group in many firms is dominated by men who have spent many years working together and who have built up close personal relationships. In the absence of a factual basis for evaluating their colleagues, top management uses subjective criteria of evaluation. It has been observed that, even if the functional structure gives way to an arrangement of product divisions, the basic tendency to rely on personal judgments and to put faith in values rather than facts persists.[21] Promotion to the highest levels in the firm can readily be justified on a class or educational basis if the subjective values of senior men are preferred to an objective assessment of a man's performance.

The men at the top of these structures are often relatively free to behave in the tradition of the merchant trader. They make alliances for business purposes, but their stock in trade is a capacity to outbargain and out-manœuvre other businesses.[22] Their freedom stems in part from a sophisticated application of the principle of divide and rule. Their subordinates are experienced in only one part of the general management task, and they cannot do much more than carry out orders.

Once decisions have been made at the top, the functional departments can be enormously efficient in undertaking the necessary actions. Close coordination is possible by means of established hierarchical procedures. Such close coordination is essential in the management of vertically integrated chains of production. Many firms with functional structures have as a result relied on vertical integration as their principal means of growth.

The cohesiveness of the functional structure makes it an inefficient vehicle for the management of diverse activities. The structure has only a single general manager, the president or managing director. It tends therefore to behave in the manner of a single problem solver; problems are dealt with one at a time in some order of priority. When the activities of the firm become diversified, the number of problems requiring decision exceeds the available decision-making capacity. Serious delays and inefficiencies are created as the queue of problems awaiting decision lengthens.

Firms typically respond to this situation by breaking the structure into separate divisions or subsidiaries. Many firms have established a holding company arrangement; the subsidiaries have almost complete autonomy and share with one another only ties of ownership to a common parent firm. Some firms have established divisions in the American fashion, and control the activities of the division through the financial function and procedures for allocating resources on a company-wide basis. This latter group of firms has been a small minority among diversified European firms, but may be expanding.

Integration of the different functions or product divisions is commonly achieved in European firms by means of group or 'collegial' management at the top. These firms have not placed any store on the notion of unity of command. In Germany, the 'Vorstand', and in Holland the 'Directie', are examples of collegial management. In the United Kingdom, it is becoming increasingly common in large firms for members of the Board of Directors to wear 'two hats'; one 'hat' is responsibility for a functional department, the other is responsibility for a product line, group of subsidiaries, or an area of operations.

Decisions in these groups are reached by consensus rather than by personal decision. The individual, however, has considerable negative decision-making powers through the use of the veto. Such a management system tends to slow down decision-making, to favour compromise solutions, and to diffuse responsibility.[23] Yet it can work extremely effectively. Why? The answer appears to lie in well-established personal relationships between the managers so that they can operate on the basis of mutual respect and trust.

The reader should note that 'collegial' management in European firms is fundamentally different from the use of executive committees of senior officers in American firms. In American executive committees, many of the committee members are divisional managers, each held personally responsible for the economic performance of his division. These men have, of necessity, to defend their own interests. The most successful of them have enormous power. Their 'track records' of superior past performance allow them to predetermine to a considerable extent the outcome of the deliberations of the committee. In other words, they have an authority based on achievement that can reduce the function of the committee to that of a rubber stamp. In contrast, the members of a 'collegial' group do not have to defend so vigorously their personal performance. There is the possibility of a much greater exchange of opinion before a collective decision is reached; the committee can act as a decision-maker with far fewer constraints than in the American case.

From a base of centralised, functional structures, many European firms have established large and successful foreign operations. Before the Second World War the bulk of European foreign investment was portfolio.[24] Direct investment, even where 100 per cent of the equity was owned, was not concerned so much with management control as with profitable entrepreneurial ventures. Men were sent abroad and expected to run the business independently, maintaining little more than a dividend relationship with the head office. Until recently it was common for European firms to manage numerous foreign subsidiaries in this way. Uncoordinated arrays of more than fifteen foreign manufacturing ventures were not uncommon in the United Kingdom. Joint ventures abroad were far more prevalent among these firms than was true for the Americans who required greater degrees of control.

The absence of direct control mirrored the pattern of the holding company arrangements for diversified activities in the domestic market; there was no organisational pressure to establish a management system equivalent to the international division. The managers of these foreign subsidiaries were exposed to the general management task far earlier than they would have been had they stayed within the domestic company. With no one at an equivalent level in the parent organisation performing an equivalent function, the managers of the foreign subsidiaries were seldom overmuch constrained by directives from the head office. Although they were often subjected to a constant stream of directives, they could ignore many of them. Many had considerable latitude in pursuing their own product policies, a characteristic that is seldom found in American companies. Training, however, was virtually non-existent; men had to learn from their own mistakes how to run a business.

Recently there have been major changes in the domestic and foreign structures of many European firms. Increasing competition, greater product diversity, the development of foreign manufacturing bases serving more than a single national market, a greater awareness of American methods, and many similar factors have acted to make Europeans start introducing controls, planning, and general management centres at many levels in the firm. They have been adapting the American techniques to suit their style of doing business.

The tradition of working in management groups and the acceptance of multiple responsibilities have allowed firms to introduce new management techniques without building up elaborate staff groups for coordinating purposes. For example, one highly successful and large United Kingdom firm has diversified into six major industry groups and has three-quarters of its turnover outside the United Kingdom. Yet this firm has less than thirty executives, line and staff, in its head office. The long-established working relationship among management groups helps to reduce the need for staff groups, because relevant information can be exchanged rapidly on a personal basis.

The effect of these domestic changes on the international organisation has been pronounced. The increasing awareness of the need for planning, especially on a global scale, has acted to integrate the foreign subsidiaries into the emerging domestic corporate structures. Managers of the foreign subsidiaries are being bombarded with more and more orders, which they can no longer afford to ignore.

The common denominator among these changes is that the links established between domestic and foreign activities do not conform to a consistent pattern in any one firm. They are tailored to the needs of each subsidiary without a single priority among area, product, or function being assigned equally to all subsidiaries.

Naturally the form of the domestic organisation affects the shape of these foreign linkages. For example, where there is dual responsibility between functions and areas in the head office, the subsidiary manager may report direct to several executives. The frequency of his reports is determined by the extent of the operating problems and changes he encounters. The budgets and targets for the subsidiary are established by consensus between the subsidiary manager, the area executive, and the functional executives. The manager of an African subsidiary of a British oil company commented recently that he never knew to whom he was directly responsible. This diffusion of responsibility, he added, did not matter; the system worked efficiently to provide him with all the support he needed for expanding his business profitably.

Flexibility and strong personal working relationships among the executives are critical features of the new structures. They are particularly important in the international sphere where the appropriate responses to events may not be determined easily or rapidly by formal, objective analysis. On this aspect of international management one executive commented: 'There have been moments in our company's life, and they may come again, when the cohesion of the group depended on such [personal] links more than on anything else.'[25]

A further example of how personal relationships can affect the workings of the formal organisation is provided by the case of a German electrical goods firm. Superficially, the structure resembles the American international division alongside domestic product divisions. The divisions, however, share an equal status with the functional departments and there are elements of dual responsibility and authority. One observer commented:

> Rationalising production within the EEC or worldwide is simply not a major problem. The company does not as yet see any need to tie the foreign operations to the domestic product divisions. And the equality of the functional and product divisions, with the lack of clear responsibility lines, causes no particular strains among a management that has worked together for many years.[26]

Although such systems of shared responsibility are probably restricted as yet to the largest of the European-based multinational enterprises, the manner in which they are being developed provides a pointer for the future. The multiplicity of informal links of different kinds allows a firm freedom to expand the many directions simultaneously. Furthermore, the systems appear to be able to tolerate a wide spectrum of different kinds of management procedure. They are based on skills in international management that were acquired many years ago, and do not have to depend on efforts to communicate newly acquired knowledge throughout the organisation. As a result, they have been able to concentrate relatively more attention on developing less formal structures. There is much less need to institute the type of standardisation in management practice that characterises most United States based multinational firms; the adaptations of domestic practice to the needs of complex multinational operations are in some ways less for the Europeans than for the Americans.

To be sure, there are many difficulties in making the adaptations. As European firms expand further abroad and continue to diversify their product lines, the present organisation practices may not continue to prove equally effective. Increasing size and complexity place a heavy burden on informal and personal methods of achieving communication and coordination. The growing body of ambitious young men who do not share a common set of attitudes with their superiors may also help to spur further changes. The establishment of more clearcut allocations of responsibility seems likely to occur.

It is interesting to note that these changes have been occurring during a period when European multinational firms have been growing fast. Although no cause and effect relationships can be established, one can speculate that the ways in which Europeans have traditionally managed their businesses will be an important source of strength for them in managing multinational operations.

Conclusions

Many American-based multinational enterprises are beginning to find that the difficulties of managing complex, multiproduct operations in many countries pose new managerial challenges. For a few firms, these challenges have induced responses that are beginning to break down their adherence to traditional ways of organising and managing a business. By working out ways of sharing responsibilities among managers, by learning how to manage multiple reporting relationships, by modifying standards of measurement to include some of the intangible factors that affect performance, and by increasing their dependence on informal relationships, these firms are moving in a direction in which they are becoming, at least superficially, more akin to their European-based multinational competitors.

At the same time there is evidence that European-based enterprises are themselves changing. They are beginning to adopt many of the American methods of management. Among European firms, those that have expanded widely abroad appear to have moved furthest in the direction of resembling American firms.

Do these directions of change mean that there is a convergence of management practice among United States and European multinational enterprises? At best, the answer to this question appears to be a qualified speculation that, for a handful of the multinational giants, some convergence is likely. Those that have undertaken the strategy of diversifying widely both by product and by area face common problems in their world markets. These common problems will probably induce some common responses, regardless of the national origin of the firm.

Nevertheless, there are many constraints on the extent of any such convergence. National origin will be most likely to continue to affect behaviour no matter how widely the managers are experienced in international business. Besides, the changes observed in the organisation of the diversified giants are experiments; it is by no means certain that they will succeed. Faced with difficulties in implementing new solutions to their problems, some firms may pull back and attempt to use the old methods in management.

Differences in strategic choice will add further constraints on any general movement towards convergence. There is no intrinsic reason why firms facing the same changes in their markets should all choose the same strategies; European enterprises have a perspective that differs from American ones simply because of the location of their headquarters. Very few firms will become so totally multinational in outlook that the location of the headquarters becomes of no consequence in their decision-making.

Although the constraints are formidable, the pressures for some convergence are strong. No United States multinational enterprise that attempts to coordinate the activities of multiproduct subsidiaries scattered around the world can escape altogether the dilemma of how to establish the appropriate blend of policies that allow adequate local autonomy and at the same time provide for adequate control. As they search for ways to resolve the dilemma, these firms would be well advised to take a long, hard look at how European-based firms have approached these problems in the past.

To be sure, the European approaches have not been wholly adequate or successful. The lack of complete success, however, does not mean that such approaches are worthless. On the contrary, they are capable of adaptation on some selective basis to American needs. By learning from European experience and practice, United States multinational enterprises may find ways of dealing with their problems more quickly than might otherwise be the case. Solutions, however incomplete, that are generated in this fashion might also hold a greater promise of success than those generated solely from an internal process of trial and error.

7

Problems in the decision-making process

Objectives and decisions

Consider the following statements:

- A great problem here is that subsidiary managers are barred from promotion outside their national frontiers.
- My plant managers will not observe the rules; they keep bypassing us and going straight to head office.
- I am put in a very difficult position when head office demands that I use my ingenuity to move funds out of this country at a time that is bad for the national economy.

These answers have all actually been given by chief executives of the foreign affiliates of multinational firms in reply to enquiries about their problems. One feature of the three mentioned above is the mixture of motives implied. Ask any of the managers concerned about the principal purpose of their jobs, and they will talk about growth or about the return on the investment at their disposal. Ask them how they think they are being appraised, and nine out of ten reply in terms of similar objectives. But ask them about their problems and many of the replies, like the ones quoted above, have little to do with these purposes and may be at variance with them.

Of course one can argue that, in the long term, to provide greater personal promotion prospects will make the company more profitable. It can also be argued that ultimately the firm's prosperity is bound up with the wellbeing of the countries in which it operates. Notoriously any argument can be turned to any effect by juggling with the time scale. But the problem is often not identified in the same way as the objective. When the manager states that helping to move money out of his country is a problem, he is not thinking of his return on investment, he is thinking of his position as a citizen of a country whose currency is under threat. When he speaks about promotion prospects, he is thinking about his own personal objectives and those of his colleagues whom he has to stimulate. He is talking as an administrator, or at least as a holder of authority, when he talks about problems of communications which do not pass through the prescribed channels.

This conflict of objectives, familiar enough in the domestic company, is considerably exacerbated in the multinational firm. Some of the various goals implied in the quotations may be set out thus:

Objectives of the manager
as company executive—high return on investment; improved growth rate; increased market share.[1]
as local national—the well-being of his country; the promotion of local nationals.
as administrator—the establishment of a neat and efficient system.
as technical expert—contact with the sources of knowledge.

A pressure that is contradictory to any of these different types of objective can constitute a problem in the eyes of an individual manager. The problems here discussed are those that are perceived as such by managers themselves. For present purposes we will assume that a problem exists because someone says it does. In other words, if someone perceives a difficulty, he is in fact indicating that some objective is being thwarted. The objective may be either official or personal, and it may be hard to detect. The purpose, after all, of so much management effort is to reduce the gap between the objectives of the company and those of the individual. Many distortions in the planning and decision-making process arise from this gap. The complications involved in identifying these distortions are greatly increased in the foreign operations. One obvious reason for this is that personal objectives may change from country to country, company objectives will remain the same. But even such a way of stating the issue is oversimplified, because of the difficulty of isolating 'company objectives'. These will themselves emerge as the result of conflicts and pressures within the company. They may be defined by the board, or appear from the firm's activities. They may vary from time to time according to the spokesman. Some judgment, as well as careful investigation, will be involved in any definition of the objectives.

The significance of the conflict of objectives is well illustrated by a firm which will be called for present purposes New World Engineering. This company operated that most obvious attempt to bring together personal and official objectives—an executive bonus scheme. This particular scheme could add anything up to 40 per cent to a man's salary, and was wholly linked to the return on investment recorded by the subsidiary in which he was a manager. The same firm had a global financial policy aimed at minimising taxes and reducing the risk of exchange losses. The policy was carried out mainly by manipulating transfer prices and credit terms between members of the group. Thus the subsidiary in Ruritania, a country with high taxes and a weak currency, was instructed to export components to affiliates in other countries at little above cost price and with a long payment period. The reverse would apply where New World Ruritania SpA was the purchaser from other members of the group. A special allowance was made to compensate for any loss of bonus that would result.

In the event the system appeared to work well, the profitability of the subsidiary was largely maintained while funds were moved out of the country. The local management constantly achieved a high bonus. This continued for some time until the finance director of the parent company became suspicious when a reported drop in Ruritanian prices did not seem to be reflected in the accounts. He sent a team to investigate, and as a result it became clear that the transfer pricing policy had hardly been followed at all, although the instruction about credit terms had. In other words, the local management had made use of an inflationary situation to maintain margins which earned a good bonus for themselves and incidentally satisfied the Ruritanian tax authorities. The instruction about credit terms was more difficult to circumvent, but avoiding the price regulation only came to light in a recession.

What in fact happens in a case like this is that there are two different types of decision-making involved. The *rational*, that is the decision that is thought out in accordance with official company objectives, and the *natural* which develops from other personal aims.[2] These represent two systems of decision-making which together make up the total company system. This distinction between natural and rational systems dates back to two well-known studies of bureaucratic structures.[3] How policies translate into rules and how these rules change, in the furtherance of personal objectives, have been conscientiously traced out in numerous studies. When a business organisation goes international, several new factors exacerbate the interactions which take place between the two systems. The example just given is an extreme one; the rest of this chapter will contain some less sensational but also more common issues.

In the New World Engineering case the process called *rational* results from decisions taken in accordance with stated company policies. The objective was to minimise risks and to reduce the impact of taxes in a difficult market. The other process is called *natural*, because it has arisen without a conscious decision being taken, but in accordance with personal objectives and interests which conflicted with the original intention. The result of this process can be either of two developments. One is the reversal of the original decision in practice, even though the theory may remain the same. The alternative, as in this case, is where the rule is reformulated to block more effectively the natural process. A further effect, in some companies, has been the establishment of yet more coordinators. This seems to underline the point that the natural systems are cheaper than the rational, if they can be made to work to the company's advantage. The coordinators are apt to appear as an expensive way of making a formal system work, with little evidence that to do so promoted any other purpose than administrative tidiness.

Elsewhere in this book strategies of organisation are discussed. Some characteristic problems of different organisational procedures are related to the interaction between the two systems just described. Thus the rational system throws up the international division. This will develop the company's activities abroad, and provide support in the head office for the foreign manager. As so often happens when a specialised department of the company is formed to take over one area of the decision-making process, the natural systems operate to undermine these plans. In this case, the product group managers who are appraised on the performance of their products attempt to sabotage the international division, thus producing expensive problems. In spite of these, the international division may still be the most effective way to promote the growth of the firm abroad, and some statistical evidence suggests this.[4] For where the company operates worldwide by product groups alone, the foreign ventures find themselves with inadequate support.

Hence many firms enter a cycle of organisation and reorganisation, the reasons for which are imperfectly understood. References to a 'shake up' that is alleged to be required 'at regular intervals' may mask a complete bewilderment about how the organisation does in fact respond to change. The case being made here is that much of this bewilderment can be clarified by an understanding of the relationships that develop between the two decision-making systems. Naturally this applies to domestic as well as to multinational firms. But this means of analysis is especially relevant to the firm that operates across frontiers. Reactions to plans and policies can be much more unpredictable abroad than at home, and efficient and economical methods of correcting the problems that arise are harder to find.

The 'decision-making process' is understood to mean all the activities that precede an action within the group, both domestic and foreign. These activities include the making of the first proposals, their examination by the various interests concerned, and the meetings, committees, lobbying, and other pressures involved. Let us assume, for instance, that New World Engineering's Italian subsidiary, NWE Italia SpA, seeks to build a new plant in Palermo. Presumably this has been suggested locally on the basis of criteria that would fit a domestic company, the considerations of a multinational firm are now brought to bear. These will be different in kind. For the rational systems will involve global considerations concerning markets and their likely development, concerning finance together with its availability and cost, concerning production and labour considerations, and concerning other matters like the confidence of the parent company in the local management. The final decision, however, will be strongly influenced by career structures, relative power positions, national aspirations, and pressure groups in the various offices concerned, as well as the lines of communication. This subject will be examined principally in terms of the locus of decision-making; but some attention will be paid to structural issues such as the monitoring systems, the staffing policies, and the planning procedures.

Centralisation and local autonomy

Nothing better illustrates the complex interaction between the rational and the natural systems than the sustained discussions that are held on the subject of the autonomy of the foreign operations. Cases where the rational, thought out, systems decentralise will be examined first. The assumption here is that a decision has been made in the parent company that more autonomy is to be given to the foreign firms. Three questions then arise: Why has this decision been taken? How is it implemented? What are the consequences?

Among a number of firms that had taken such a decision, the most common reasons given were connected with the effectiveness of local management; one firm, for instance, spoke of high turnover in one subsidiary, while four others mentioned lack of initiative and time wasted by unnecessary consultations. Elsewhere problems of recruitment had produced a decision for decentralisation. Some of the companies questioned about this went further in saying that their problem was not to allow managers abroad to take more responsibility, but to force them to do so. Too many decisions were being referred back to head office.

The expenses of communication, the danger of slowing down essential decisions, increasing sophistication in the local subsidiary, and the need for more sensitiveness to the local market were among other reasons given for a measure of devolution. In our original sample, directors and senior executives at head office almost invariably said that their policy was to decentralise. However, a smaller number of companies have since come to light which have said 'centralising' and said it convincingly.

There are several ways of implementing a decision to decentralise. One of these is to notify local managers that the discretion limits on their spending have been raised. This is simple and straightforward, but may not achieve its objectives. Another way is to produce a manual setting out precisely which decisions still have to be referred to headquarters. This appears to some, especially British, executives to be an unnecessarily elaborate and time-consuming exercise; but at least a clear statement of which decisions are to be taken where allows further changes to be made as they become possible or desirable. Experience has shown that unwritten procedures can be more inflexible than written ones. The manual can be amended; whereas rules that are known but not codified in this way can be much harder to change. It has also been observed that a manager's autonomy can be very tenuous if it is not underpinned by a written agreement. This may be a point in which the foreign is in a different position from the domestic manager.

Where rational systems decentralise and natural centralise

The situation whereby head office decides on decentralisation, and what happens in fact is a greater measure of centralisation, is more common than the opposite state of affairs. This has been suggested in other studies. For instance a report of the British Trades Union Congress has said: 'Subsidiary companies may often say that decisions are taken at the centre (overseas), and at the centre, companies often claim that decisions are taken by their subsidiaries.'[5] One reason for this could be bluff. A company usually has to present an appearance of dealing at 'arm's length'[6] with its subsidiaries for a number of legal and taxation purposes. It may be necessary to establish, among other things, that the foreign affiliate is a subsidiary and not a branch. But this appearance of delegation is not always intended to be taken seriously by the foreign managers. Indeed one of the problems of studying how the decision-making works is precisely the difficulty of knowing when to take words at their face value. Many firms have some sort of code whereby the subsidiary can recognise what is a mandatory instruction in a letter that is couched in terms of advice. While it is necessary for the researcher to learn this code, it is not always clear to the foreign company just how strong some recommendations are.

Apart from the possibility of bluff, there are many reasons why centralising trends develop where the reverse is intended. Many of these arise through officials in the subsidiary seeking a closer link with the parent company. But, whether they arise at home or abroad, most of the reasons point to some specialist 'central services' department as being involved, and taking decisions at home that are supposed to be taken abroad. This can arise because the local expert is more interested in having contact with the source of knowledge, and with those who share his skill, than with those who share his nationality. This is the issue that has been called the 'problem of the two headquarters',[7] and arises when a company establishes a strong national organisation in a foreign country as part of a policy of decentralisation. This is a policy which has many advantages. The local company operates with the minimum of expensive supervision, it develops close to the market, it recruits able local nationals, it is not a foreign firm to the government, and it has a better chance to build a secure place in the local industry. But it can only be a strong national subsidiary if communications and control links with the group are channelled through the national headquarters. This means limiting the right of the operating units, both manufacturing and marketing, to make direct contact with the foreign centre of the company. But as soon as these units begin to grow, they will outgrow the scope of the local headquarters. As a result the systems will become inadequate for the managers in the operating units, who will be faced with two headquarters to deal with. The procedure is sketched out in Fig. 7.1. They are likely to prefer the international for reasons

(a)

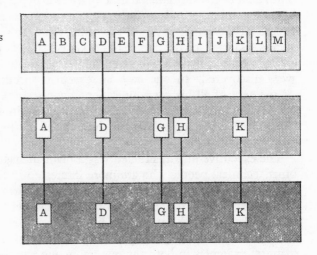

Head office	contains numerous technologies for products and for production
Foreign Subsidiary Head office	of which some are available here
Operating units	and are used here

(b)

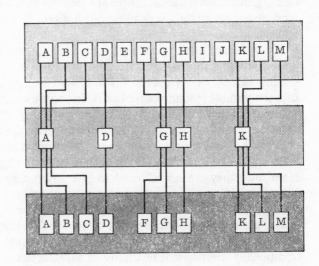

Head office	
Foreign Subsidiary Head office	
Operating units	

A B C = product groups in a company

7.1 (a & b)   The problem of the two headquarters: This system may be adequate and workable but it will always be under strain, for the managers in the operating units may well wish to contact the international headquarters. The system begins to break down as the number of technologies used abroad grows, see (b).

already suggested, the knowledge and skill they need are to be found there. The result is that the national headquarters is bypassed and weakened, and the operating managers are referring decisions to the parent company which should have been taken locally according to the rules. A process of centralisation is taking place in spite of the declared policies of the company.

The evidence for this will be examined again later, but numerous examples were discovered. In one case an executive produced evidence that over 75 per cent of all his communications bypassed the national centre. He was proud of having manœuvred himself into this position which, needless to say, constituted a major problem in the eyes of his immediate superior in the national subsidiary.

The executive just mentioned was a plant manager, but examples exist of other technical people who are more interested in the links of specialisation than in those of nationality. Thus, in another firm, the industrial engineer at one plant found means of acquiring contact with his head office, and his communications with the national headquarters were eventually limited to the minimum of official reporting. This phenomenon is not limited to technical matters; examples in both the marketing and the personnel fields have been discovered. The common characteristic is that regulations about communications through the national centre are resisted as bureaucratic and irrelevant; local managers actively seek to establish direct links which gradually become stronger.

The problem of the two headquarters is naturally confined to the larger, more mature subsidiaries; but these are just the ones where head office usually affirms that a decentralised system works. The more common way that the natural systems centralise is through the activities of staff managers at head office effectively revoking an autonomy that their superiors have granted. This is a variant of some long-recognised problems of staff-line relations.[8] There are central services departments at head office with a strong interest in ensuring that techniques they have developed are used worldwide. Nominally they are not allowed to give instructions, but in practice there may be many ways in which they can bring pressure to bear on the foreign subsidiary as on the line managers at home. Frequently subsidiaries mentioned tactics used by the central services to ensure that they took part in the global use of new techniques in marketing and personnel as well as in the more traditionally centralised functions. These tactics range from emphasising that the parent company expects all the subsidiaries to adopt their methods to implying the dangers of refusal. The company which gets into trouble while pursuing head office instructions is obviously in a stronger position than the one which strikes problems when following different policies. This consideration alone makes it likely that the subsidiary will follow head office, whatever the problems caused by using large firm methods in the small affiliate.

A more subtle form of centralisation is a consequence of the information flow. In order to operate their techniques worldwide, the central service departments seek to acquire ever greater quantities of information. This collection is burdensome to the smaller subsidiary, and tends to force changes in its structure to meet the demand for information from the centre; these changes may not meet the needs of its own local market so well. The process can be seen by an examination of the subsidiary organisation, which demonstrates how alterations have occurred in response to the flow of communications from headquarters; it can also be seen in the use of foreign techniques by the local firm. Frequently it can be shown that, although the parent company denies any effort to influence these matters, the subsidiary does in fact follow the central policies. Hence its decision-making can hardly be called independent.

One example of this from outside our evidence is a survey of personnel policies in Japan. This survey brings the function which is always said to be the most autonomous together with the country that insists on local participation and other safeguards of independent decision-making. In this situation it is shown that there are yet considerable differences between the personnel policies of Japanese companies and those of foreign firms in that country.[9]

Numerous other less dramatic examples could be quoted. For instance, in one firm it was said that the local subsidiaries were intended to be completely identified with the local economy and the local culture. So long as a satisfactory account was given, showing both profitability and development, there was no interference. Nevertheless it was found that subsidiaries did conform closely to head office patterns in that company. The stated policies were reversed by the pressures of the experts at the centre, and the demands of the information system they had established.

Thus in every function examples can be found of how new management techniques influence the level of decision-making. These may be costly and elaborate, and once devised they will be placed at the disposal of the whole company. Indeed one of the advantages of the multinational firm should be that the smallest subsidiary has access to the latest innovation, which it could not possibly develop on its own. In view of this, it might be questioned why decentralisation is considered so desirable. The answer to this lies in a number of assumptions that are generally believed. One is that managers perform better when given greater autonomy, and that in particular this is true of foreign managers. This belief is the main reason why efforts at decentralisation are so commonly made in spite of the practical difficulties. The evidence is as yet unclear and the same facts have been interpreted in contradictory ways. It is likely that the relationship between autonomy or the reverse and successful performance depends on other factors such as education. This is discussed more fully in the next chapter.[10]

Sensitiveness to local conditions is a phrase which carries political as well as economic overtones. In fact it would appear that centralised decision-making is becoming a political issue in many countries. Examples have been noticed in Germany and France; and in Britain the Trades Union Congress report already quoted has queried the consequences for their members of decisions taken abroad. The ability of the foreign firm to ignore national aspirations is bound eventually to reach a limit of tolerance. Hitherto the advantages that the company brings have been far clearer than the disadvantages. Host countries have received much-needed capital, and with this has come know-how, employment and other contributions to the standard of living. But now the losses are becoming apparent too. The local capital markets are losing some of the most desirable stocks, research effort is being stifled, money is being moved out of the country at times of financial crisis, national trading policies are being frustrated. Some of our evidence suggests that where these things are happening, they may happen in spite of and not because of the official policies of the company. Hence greater attention to the short-term reformulation of official policies may well be to the advantage of firms as a hedge against political insecurity.

Where rational systems centralise and natural decentralise

This is the rarer situation simply because the belief in autonomy is strong. Nevertheless centralisation often appears to be more logical. Press an executive as to why he advocates decentralisation, and most of his answers are vague. They rest on assumptions already mentioned about the motivation of the foreign manager; only recently has the influence on political risks begun to be considered. On the other hand there are some clear and tangible advantages of centralisation, such as the rationalisation of production across frontiers. Benefits like this and the possibilities of global financial planning persuade a few companies to adopt a strongly centralised system. Where this happens resistance may be encountered within the group, but this does not change the system. Indeed the official line can be said to have been modified only when it meets government resistance in a local country. Thus General Motors operates a centralised policy throughout the world, but the attractions of the Japanese market have been strong enough to punch a hole in that policy.

In this and other ways, like the loss of skilled managers, official centralisation has its problems and may become unworkable; but the reaction to it is different from the reaction to official decentralisation as already described. Resistances are built up and strains can be identified, but there is not the same growth of an unofficial system reversing the original intention. One generalisation that also follows, but has not yet been mentioned, is the relationship between the degree of autonomy and the type of organisation. If this is geographical, that is to say the main reporting lines are through managers with regional or national responsibilities, then the decentralisation is made easier but the other problems become more difficult. We have already seen that this type of company can be shown to grow faster under certain circumstances.[11] The product group organised company normally produces a minimum of national autonomy, indeed where a substantial measure of independence is obtained this leads to other problems.

The last paragraph demonstrates one of the links between structure and centralisation. Examination of subsidiary reactions shows that usually the company with more levels of management also appears more centralised. Although organisation and autonomy come in different decision-making systems, the connection between the two must be noted. At this point, it is worth while to examine the facts which underlie these generalisations.

The measurement of centralisation

The facts on which the last two sections are based are not as precise as would be wished, and it is hoped that techniques will be developed to make them more exact. For instance, the evidence for the statements about the problem of the two headquarters rests largely on managers' perceptions. These are only reliable within broad limits. Notoriously people exaggerate some activities and understate others, and the more varied a man's activities the more likelihood there is of inaccuracy. In a study of the lower levels of a management hierarchy supervised by the present author, two different ways of measuring the allocation of time were compared. One was the respondent's own perception of how the working day was spent; the other was done by a researcher over a six-week period.[12] In this case the similarities were greater than expected, but they would be likely to diminish given the more complex programme of the senior manager.

Even allowing for inaccuracies, however, the statements about the two headquarters are clear. For instance the most recent example discovered came to light when a manager in a national head office described the difficulty of enforcing rules about communications. He pointed out exactly what has been said above, namely that a plan to decentralise the company by national unit was being frustrated and the authority of the national management undermined by the short-circuiting of the formal links. This effectively meant that decisions that had been delegated to the subsidiary were once again being taken at head office. Operating managers in the same company unwittingly confirmed this. A figure of 90 per cent of correspondence with head office, leaving only 10 per cent with their national superiors, was agreed. Even allowing for considerable inaccuracy, the extent to which the operating unit has established a close link with the parent company contrary to the declared aims of the latter is obvious.

If the perception of the managers concerned is one means of establishing what is actually happening, another way of determining the degree of centralisation is by measuring the outward communications from head office. In one firm where postal and telex messages were analysed for a specimen month, the proportion of mandatory to other communications was just short of 16 per cent ($n = 439$). The other principal categories were advice apologies, information, routine requests and acknowledgements. This type of analysis showed a higher flow of mandatory orders than had been expected, and there is reason to think that the same will be found in other firms. Two other surprising features found in this particular firm were that mandatory instructions were being sent out by five different levels of personnel at head office, and that they were not related to the degree of industrialisation of the host country.[13] On the whole this evidence confirms other indications that statements such as 'we leave them to settle their own affairs' are not justified; and hence failure cannot be ascribed to such policies.

Perhaps the most accurate way of determining the degree of centralisation is to examine where the most significant decisions are taken. This implies the resolving of two problems—how to decide which are 'significant' decisions, and how to distinguish between where the decision is officially and where it is actually taken. When these two problems have been settled there is the further problem as to whether some 'centralisation index' for a company is feasible, or whether a separate calculation is needed for each subsidiary. Since practices vary widely within a firm, it would seem that the latter is more meaningful; but this in turn leads to a problem of generalisation. On the whole it would appear that some centralisation index by country or by part of the world, based on level of industrialisation, would produce the most meaningful results. This would answer questions about how much decision-making was done outside a particular country, and it would also be possible to trace relationships between the degree of centralisation and the growth and profitability of the firm and its staffing problems.

Existing tools are too blunt to meet these requirements fully, but appropriate methods are being devised; meanwhile statements like 'more centralisation' or 'more autonomy' are bound to contain a large measure of judgment. In considering the degree of centralisation in a given firm in this study, all the relevant facts have been collected and then some assessment has been made as to what the result would be of a measurement of the degree of autonomy. The generalisations made in this section, therefore, rest on this judgment.

Monitoring systems

Methods of reporting are discussed elsewhere and the object of this section is simply to examine the effects that the different means used to watch the foreign subsidiary have on the decision-making process. The reverse of the previous part, this section deals with the feedback which can be the reverse in another sense too. A company which has developed an efficient monitoring system may feel able to allow more local autonomy. At least there is a quick awareness of the onset of difficulties, and a connection between autonomy and feedback has been suggested; but the balance of our evidence suggests that a heavy reporting load is in fact seen as a removal of independence by the subsidiary managers. They do not act independently under these circumstances. Indeed the quantity of reporting was a main complaint in local companies who frequently claimed that this distorted their activities.

A particular cause of complaint was that head office was demanding information which the subsidiary did not need for its own purposes. Like many such complaints, this was expressed strongly in a limited number of companies. Indeed evidence from forty groups, in which questions were asked about this, only showed seven where the subsidiaries alleged that they were being forced to submit information that they did not need for themselves. In four of these there was a difference of opinion between the local and the parent company as to how much information the affiliate did in fact need to run its own operation. It was said that subsidiaries were often bad judges of this, and that a reduction in the amount of reporting simply led to inefficiency.

Evidence of how concerned subsidiaries are with the reporting systems was shown in one company by the results of a questionnaire which asked how the system was working. Among replies from twenty members of the group, three said that all was well and that they had no comment to make; five others made miscellaneous points including proposals for further diversification. All the other twelve answers concerned problems with the reporting system. The complaints included comments on excessive requirements of a too detailed nature and the implied lack of trust in local personnel.

While every company has some regular reporting, at least of the most significant financial data, some companies have devised more subtle monitoring systems to give maximum results with minimum formality. One company reserved very few decisions to head office, and did not keep a large enough staff there to interfere with local autonomy, but did insist that internal auditors from the centre were used throughout the group. They regarded this as an effective and economical way of monitoring the affiliates without elaborate reporting systems. More obvious ways were visiting, meetings, and the circulation of minutes. There was also great emphasis on speed of feedback in some firms.

The use of the computer is having considerable influence on the monitoring systems and the way they affect the decision-making process. However, at the time of writing, the actual effects fall far below those predicted. Indeed the progress of computerisation has been very slow indeed. For instance a company which announced plans for global production scheduling by computer in 1966 reported in 1970 that these plans had been postponed indefinitely. By the latter year, the number of on-line links had increased enormously; but these were being used for routine communications, rather than as aids to decision-making.[14] It looks as if the latter use will have to await a new generation of managers. What can be said now is that the technology is neutral. It can demonstrate the local problems more convincingly at the centre, and give the subsidiary manager the materials for more realistic decision-making; but present evidence does not show this to be happening. On the contrary it suggests that mechanisation and centralisation still go hand in hand. Quicker feedback removes the problems of central decision-making such as the lack of relevant information. In sum, despite the claims and predictions, greater opportunity for concentrating decisions at the centre leads to just this concentration.

Whatever is likely to happen, the influence of personal contact stands out clearly. The common belief that there is no substitute for constant visiting does seem to be borne out. The companies that reported the highest growth rates usually also showed a high level of executive travel. This suggests that the real problems of a reporting system may be that it is too impersonal. The effects of the visiting are not just that the foreign managers are stimulated by personal contact, although this would follow from other research on motivation, but also that policies are more readily understood in personal terms. The depersonalisation of communications is a problem that is particularly significant in the multinational firm. But there are other ways of tackling this problem than constant visitors from head office, and one is by closer attention to staffing policies.

The influence of staffing policies

One British company in 1968 made eight appointments at board or divisional board level. All the eight men involved had joined the company as graduate trainees. That may represent a rare degree of stability these days; it also represents a long-standing tradition in a firm which has modernised itself and consistently reports higher-than-average growth and return on investment at the same time. The tradition is that knowing the company is one of the most important qualifications of a manager. This particular firm has existed for 200 years, and has been multinational for most of them. For much of its history very few other qualifications were required.

This, then, is one way to staff a company—with an emphasis on knowledge of the firm which enables informal procedures to be used. These days, of course, many other qualifications are also required; but knowing the way around is still given high priority among some of the largest concerns. The alternative is to make a proportion of appointments from outside, bringing in fresh experience and insights. This is likely to be accompanied by a more formalised system of decision-making. Both methods have their problems when applied to international operations, and both make their characteristic impacts on the overall system. Let us examine some of the ways in which this happens.

The informal method suits the company with a high proportion of expatriates. These will usually have started at headquarters and hence know the company thoroughly. Once abroad, they know the limits of their discretion and know whom to consult. The organisation works to a regular, clearly understood system which often proves to be less flexible than it looks: the heavy reliance on informal procedures may be rigid, just because of the lack of written rules which can be amended more easily. Where such systems arose without conscious thought, the reduced use of expatriates has forced companies to think out their policies. One possibility is then to go over to a wholesale decentralisation; this is unlikely to happen for reasons that have already been suggested. If a measure of centralisation is to be retained, the alternatives are either to turn to a highly formalised system with detailed operating manuals, or to move foreign managers around the company before they take charge in their own countries. A refinement of the latter alternative is the development of an international grade of management, in which successful executives in any country become globally available. There are problems to this, such as obtaining work permits in many countries, but these do not outweigh the advantages.

If centralisation is going to remain the norm, then international avenues of promotion are likely to become more and more important to enable companies to recruit and retain able personnel. Higher standards of education and competence in host countries are going to mean that foreign executives will not remain content with permanently subordinate positions. This is a constant theme among subsidiary managers. At the same time, as has already been suggested, global promotion is difficult to organise. More important for future policy-making are two predictable consequences of international promotion schemes. One is that effective decentralisation will become even less likely, as there will be greater concentrations of talent at the centre. Add this to the fact that the multinational company tends anyway to recruit internationally minded people, and the chances of problems with host countries are clearly increased. The other consequence is that what we have called 'natural systems' will produce rigid career patterns based on the initial experiences of those who benefit from the global promotion. Management development schemes are always liable to produce rigidity. This observed fact no doubt arises from the way career expectations are built up and become self-perpetuating. This is a significant difficulty of managerial planning, and ties up with other problems of forecasting and strategy.

Planning

In this chapter we are not concerned with the technical aspects of this subject, but with the part that planning plays in the way decisions are reached throughout an international group. In this context there are three types of planning:

• that which is arrived at by a process of assessing long-term prospects at head office, broken down into products and areas, and then imposed on the subsidiary. This may include more or less discussion with the local companies, but on principle the inputs to the process and the criteria for making choices are decided by the parent company.

● that which is arrived at by a process of examining and coordinating plans put up by the subsidiaries. Again the amount of stimulus and discussion may vary, but in general the initiative is expected to come from the periphery and towards the centre.

● that which is arrived at by a process of discussion and negotiation, whereby the general principles of the plans are agreed at each stage by representatives of all the units involved. Clearly the parent company stands in a position of power, indeed the chairman of one firm which operates this way found it necessary to state publicly that his company was not 'a democracy'. Nevertheless planning decisions are made as a result of formal meetings held between the chief executives of operating subsidiaries, both domestic and foreign.

The implications of these different approaches need to be examined more closely, but for present purposes it is sufficient to point out that this third method is a serious attempt to avoid undue domination from the centre. For planning, like computerisation, is usually regarded as an expert function using esoteric tools little understood by subsidiary managements. It thus becomes a strong implement of centralisation, and frustrates moves towards national autonomy. This question is examined more closely in chapter 9.

Conclusion

Some ways by which the rational and natural systems interact have been demonstrated. The discrepancies between the two systems arise as the result of differing objectives within the company, the pursuit of personal and national aims alongside the official purposes of the firm. Ways of bringing these closer together and avoiding some of the problems are becoming more sophisticated in some of the multinational companies under examination.

The facts mentioned in this study have shown the difficulty of determining where a particular decision is, as well as where it should be, taken. If the policy that decisions should be taken as near as possible to the point of implementation is regarded as a starting-point, then two considerations alter this. One is the pressure for links between skills, the other is the usual method of promoting global planning and rationalisation. Both these problems have been resolved by individual companies, and it would seem to follow from our evidence that the problems are more related to attitudes to decision-making than to difficulties inherent in the situation.

These considerations suggest that companies would do well to examine more closely the decision-making process. The recommendations that arise from such an examination need to take special account of the importance of local autonomy for a number of reasons: personal and political, the need to bring together conflicting objectives, the necessity for centralisation in decisions which involve complex technologies or the introduction of new managerial techniques. These considerations would seem to suggest a fresh breakdown of the management structures, but something along these lines is happening anyway. Many decisions cannot be contained within geographical or product group boundaries. A reappraisal of what are properly national functions and what are most suitably internationalised would still leave some political problems. The dominance of foreign firms in technologically based industries would, for instance, still place limitations on the national research effort. But at least a greater openness about this would enable an informed debate to take place as to the balance of national advantage.

Considerable ambiguity in the decision-making process has been demonstrated, an ambiguity which is not necessarily met by more formal regulations, but may be more effectively countered by changes in organisation and staffing arrangements. For instance, a restructuring of the central services departments to make them small, highly specialised teams of expert advisers may prevent some of the creeping centralisation; but then such changes also raise the question whether some of these departments are required at all, or whether their advice is not better bought from outside.

A method of overcoming many of the problems outlined would be the establishment of international project teams within the company. These could be set up to examine fresh opportunities as well as persistent difficulties. They could consist of representatives of the various subsidiaries and operating units as well as the parent company, and they would have power to carry out solutions as well as to investigate situations. One side effect of this would be more movement around the company without attendant difficulties. For appointment to a project team would need to be prestigious and highly paid enough to make the system effective. This would mean the temporary release of senior managers from the subsidiaries. They could be replaced from elsewhere in the company on a fixed term basis. Like other situations where project groups have been developed, these would be oriented towards action rather than inaction. Hence they would also help to overcome the forces of inertia within the large organisation.

This system would produce its own problems, for instance company politics might be reflected in the project groups and make agreement sometimes difficult. But these and other likely difficulties should not be insuperable, and a skilful construction of the teams should be possible to meet them.

8

Communication, culture and the education of multinational managers[1]

France, Britain, Israel and the United States: different communication patterns

The existence of different patterns of communication in different countries has often been suggested, but seldom systematically investigated. For greater precision it has been necessary to develop a new analytical tool—the *communication diagram*, or *communicogram* as it is now called. This makes it possible to discern and analyse one of the basic differences in managerial structure between different cultural environments, namely that of communications behaviour. This use of the communicogram became evident by coincidence rather than through testing hypotheses concerning management communication. In 1966 a group of students carried out a communicogram study under the supervision of the present author. The study was conducted in three organisations, one British, and two French; this was done simultaneously with another which explored the relationships and attitudes of the same managers of these organisations who were included in the communicogram study. The chief executives of all three organisations had been promised that they would receive not only the results of their own respective studies, but also a comparison between themselves and the other two organisations. However, when the recorded interactions were fed into the computer, it turned out that while the total number of interactions in the British organisation for the fifty participants during two weeks was 2639, the equivalent number of interactions for the 21 and 26 participants of the two French companies were 128 and 215 respectively, too small for analysis.

When the British chief executive was presented with the results of his organisation, an apology was made for not being able to provide him with a comparison with the two French organisations, on the grounds that the French managers failed to report their interactions. He replied: 'The reason is quite clear to me—they just do not interact orally.'

He was right. Going back to the individual Daily Interaction Sheets, it was discovered that while on each British sheet there was an average of some 15 interactions per person per day, only 2–3 interactions per person per day

Table 8.1 Comparison of self-recorded interaction studies in six organisations in four countries

Type of organisation	Industrial: plastics	Marketing: pharmaceutical consumer	Industrial: electronic components	Industrial: aircraft production	Army: ordinance	Education: management development
Data studied Country Year	USA 1959	UK 1966	FRANCE 1966	FRANCE 1966	ISRAEL 1969	UK 1971
No. of managers approached	50	60	26	21	48	32
participated	34	50	26	21	41	27
Length of study (no. of days)	10	10	10	10	10	10
Oral interactions with other participants Total reported	1708	2639	128	215	672	1272
% mutually perceived	26%	14%	17%	21%	7%	38%
Daily average per person	5·0	5·3	0·5	1·0	2·6	4·7
% of interactions by telephone	22%	45%	73%	29%	19%	14%
Face to face	78%	55%	27%	71%	81%	86%
Consensus as to type in mutually perceived interactions	47%	35%	46%	73%	50%	43%
Source	(Weinshall 1966 and 1968b)		(Weinshall, 1970)		(Tzirulnitsky 1969)	(Weinshall, Beal and Silver, 1971)

appeared on the sheets of the managers in the two French organisations. The number of reported interactions with other managers participating in the study being usually about one-third of the total recorded interactions, corresponds with the results of 5·3 interactions per person per day in the British organisation and 0·5 and 1·0 interactions in the two French organisations. The results of the studies in four countries are shown in Table 8.1. It can be assumed that the degree of oral communication is not only a function of the cultural environment but likewise of the managerial structure, as well as of the type of business. The communicogram results are considered separately for the individual organisations in each of the four cultural environmental settings, trying to segregate the cultural effects from the effects of managerial structure and type of business.

THE UNITED STATES

The study was carried out in the Devon Corporation which has been described in detail elsewhere.* A surprising discovery, demonstrated by the 'Industrial plastics' column in Table 8.1, was that only 26 per cent of the recorded interactions were mutually perceived. In other words, only 26 per cent of the recorded interactions with other participants in the study were reciprocated by those other participants. However, this low rate of mutually perceived interactions turned out eventually to be the normal rather than the unusual.

We can see that 26 per cent is exactly the average between the two British organisations (14 and 38 per cent), somewhat higher than the rate in the French organisations (17 and 21 per cent) and much higher than the Israeli organisation's rate of 7 per cent.

We shall see in the ensuing sections that other communicogram results of the United States organisation were also similar to the results in other organisations, except for the 'Daily average oral interactions per person', on which we shall elaborate in the following section regarding the French organisations.

FRANCE

All comparisons as to other data studied in the United States, British and Israeli organisations are overshadowed by the relatively very small amount of oral interactions in the French. Indeed some of these comparisons are invalid because of the small and statistically insignificant numbers of interactions. Nevertheless it is interesting to note that in the Aircraft Production organisation, where the variations in the manufacturing were larger than in the Electronic Components one, the per cent of face-to-face interactions (71 per cent) was significantly higher than in the other French firm (27 per cent). This should give us some indication as to the effect of the type of organisation on communication behaviour.

THE UNITED KINGDOM

The two organisations studied were of completely different types, one in education and the other in marketing. Nevertheless both were service organisations and both had a strong research orientation. It seems that the difference in type of organisation between the two explains the significant difference in the face-to-face interactions (55 per cent as against 86 per cent). The significantly lower rate of those mutually perceived in the marketing (14 per cent) when compared to the education (38 per cent) follows the pattern noticed in the United States company, namely that agreement as to the occurrence of interaction is higher in face-to-face interactions, when the participants see each other rather than only hearing each other's voice on the telephone.

*(Weinshall, 1960)

ISRAEL

The figures in this column seem to be dominated by the fact that this is a military organisation. This is especially evident when one considers the daily average oral interactions per person (2·6). The managerial structure of this organisation, measured by an informalogram,[2] was discovered to be similar to the structure of the French industrial aircraft production organisation—to which it is closest in the rate of oral interactions (1·0 as against 2·6). Based on various phenomena of organisational and social behaviour, one could expect Israeli oral communication to be as high as that of the United States. Indeed in both the percentages of face-to-face interactions and in the consensus as to the mutually perceived interactions the Israeli organisation's results are the closest to the United States. This is why the results in the Israeli organisation seem to indicate strongly the effects of the type of organisation, rather than the cultural effects on communication behaviour. It could be that the low percentage mutually perceived in the Israeli organisation is indicative of the high bureaucratisation of the military which is used to written communication and therefore perceives low oral communication.

COMPARISON

Looking at Table 8.1 as a whole and comparing the six organisations to each other, one is repeatedly drawn back to the 'Daily average per person' row. This seems to be the most meaningful measurement by which to compare one organisation to the other.

The cultural effects on communication are not measured by themselves, and there is a relationship to the type of organisation and to the type of managerial structure. However, even in the communication behaviour of people in this small sample of organisations, different from each other in type and structure, the difference between the United States and British organisations on the one hand, and the French organisations on the other, is unmistakable. So it is useful to discuss the difference in the oral communication between the French organisations and the Anglo-Saxon ones.

A low rate of oral interaction is indicative of the high rate of written communication. Indeed, the higher the bureaucratisation of the structure the more the written communication. However, bureaucracies in different cultures such as those of the United States and of France behave differently and have different rates of oral and written communication. The reasons why such cultural differences evolved have probably to do with the fact that French organisational culture has been influenced by and derived from organisations such as the Catholic Church, the army and the government. In the United States, on the other hand, organisation culture has been more affected by the development of business organisations which have influenced the Church, the army and governmental organisations, rather than the other way round.

Therefore, while the degree of formalisation is an indication of managerial structure, it is also an indication of the cultural effects on management. This is to say that if two identical organisations had been compared as to their scope of decision-making and as to their managerial structure, but operating the one in France and the other in the United States, a significantly higher oral communication would have been found in the latter. The other finding is that comparing oral communication in the three Western countries of the United States, the United Kingdom and France, the United States and the United Kingdom figures are found to be similar to each other (4·7, 5·0 and 5·3 interactions per person per day, respectively), while the French figures (0·5 and 1·0) are significantly different.

The proximity of Britain to the United States rather than to other European countries with regard to managerial behaviour has already been found by others in connection with managerial attitudes and decision-making processes.[3] The almost indentical rate of oral communication in Anglo-Saxon organisations on both sides of the Atlantic Ocean is another indication of the cultural affinity between the United States and Britain.

These differences in oral versus written cultures appear in other areas related to the manager's work, whether within or without the organisation. Education and teaching is an example. The learning processes in the United States are much more participative than those in continental European countries. Professors in France or other continental European countries hardly ever see students out of the classroom, and within the classroom hardly ever hear what the students have to say. Britain, again, is more like the United States than its European neighbours in that the faculty is closer to the students, through tutoring and other means. Indeed even the ability of the Anglo-Saxons to spread among the nations and the emergence of the English language as the universal tongue could be attributed to a great extent to their abilities and aptitudes in oral communication. National differences in communications patterns would seem to be the basic and probably the most important cultural characteristic to be overcome in the education of multinational managers.

Let us now turn to some other cross-national differences bearing on multinational management.

Other national differences bearing on multinational management

Four areas in which national differences occur are education, social stratification, organisation structure and spoken language. These are not the only areas which affect management and in which one would find national differences; nevertheless these four, along with communications, seem to be the most predominant in so far as they affect multinational management.

Other areas influenced by cultural values, though sometimes crucial for multinational managers, seem to be of secondary importance when compared to the ones chosen for discussion. One such additional area is that of competition and profits, the attitudes to which differ substantially from one culture to another. Attitudes would, likewise, differ substantially with regard to what one might call business morality. This includes such matters as bribery, which in some countries is regarded as outright corruption and in others is accepted. The degree of government intervention and the extent to which this is considered tolerable is another factor which it is important multinational managers should take into account.

The national differences discussed concern primarily countries which belong to what one could refer to as the 'Western culture countries'. This excludes completely different types of culture like, for example, that of Japan. If we had included Japan we would have had to consider the totally different 'business ideology' of that country, when 'ideology' is defined as 'any system of beliefs publicly expressed with the manifest purpose of influencing the sentiments and actions of others'.[4] This term 'business ideology' is used throughout one recent description of the Japanese managerial system.[5] In this the personal and cultural background and practices of Japanese management are summarised for a period of over one hundred years. Communications, education, social stratification and organisation structures are covered together with a comprehensive discussion of the historical development of Japan's business ideologies. This whole study shows that the ways of thinking and the decision-making process are being conducted in an environment that is in no way derived from Western culture. Hence the following discussion will only be concerned with Western types of behaviour, to which the references to Japan are incidental.

EDUCATION

The suggestion has been made that the availability of higher education in a country determines its economic growth.[6] This theory is hard to verify because of the differences in educational methods between different countries. Some of these differences affect management style more clearly than the general amount of education available. For instance the difference between the French approach and that of the United States can best be described by saying that one is dogmatic and the other is pragmatic. The French approach is Cartesian, and stands for the most systematic and quantitative assault possible on every problem, while taking into consideration all factors which may influence it. The Americans, on the other hand, are more interested in the usefulness of the result than in the theoretical side of the method used to approach the problem.

Thus, if the same problem is presented to a French and to an American businessman, the former is liable to discover, say, twenty factors which influence it, think of about fifty alternative solutions and attempt to find the connection between them. Each alternative would be weighed in the light of the conditioning factors. The American, by contrast, would probably look for the three main factors which influence the problem and take these into consideration. He would then decide on, say, five alternative solutions and evaluate them in the light of these factors. This simplified description points, to a certain extent, to two different ways of thinking; but first and foremost it shows that there is a basic difference of approach to problem analysis, which has its source in the differences in the social, cultural and educational values of the two peoples. Many Frenchmen regard the Americans as efficient and successful economically, but they despise them for what they consider to be their superficiality. Many Americans, on the other hand, regard the French as being highly cultured and educated, but despise them for their supposed inefficiency, disorder and uncleanliness. It is precisely their tendency to specialise—which is so often incompatible with a broad outlook—which seems to enable the Americans to attack their business problems so efficiently. A broad outlook, on the other hand, and a knowledge of the culture of the world, while they may confer an ability to see the whole picture, also give rise to a tendency to include more and more factors in the analysis of a problem.

The separation between faculty and students, of which the French universities have been an extreme example, has been made possible by both the teaching method and the design of the physical facilities. The professor enters the lecture hall from another door than that used by his students and confronts a crowd of hundreds, usually in a hall originally designed to contain a much smaller number. He delivers his lecture, often read from the paper and repeated from year to year with modifications, without enabling subsequent discussion. The students perceive this way of teaching, in many instances, as the pronouncement of the gospel in whatever field of learning this may be.

The physical design of many French universities prevents the faculty from meeting their students out of class, even by chance. Separate facilities exist for faculty and students in their restaurants, toilets and even in their lifts and staircases.

While continental European universities prefer a separation between faculty and students similar to the one described in France, British universities advocate a certain degree of cooperation. This is mainly practised out of the classroom in the so-called 'tutoring'. Members of the faculty, usually junior members, coach the students on the material covered in class, or any other additional material. The consequence of this cooperation *out* of the classroom is that there is also a fair amount of participation inside the classroom.

The third learning method advocates, in principal, cooperation between the faculty and the students both in the classroom and outside. This method originated in the United States, but is spreading quickly to other countries, especially countries like Israel where the ties with cultural tradition are not as strong as those in western continental Europe.[7]

The purpose of graduate studies in management and business administration is the academic training of managers for middle and higher management levels in economic and public organisations. The former include industry, agriculture, banking, insurance, transport, tourism and other services. The public organisations are governmental, military, municipal, other public services and trade unions. Graduate management studies are not for the training of professional people who might serve public and economic organisations in fields such as engineering, chemistry, law, economics and others. Their purpose is to train people who might fulfil management functions. The training includes finance, control, production, marketing, research and development, personnel, as well as a synthesis which combines all these and is called 'business policy'. As every one of the managers in charge of each of the above-mentioned functions has to be in a permanent relationship with the other functions of the organisation, every manager has to receive a thorough and all-round training in them all. In the modern organisation the proportion of professional people is increasing from year to year. There are those who believe that within twenty years the number of professional people in an industrial organisation will exceed the number of non-professional.

The manager, who has to be a professional himself, finds himself in charge of one or more functions, each of which involves knowhow at an academic level, and many of his subordinates are professionals too: auditors report to comptrollers, economists to finance managers, marketing and research people to sales managers, engineers and scientists to the research and development and production managers, sociologists and psychologists to personnel and manpower managers.

This means that the manager in the modern organisation has to have a profession *before* he becomes a manager. In many cases, a man acquires a managerial position by working himself up one of the 'functional channels'. Thus, for example, a man starts as a junior engineer in a certain organisation, progresses through the various stages of engineering and production and becomes manager of the production or research and development division. When he reaches management in this way, he is well acquainted with his function but does not always know how to manage it. This is why we sometimes lose a good engineer and gain a bad manager. In other instances, an old-time engineer (or old-time auditor, economist and so on) will receive management training through advanced management courses or by way of a graduate school for management, usually being sent and paid by his company for this long leave of absence. Yet not every student training for management has to travel through this lengthy practical route along one of the 'functional channels'. He has to have previous academic training, meaning a bachelor's degree, so that he will have the educational ability to know how to study what is going on in the organisation. His bachelor's degree might be in any field.

The case studies included in the learning programme are usually chosen so as to ensure coverage of various situations that have occurred in recent times in business and other organisations which might employ new managers after their graduation. The length of the 'recent times' depends on the circumstances and especially on the rate of the technological changes which dictate the conditions under which the executive operates. The cases studied today in good graduate business schools generally describe situations which have occurred since the Second World War, namely during the last thirty years. Most of the cases cover a period of the last ten, and sometimes of only the last five years.

The background material, readings, seminars, reports, business games and all other teaching media complementary to the case method, are usually based on the problems to be encountered in the cases. This is why the material studied is very rarely out of context with the situations in which the manager might expect to find during his career. In addition it has been suggested that there is a need for fictional cases, based on expectations of future managerial situations. Such opinions are prompted by the increasing rate of change occurring in organisations today. Thus, for example, even the study of business history is only carried out in relation to those themes that have a direct bearing on what is happening in present situations, and are important for the actual performance of the manager's functions. Such an approach results in a large economy of the students' time. These points are relevant to the training of all managers. However, the participative learning method is of special importance in the training of multinational managers, who will have to operate in different sociocultural environments.

The possible effects of higher education on multinational management have already been discussed. We have, however, to realise that management is composed of and assisted by people who do not necessarily have a university education. Let us therefore consider the degree of secondary education, in several countries. Table 8.2 shows the percentage of seventeen-year-olds in secondary education in different countries.

The following table means that many jobs which are held in Western Europe

Table 8.2 Availability of education in various countries

	% of 17-year-olds in secondary education* (in early 1960s)	% of 20–24-year-olds in higher education (in 1966)	% in higher education of those with secondary education (2) (1)
Britain	56	5	9
Holland	41	n.a.	n.a.
Israel	27	13	48
USA	70	24	34

* including secondary vocational education

by those with secondary educations are held in the United States by university graduates. In Israel, on the other hand, there is a severe shortage of secondary school graduates. A typical example of the different type of people used for the same type of job in the various countries is to be found in secretarial work. Following the differences appearing in Table 8.2, in Western Europe secretaries generally have a secondary education; in the United States they have at least a secondary education and there are many who have had a higher education. In Israel, however, the secretary with higher or even secondary education is the rare exception and most of them have only finished elementary school.

SOCIAL STRATIFICATION

The differences in learning methods in different countries seem to be related to the degrees of social stratification existing in the countries. Israel, which could be considered to be the least socially stratified country in the world, has also democratic and participative learning. This follows the United States, which is the least socially stratified of the larger Western democracies.

One way to measure social stratification in a country is by considering social mobility in that country. Table 8.3 presents the inequality of opportunities in various countries. The countries can be divided into five groups, moving from those with the lowest to those with the highest inequality ratio.

Table 8.3 Educational inequalities

Inequality ratio	Countries
Less than 250	Israel (Haifa), Great Britain, USSR (refugees)
250–299	Australia, Denmark, France, India, United States, Brazil, Sweden, Holland, Japan
300–499	Norway, West Germany, Puerto Rico
500–799	Hungary, Finland, Italy
More than 800	Belgium

$$\text{Inequality ratio} = \frac{\text{Non-manual worker sons of non-manual worker fathers}}{\text{Non-manual worker sons of manual worker fathers}}$$

Source. Bendix and Lipset 1966, pp. 582–601.

The effects of social stratification on the management of national and multinational companies in the different countries are dramatic. Some of these effects carry through from elementary, secondary and higher education right to the positions into which people are hired in business organisations. Let us consider the cases of Britain and France.

There is still a correlation between the social class of candidates in both countries and their chances of being admitted into Oxford and Cambridge or the *grandes écoles*. Nevertheless, the admission to these universities is based more and more on achievement rather than on family background.

Similarly to those who graduate in the United States from, say, Harvard, the graduates of Oxbridge and the *grandes écoles* are preferred over other university graduates. At this point, however, the similarity between Oxbridge and the *grandes écoles* ends.

In Britain and in the United States the companies are seeking to employ the top graduates. In France those who are recruiting from the *grandes écoles* are the previous graduates hired by the same organisations, and they usually go all out to hire from the same school as the one from which they themselves graduated. Thus if you meet in a certain organisation with a top executive from, say, the Haute Ecole de Commerce, there is a good chance that most of the graduates in the organisation are from that school.

Another difference between university alumni in the United States and British as against French organisations is an extension of this relationship between university and job. In the Anglo-Saxon countries a degree from a 'good' university helps to get a first 'good' job, but from then on performance is more important for progress; in France, on the other hand, previous performance has a much smaller significance throughout a person's career. Once a person has graduated from a *grande école* he has in the great majority of cases made it for life. He could be a complete failure, but usually the alumni of his own school would make sure that his career progresses as if nothing had happened. Thus in France one's objective chances to succeed throughout life are much more related to one's education than in Britain.

In Britain the custom of many companies of placing in positions like the board of directors only members of the higher social classes has been gradually disappearing, while it is still common in France. There are still in existence French companies who would not hire a top executive into formal positions of 'directeur', somewhat parallel to a vice-president who is a member of the board of directors, unless he belonged to one of the so called '200 best families' of France. Strong social stratification is evident in other Western European countries as well. In some of them this social stratification seems to be even more polarised.

In most of these countries such things as the way of addressing people in business organisations, and the times at which these people arrive at work and leave it, change according to their social and organisational positions. Thus, while in the United States people usually address each other by their first name whatever their rank, in Western Europe the form of address usually changes from level to level, and is different in both directions between two people in two different organisational levels. Again, while it is customary in the United

States for everybody to arrive at work at the same time, though higher ranking executives may leave later, in Europe the higher the person in the organisation the later he often arrives at and leaves work.

ORGANISATION STRUCTURES[8]

Organisation structures are related to the sociocultural environment and the emerging educational patterns in the different countries. There is a direct connection between the ability of the organisations to grow, to innovate and absorb new technologies and their propensity to change and adapt their managerial structures to the growing need to absorb broader decision-making processes. However, every managerial structure requires a different type of manager and therefore managers have to move from one company to another. Alternatively they could be transferred from one part to another, if the organisation is large enough to contain different types of structures within it.

The sociocultural environment affects the processes of growth, change and mobility in several different ways, but primarily in the way that new generations of managers are being educated and formed. The preparation of the new type of leader required for a new type of managerial structure takes at least one generation. Fifty years ago the United States had a very few people who could become chief executives of decentralised structures. However, as the educational system became more participative and to some degree permissive, more and more decentralised leaders were emerging out of American families and educational institutes.

Taking France again as an example, there are few of what might be called 'decentralised leaders' in the country and therefore few decentralised structures. As a result organisations cannot absorb broader decision-making processes than their functional structures permit. This fact hinders developments in more advanced technologies, more diversified product lines and more international activities.

Another environmental effect on the dynamics and adaptability of managerial structures is the 'anti-mobility value' to which we shall return at some length. This anti-mobility value is a constraint on the interorganisational mobility which is required in order to enable the progression of management from an entrepreneurial structure to a functional one and from there to a decentralised system. The anti-mobility value is quite powerful in European countries. It, likewise, almost completely freezes any movement of managers between organisations in the large corporations of Japan.

However, the appearance of the so called multistructure organisation has enabled countries with strong anti-mobility values to bypass the necessity of interorganisational mobility. It is interesting to highlight two points regarding the anti-mobility value and the evolution of large Japanese multistructure organisations. The anti-mobility value was inculcated into Japanese business only just before the First World War, in order to stop the enormously high interorganisational mobility which existed at the time and thought to be contrary to the Japanese aspirations of growth and technological progress.[9] Until now a very strict anti-mobility value has been preserved only among large Japanese organisations. However, in the smaller ones, where interorganisational mobility is a condition for their survival through a progression from one managerial structure to another, such a mobility exists.

Countries with cultures permitting the establishment of multistructure organisations are able to bypass the anti-mobility value by means of arranging a systematic managerial mobility not between one organisation and another, but rather within the various parts of the same organisation; such multistructure organisations are in existence in both the United States and Europe. However they are of special importance for European countries where the anti-mobility value is quite strong. Not all Western European countries have welcomed the appearance of very large business organisations through growth, merger and acquisition.[10]

Managerial structures can be measured and established by way of the degree of autonomy, centralised or decentralised, and the degree of clarity, informal as against formal, in the existing relationships between the managers of organisations. However, the degree of clarity is not only related to the managerial structure, but also to the culture in which the organisation operates. This culture is determined by the country in which the organisation functions and the field—business, political, military and so on—in which it operates. Therefore when one is measuring the relationships in order to establish the managerial structure of an organisation, one should be aware of different flavours of relationships describing essentially the same types of managerial structure. Thus an entrepreneurial structure of a French organisation could be expected to be more formalised than a similar structure in an American organisation; and functional structures in France would be more 'bureaucratic' than the same structures in the United States. One of the reasons for these differences is the relative degree of usage of oral and written communication in the different countries, which has already been discussed.

CONCLUSION

The differences in education, social stratification, organisation structure and spoken languages are interrelated with each other and connected with the differences in communication patterns in the various countries which we discussed in the previous section.

Generally speaking we could say that the more democratic the culture of the country is, the more one would expect to discover in it participative learning methods, low social stratification, decentralised organisational structures, free mixing with other nationalities and linguistic ability. The world is moving very fast to the merging and unifying of cultural behaviour, social structure, organisation practices and language. However, some countries are moving faster than others.

Cross-national values, norms and attitudes

Certain values, norms and attitudes arise from the communication patterns just described, and are in turn subject to influence by multinational education. When a group of people from a variety of countries are gathered into the same formal organisation, they bring along with them all the differences in communication behaviour, education, social stratification, organisation structure and national spoken languages which have already been discussed. Nobody could better describe the consequences of such a gathering than the author who wrote about the construction of the Tower of Babel:

> Once upon a time all the world spoke a single language and used the same words. As men journeyed in the east, they came upon a plain in the land of Shinar and settled there. They said to one another, 'Come, let us make bricks and bake them hard'; they used bricks for stone and bitumen for mortar. 'Come,' they said, 'let us build ourselves a city and a tower with its top in the heavens, and make a name for ourselves; or we shall be dispersed all over the earth'. Then the Lord came down to see the city and tower which mortal men had built, and he said, 'Here they are, one people with a single language, and now they have started to do this; henceforward nothing they have a mind to do will be beyond their reach. Come, let us go down there and confuse their speech, so that they will not understand what they say to one another.' So the Lord dispersed them from there all over the earth, and they left off building the city. That is why it is called Babel, because the Lord there made a babble of the language of all the world; from that place the Lord scattered men all over the face of the earth.[11]

One has only to consider a 'language' in its wider meaning and exchange the type of organisation from one of construction to, say, a military one defending the Western democracies or to political ones preserving the health and culture of the world. This quotation would then be transplanted from over twenty centuries before Christ to the twentieth century after.

The educational study for this paper was among the students of the European Institute of Business Administration at Fontainebleau (INSEAD). This began with an attempt to find out how they differ from each other when they come in. The differences examined were partly their background characteristics: age, nationality, marital status and first university degree. They also included attitudes towards problems related to multinational management, to business and to business education. The differences in values, norms and attitudes of the students were found to be mainly the consequence of their national background, and only to a lesser degree related to other background characteristics.

The data relating to the pre-INSEAD values, norms and attitudes have been collected by way of two methods:

- General attitudes—gathered through a so-called INSEAD motivation questionnaire.
- Attitudes regarding the anti-mobility value—gathered through reactions to the Jim Fairfax case.[12]

Let us consider each of these methods and their findings separately.

GENERAL ATTITUDES

A motivation questionnaire has been administered to the INSEAD students at varying intervals in every academic year since 1965–66.

Table 8.4 includes an analysis of responses to six selected alternative answers, analysed according to the dependent variables of national complexity,[13] age and marital status. Thus, for example, the first answer selected is that of the 'American ways and approach to business administration', which is one possible answer to the question 'What attracted you in coming to INSEAD?' This was the first choice of the respondents when choosing from among nine possible answers. While age did not affect the answers and marital status affected them only to a small degree, the responses were significantly affected by national complexity. Seventeen per cent of those not nationally complex chose this answer, while only 11 per cent of the nationally complex group did so. The explanation for this difference seems to be that the nationally complex group is less interested in the career aspects of the INSEAD studies.

Table 8.4 suggests that the background characteristic which most affected the participants' attitudes was their national complexity, marital status came second and age last. It can likewise be seen that the more nationally complex the participant's family, the more he expresses international attitudes and is inclined towards multinational companies. Married participants generally manifest the trend in their attitudes as participants with nationally complex families; but this does not always happen as is shown by attitudes towards the 'International composition of participant body' where the trend is reversed. Similarly, young participants express more internationalist attitudes than older ones.

The other background factor which was tested as to its effects on the attitudes and motivations of the students was their length of stay outside their native countries. It was discovered to be an important factor in that the longer the stay of the participants outside their countries, the more 'international' their attitudes. However this finding, as well as the previous ones, was based on a comparatively small sample; it requires additional exploration.

Table 8.4 Selected answers from 'The motivation of INSEAD students', questionnaire according to national complexity, age and marital status

Question	Selected answer	National complexity		Age		Marital status		Total student body	
		None (%)	Complex (%)	Low (%)	High (%)	Single (%)	Married (%)	This Ans.	Out of (no. of choices)
a. What attracted you in coming to INSEAD?	The American ways and approach to business administration	17*	11*	16*	15*	16*	13*	1st choice	9
a. What attracted you in coming to INSEAD?	International composition of participant body	11*	15*	14*	10*	16*	4*	2nd choice	9
d. When you chose INSEAD, what did you primarily want?	Go to an international school	23	35	28	25	24	38	2nd choice (26%)	2 (100%)
e. When you find basic fault in things that happen in your country—what do you do?	Non-conformists ('Speak to people in my own country about it even if they are not close friends', and more drastic reactions)	69	61	70	66	70	64	4 last choices (68%)	7 (100%)
f. What do you really want to do in the future?	Work in a large organisation†	8*	12*	8*	6*	8*	2*	3rd/4th choice	9
h. How much of your spare time did you spend with those participants not from your country?	The greater part (during the last term)	43	50	46	40	45	38	1st choice (44%)	4 (100%)

* This is a 'positive percentage', which is arrived at after the percentage of 'Least attractive' is subtracted from the percentage of 'Most attractive'. The percentages in this row are also 'positive percentages', arrived at after subtracting 'the least' percentage from 'the most' percentage.

† Perceived by many participants to be a multinational corporation.

ATTITUDES REGARDING THE ANTI-MOBILITY VALUE

Differences in interorganisational mobility are likely to account in some degree for the varying amounts of success that business and other organisations have in absorbing innovations and new technologies, as well as in competing and surviving. Interorganisational mobility has to occur within all the human factors comprising the organisation which include the customers, the shareholders, the bankers and the workers. However, the most crucial human factor as far as interorganisational mobility is concerned is the management. It is important that the styles of leadership of the managers should comply with the structure required to handle the full range of the decision-making process

Table 8.5 The anti-mobility value—reactions to the Jim Fairfax case

a. The original results

	Distribution of choices	
	French (managers) %	American (board-members) %
a. Fire (sack) Jim Fairfax	2	80
b. Appoint him as chairman of the board of directors	28	—
c. Leave him in his present position but appoint one or more deputy managers	22	—
d. Remove him from post and appoint him as consultant to the company	26	—
e. Other alternatives	22	Almost none were mentioned

b. INSEAD'S results at the beginnings of academic years*

Class	Total of participants	Those who decided to 'fire' No.	%
1969–70*	214	11	5
1970–71*	223	20	9
TOTAL:	437	31	7

* The statistic u of the Poisson Approximation to the Normal Distribution is 2·279, making the difference between the two classes (1969–70 and 1970–71) in those favouring firing significant at better than the 5 per cent level.

c. Reactions at INSEAD—arranged by countries (ordered by favourability towards firing Jim Fairfax)—for the two groups at the beginning of 1969–70 and 1970–71

Country	Total of 1969–70 and 1970–71	
	Total of participants	Those who decided to fire (%)
Subgroup 1		
1. USA	7	29
2. Israel	8	25
3. Spain	8	25
4. Italy	9	17
Subtotal:	32	Subtotal: 25
Subgroup 2		
5. Sweden	9	11
6. Great Britain	43	9
7. France	104	9
8. Norway	16	6
9. Germany	78	5
10. Holland	29	3
11. Switzerland	39	3
Subtotal:	318	Subtotal: 7
Subgroup 3		
12. Belgium	23	0
13. Austria	15	0
14. Denmark	7	0
15. Lebanon	7	0
16. Luxembourg	7	0
Subtotal:	59	Subtotal: 0
Total:	437	7

Notes. Only those countries with seven or more participants have been included; this accounts for the totals not corresponding with the subtotals. The statistic u of the Binomial Approximation to the Normal Distribution is 4·76 for the difference in the subtotal for groups 1 and 2, making it significant at better than the 1 per cent level, and for the difference between subgroups 2 and 3, tested by the Poisson Approximation, $u = 4·86$, and the difference is therefore significant at better than the 0·5 per cent level.

at every stage of its development. Companies are constantly growing, in terms of the scope of their decision-making process, in order to meet their competition. They therefore have from time to time to adapt their managerial structures. These changes involve an exchange of managers, because the styles of leadership required in each managerial structure are different. Often this means managers changing companies. However, when the firm is very large in its scope, it can adopt several different managerial structures at once. This multistructure system makes possible mobility within itself and does not require movement from one company to another.

The difference in the rate of managerial mobility as between the United States and Western Europe has already been discussed earlier in this chapter. Differences in the rates of managerial mobility extend from countries with almost no mobility at all, like Japan, through countries with very little mobility, like France, and those with growing mobility, like Britain and Germany, to countries where the anti-mobility cultural value almost does not exist, like the Soviet Union and the United States.[14]

A test of the anti-mobility value in French culture occurred when the case of Jim Fairfax was given to a group of French managers. The results appear in Table 8.5*a*.

Next to the distribution of the responses of the French managers appears the *actual* vote of the American members of the board of directors of this company, who considered all the four first alternatives, but voted only on whether to fire Jim Fairfax, a motion which obtained approval from 80 per cent of those present. The French managers gave to this alternative only 2 per cent while the remaining responses favoured almost equally any one of the other four alternatives: (appoint as chairman—28 per cent; appoint as consultant—26 per cent; leave him, but appoint deputy managers—22 per cent; other alternatives—22 per cent). This is almost as if the French respondents were saying—'as long as you do not fire him, we don't care what you do. We have therefore chosen at random one alternative from among the solutions which would enable us to retain Jim Fairfax.'

This case study was therefore chosen as a tool for measuring the attitudes of the INSEAD students towards the anti-mobility value. When this was first used at INSEAD, it was only towards the *end* of the academic year 1968–69 and it constituted part of an examination in the field of business policy. However, since then the Jim Fairfax case has been administered to the students at the very beginning of every academic year.

Table 8.5*b* presents the results for the INSEAD classes of 1969–70 and 1970–71. The main finding to be drawn from this table is that the 1970–71 class had a significantly higher percentage of students who chose the solution of 'Fire Jim Fairfax' (9 per cent), than the class of 1969–70 which preceded them (5 per cent). Assuming that these two classes were equally representative of the cultural values existing among the nations from which the INSEAD students are drawn, one can discern a shift away from this anti-mobility attitude. More people were ready to accept interorganisational mobility in 1970 than in 1969.

The second analysis which was made of the same figures was by lumping the 1969–70 and 1970–71 figures together and dividing them according to the students' national origins. The countries were grouped into three subgroups, according to the percentages of those who chose the 'Fire Jim Fairfax' alternative in each group (17–29 per cent subgroup; 3–11 per cent subgroup and 0 per cent subgroup). When doing so it was found that the countries in subgroup 1 included the United States and three out of four Mediterranean countries. The one excluded was Lebanon, which could be because of the influence of French culture in that country. Subgroup 2 included some of the more economically advanced and more homogeneously cultured countries of Europe, while subgroup 3 included countries with somewhat mixed cultures like Belgium and the Lebanon as well as subcultures of countries in the previous group. These explanations should be regarded as hypothetical and to be explored in future research, in which the growing numbers of respondents from individual countries would enable statistically significant comparisons between single countries, rather than between subgroups of countries.

SUMMARY

One dominant factor which accounts for the differences in the attitudes between a conglomeration of human beings gathered from a variety of nation states is their affiliation to the culture of their countries. The difference between people with regard to communications, education, organisation structures, and spoken languages originates from the different cultures of their countries of origin. We have surveyed in this chapter some background characteristics of people which tend to *counter* their national attitudes. This we did by exploring the characteristics of those who manifest internationalist attitudes, as distinguished from attitudes one would expect from non-internationally inclined students who come to INSEAD. The small sample which has been analysed hitherto could only lead to some indications rather than to definite conclusions. The findings of this small sample indicate that two of the most important background factors which are conducive to internationalist attitudes are the national complexity of the student's family, usually when his wife comes from a different national origin, and the length of time he has spent outside his own country. We then regarded the attitudes of the students at the very beginning of the year towards the anti-mobility value, by way of asking for their reactions to a case study in which the attitudes towards interorganisational managerial mobility are cardinal when the student's decision is made. We found that the average anti-mobility attitudes decreased from 95 to 91 per cent, from September 1969 to September 1970. We likewise analysed the subgroups of countries from which the students expressed similar degrees of anti-mobility attitudes. These ranged from the sub-group including the United States, Israel, Spain and Italy, which averaged 75 per cent with anti-mobility attitudes, to the sub-group including Belgium, Austria, Denmark, Lebanon and Luxembourg, which expressed 100 per cent anti-mobility attitudes.

The effects of multinational education

Having discussed the cross-national values, norms and attitudes of the students who come to a school like INSEAD for multinational education, let us now consider the effects that this type of multinational education has on both their attitudes and social relationships.

In spite of the relatively short period of exposure to the educational and social experience of INSEAD, the findings of the research project show a marked effect on the attitudes and relationships of participants. The findings concerning these attitudes and relationships towards the end of the year at INSEAD will be presented separately for the three phases of the research: general attitudes, attitudes towards the anti-mobility value and the social structure of the students.

GENERAL ATTITUDES

In part B of the questionnaire the respondents were asked to rate the various countries and fields of study represented at INSEAD with regard to the degrees of mixing with students from different countries and backgrounds, their contribution to the learning process and how much they benefited from it.

The various countries and professions were subsequently ranked on each of the three scores: mixing, contributing, receiving. The results are presented in a graphic way on the two parts of Fig. 8.1. Thus, for example, in Fig. 8.1a Belgium scores the highest on mixing, is the third in ranking on contributing and in sixth and seventh place together with Italy on receiving. The average rank order of Belgium is therefore 3·5.

Because of the small size of the class of 1965–66, there were only 100 respondents. This is why the findings presented on the two charts of Fig. 8.1 should be considered as tentative rather than conclusive. Examining only the three largest groups represented that year at INSEAD—France, Germany and Great Britain—in their rank orders on the three parameters we find:

| | Detailed rank orders (RO) | | | Average RO |
	Mixing	Contributing	Receiving	
Great Britain	3	1	1	1·7
France	11	2	5	6·0
Germany	12	4·5	3	6·5

While the British students were perceived to be very high on all three parameters, the French and German students were perceived as the lowest

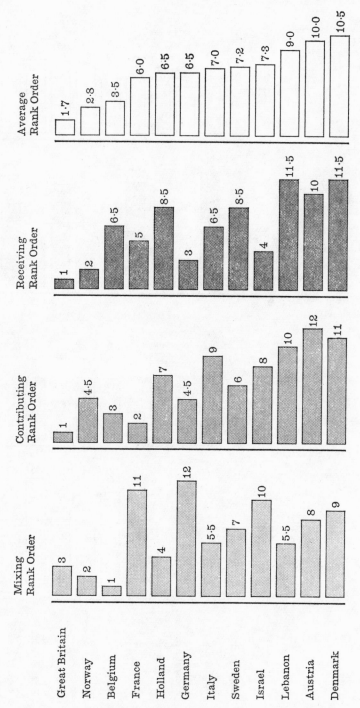

8.1 (a) The effects of the participants' mentioned origins on their studies.

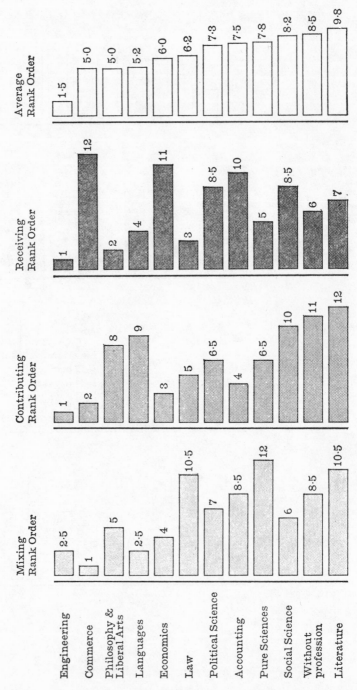

8.1 (b) The effects of the participants' professions on their studies.

on mixing, but relatively high on contributing and receiving. On the whole contributing and receiving are perceived as more closely related to each other than either of them is related to mixing. Generally speaking when students from one country are perceived to be highly contributing, they are likewise perceived to be highly receiving (profiting from the educational process). Mixing is not perceived to be necessarily related to contributing or receiving.

These tendencies do not recur when the mixing, contributing and receiving of the professions are charted. The largest student groups were those with degrees in engineering, commerce and economics. The following are the rank order scores of these groups:

	Detailed rank orders (RO)			Average RO
	Mixing	*Contributing*	*Receiving*	
Engineering	2·5	1	1	1·5
Commerce	1	2	12	5·0
Economics	4	3	11	6·0
Average commerce–economics	2·5	2·5	11·5	5·5

Comparing the engineering with the average of the commerce–economics groups, we see that in mixing the engineering graduates are just between those with commerce degrees and those with economics degrees. The engineering graduates contribute more to the educational process than their colleagues with commerce and economics degrees, who immediately follow them in the highest contributions. As to receiving, profiting from the studies, the engineering graduates are perceived to be the highest. Those with degrees in economics and commerce are ranked lowest on receiving. This probably means that the INSEAD studies were perceived to be closely oriented towards commerce and economics, but also to require a high degree of knowledge in quantitative techniques.

These were the perceptions of the 1965–66 respondents as to the relative positions of the three largest national groups (France, Germany and Britain) and the largest professional groups (commerce, economics and engineering), when measured by the parameters of mixing, contributing and receiving. When asked 'To what background factors do you think that mixing or not mixing internationally could be attributed at INSEAD?' they ranked the six alternative factors presented to them in the following order:

1. Mastering the required languages.
2. Being married to another nationality.
3. Having parents of two different nationalities.
4. Social class.
5. Nationality.
6. Profession.

We have already seen that 'being married to another national' does indeed account to a large extent for the 'international' attitudes and motivations of the INSEAD students. As for the national origin having a larger effect than the professional background on mixing or not mixing internationally, we shall see that this is borne out by the social structure which will be discussed later.

IDEAS ABOUT THE ANTI-MOBILITY VALUE

The Jim Fairfax case was first applied in research with the INSEAD students at the end of the academic year 1968–69, as part of a written examination. The results of this were compared with the results of the administration of the Jim Fairfax case to the students at the beginning of the following year, 1969–1970. It was found that the percentage of those who chose to fire Jim Fairfax at the *end* of 1968–69 (33 per cent) was almost *seven times* more than those who chose to fire him at the beginning of 1969–70 (5 per cent). This comparison appears on Table 8.6a country by country.

Table 8.6 Changes in the anti-mobility value—changing reactions to the Jim Fairfax case

a. From the end of one year to the beginning of the following year

Country	End of 1968–69		Beginning of 1969–70	
	Total of participants	Those who decided to 'fire' (%)	Total of participants	Those who decided to 'fire' (%)
1. Norway	3	67	7	0
2. Germany	35	37	39	3
3. France	50	34	45	7
4. Austria	6	33	8	0
5. Switzerland	12	33	23	4
6. Great Britain	16	31	21	10
7. Holland	9	29	14	17
8. Italy	9	29	3	0
9. Belgium	8	13	15	0
Total	164	33	214	5

Notes. Only includes countries in which there were at least three participants in each of the two years. Hence 'total' varies from sum of countries shown.
  The difference between the 1968–69 and 1969–70 totals gives a value of 6·8 for the statistic u of the Binomial Approximation to the Normal Distribution and it is therefore significant at better than the 0·5 per cent level.
  In the cases of France and Germany, the differences between the two classes in those favouring firing, when tested by the Binomial Approximation to the Normal Distribution, give u values and significance levels the same for both countries namely 5·7 and better than the 0·5 per cent level respectively. The differences could not be tested for other individual countries, because the numbers involved were too small.
  The total includes all thirty-seven countries.

b. From beginning to the end of same academic year

Country	Beginning of 1970–71			Towards end 1970–71		
	Firing		No. of	Firing		No. of
	%	No.	participants	%	No.	participants
1. USA	50	2	4	50	2	4
2. Israel	33	2	6	50	3	6
3. Britain	9	2	22	39	7	18
4. Luxembourg	0	0	3	33	1	3
5. Sweden	0	0	3	33	1	3
6. Italy	22	2	9	29	2	7
7. Norway	11	1	9	29	2	7
8. Germany	8	3	39	21	5	24
9. Switzerland	0	0	16	20	2	10
10. Austria	0	0	8	17	1	6
11. France	10	6	59	12	5	43
12. Holland	0	0	15	8	1	13
13. Belgium	0	0	8	0	0	5
14. Denmark	0	0	4	0	0	4
	9·1%	20	220	20·3%	35	172

Notes. Only countries with at least three participants in beginning and end of year; arranged by the percentage of the 'firing' at the end of the year.
The total includes also participants from another eleven countries with less than three participants at the beginning and/or end of year.
   (a) Difference between beginning and end of 1970–71 is significant at the 2 per cent level when treated by the Binomial Approximation to the normal and at the 1 per cent level when tested by the Sign test for two related samples.
   (b) Difference between beginning and end of year—significant at better than the 3 per cent.
   (c) Difference between beginning and end of year—significant at better than the 0·5%.

The following academic year of 1970–71 enabled the researchers to compare the change which occurred within the same class over a period of about seven months' studies at INSEAD. The findings appear in Table 8.6b. We can see from Table 8.6c overleaf that the distribution of 'firing' by countries at the ends of the two years are of a bell-shape around an average, while the beginnings of years are moving from about half of the countries at 0 per cent firing to a gradual increase of up to 17 per cent in 1969–70 and 50 per cent in 1970–71. This suggests that education at INSEAD leads to a change in the anti-mobility value for students from different cultural backgrounds. The table also shows that the amount of change varies from year to year.

Analysing in more detail the changes which occurred among students of different countries, we could divide the countries according to the levels of 'firing' responses at the end of the year and find out the rates of change which occurred in each group (Table 8.6d). We see that in the group which regis-

c. Distribution of 'firing' responses in beginnings and ends of academic years

| | 1968/69 (end)–1969/70 (beginning) | | | | | 1970/71 (end and beginning) | | | |
| | No. of countries | | % of countries | | | No. of countries | | % of countries | |
% Firing	End	Beginning	End	Beginning	% Firing	End	Beginning	End	Beginning
More than 37	1	—	11	—	more than 39	3	1	21	7
29–37	7	—	78	—	17–39	7	2	50	14
less than 29	1	9*	11	100	less than 17	4	11†	29	79
Total	9	9*	100	100	Total	14	14†	100	100

* including four countries with 0% 'firing'
† including five countries with 0% 'firing'

d. Rates of change in 'firing' responses of country groups from beginning to end of 1970–71

| Level of firing at end of year | | Country group | Beginning | | | End | | | Rate of change (% firing) |
%	level		% firing	No. of pts* firing	total	% firing	No. of pts* firing	total	
39–50	Very high	USA + Israel + Britain	19	6	32	43	12	28	×2·3
29–33	Medium	Luxembourg + Sweden + Italy + Norway	12	3	24	30	6	20	×2·5
17–21	Low	Germany + Switzerland + Austria	5	3	63	20	8	40	×4
0–8	Very low	France + Holland + Belgium + Denmark	7	6	86	9	6	65	×1·3

* participants

tered high on firing (39–50 per cent) and comprised the United States, Israel and Britain, the rate of change was more than doubled (from 19 to 43 per cent). These countries have also been found to be similar to each other in their managerial communication as well as in other aspects of organisational behaviour. The rate of change of the next group, which consisted of Luxembourg, Sweden, Italy and Norway, was at a similar rate (from 12 to 30 per cent). The largest rate of change (from 5 to 20 per cent) occurred in the German group, which included Switzerland and Austria; the smallest (from 7 to 9 per cent) in the group of France, Holland, Belgium and Denmark. The grouping of the countries could be of some significance, considering that the more centrally situated, non-German-speaking countries of Europe behave differently from those located on the outskirts of Europe.

SOCIAL STRUCTURE

The students gathered at INSEAD came from a variety of national origins, had gone through different fields of study for their first degree and had various other different personal characteristics including age, marital status, degree of national complexity and length of time spent abroad. Had INSEAD let its students structure themselves freely, without any institutional intervention, it is probable that they would have structured themselves along one or more of their personal characteristics. In 1966–67 the students were divided as follows:

National language:	12 groups of countries, with an average of 12 participants in each.
Profession:	9 first university specialisations, with an average of 16 participants in each.
Family status:	bachelor and married groups, with an average of 72 participants in each.
National complexity:	nationally complex and non-nationally complex groups with an average of 72 participants in each.
Age:	young and old (divided by medium) groups, with an average of 72 participants in each.
Time abroad:	long and short term abroad (divided by medium) groups, with an average of 72 participants in each.

However, the formal structure of INSEAD has been set up so as to counteract the possible effects of the personal characteristics of the participants on their social structure. In other words, the objective has been to mix the students as much as possible. Many other graduate schools of business administration have a similar objective in that they try to mix the students by profession, in order that their different academic backgrounds would contribute to each other, or by age, so that the more experienced will contribute to the less and vice versa. INSEAD adds one other important mixing factor, namely that of mixing the culture, nationalities and languages of its students. This mixing is done through both the learning organisation and the living organisation of the students. In 1966–67 they were divided as follows:

Case discussion group: 20 groups, with an average of 7 participants in each.
Floor in the residence: 15 floors, with an average of 8 participants on each.
Residence: 6 residences with an average of 20 in each.
Class at entry: 3 classes in the first half of 1966–67 with an average of 45 in each.
Class at end of year: 3 classes in the second half of 1966–67 with an average of 45 in each.

About 17 per cent of the students did not live in INSEAD residences.

The researchers, therefore, set two possibly conflicting hypotheses for their research:

• that the personal characteristics of the students affect their social structure.
• that the formal structure affects the students' social structure.

The social structure was investigated by means of four sociometric indicators, measuring the perceptions of participants as to their relationships with other participants: whom they had meals with, met during leisure time, would like to work with, would like to meet socially. The choices of participants in each of these four indicators were matched and only mutually perceived choices were taken into account. Two sociograms (Figs 8.2 and 8.3) were drawn to demonstrate the network of the closer social relations between participants. The lines between participants in these two sociograms indicate mutual choices according to more than one indicator. For the purpose of clarity only those participants who had such social relationships among themselves namely having mutual choices according to more than one indicator appear. All the isolates according to this definition, those participants who had no mutual choices or had them only on one indicator, were omitted from the sociograms. Fig. 8.2 shows the social network superimposed on the geographical map of the different countries. Fig. 8.3 shows this network in relation to the accommodation of the INSEAD participants at Fontainebleau.

In both sociograms the types of lines designate the degrees of closeness of social relations between participants. The closest social relation is found to be between participants who chose each other on all four indicators for social relationships and is represented in the sociograms by the thick black lines. Thus on Fig. 8.2 two thick lines are inside one country, France, while the other three thick lines cross borders between the following pairs of participants— Austrian and Finnish, British and French, French and Lebanese. In Fig. 8.3 we see that four thick lines are inside the residences while only one thick line passes outside.

A visual analysis of the sociograms points again to the fact that the school's framework, the residences in this case, affects somewhat more social relations between participants than the background characteristics, the countries of origin.

Finally, the conclusion of the whole analysis supports hypotheses about the effect of imposed conditions and given conditions on social relations between participants. There is also a clear indication that the imposed conditions had a larger effect on the social structure than the given conditions. This last finding puts a special emphasis on the importance of international schools such as INSEAD, which by its formal structure and teaching methods encourages social relations among participants from different nations and different backgrounds.

An analysis of the correlations between the social structure and the personal characteristics of participants on the one side and the formal structure of INSEAD on the other is presented in Table 8.7. The analysis presented in this table reveals that the effect of INSEAD'S formal structure on the students' social structures is much more dominant than the effects of their personal characteristics.[15]

The most significant factor affecting the social structure was found to be membership of a discussion group. The relationships *between* members of discussion groups exceeded by six their randomness. Next in its effect on the social structure in Table 8.10 is the residence: relationships between students living on the same floor exceeded by 5·5 their randomness. The next two factors affecting the social structure, exceeding by three their randomness, were the residence itself, as opposed to the floor, and the national origin. The following two factors which had an effect on the students' social structures were their first degree, and the class in which they studied at the beginning of the year. Such a class was usually composed of seven discussion groups. The last two factors appearing in the Table 8.7, as having an effect on the social structure, were the students' class at the time of the research and their marital status.

All other factors tested were below 1 per cent per participant and very close to the random 0·7 per cent per participant. It can be seen from the tables that the factors imposed by INSEAD were predominant in their effect on the social structure both in their number, five factors imposed by INSEAD and only three personal characteristics, and in their variance from random, as follows:

Imposed factors: membership in a discussion group, 6 times more than random.
living on the same floor of residence, 5·5 times more than random.
living in the same residence, 3 times more than random.
belonging to class at beginning of year, 3 times more than random.

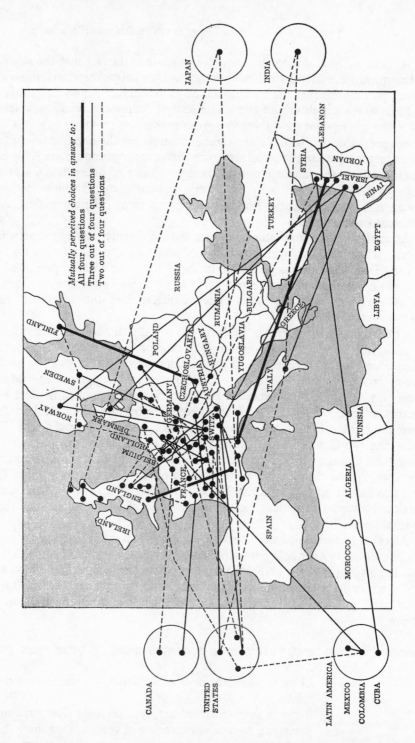

8.2 The social structure: mutual relationships between INSEAD participants by countries of origin. The four questions were as to choices regarding having meals together: meeting during leisure time: working together in future: meeting socially in future.

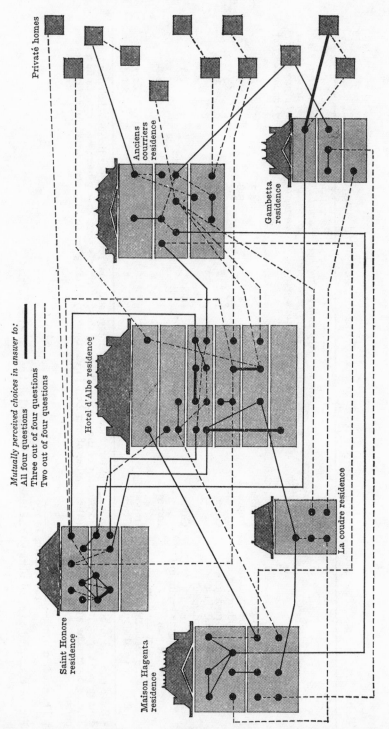

8.3 Mutual relationships between INSEAD participants by distribution of residences and homes in Fontainebleau, 1967. The four questions were as to choices regarding having meals together: meeting during leisure time: working together in future: meeting socially in future.

Table 8.7 The social structure: summary of effects of independent factors on social structure

Rank order	Factor	Imposed or given conditions	% of mutual choices within own factor group	Approximate average no. of participants in a group	Percentage of total mutual choices per participant within own factor group* (%)	Relation between % of actual choices within group and % of random choice†
1	Discussion group	Imposed	30	7	4·3	×6·1
2	Floor in the residence	Imposed	31	8	3·9	×5·5
3·4	Whole residence group	Imposed	44	20	2·2	×3·1
3·4	National origin group	Given	26	12	2·2	×3·1
5	Professional (first university degree) group	Given	31	16	2·0	×2·9
6	Class at the beginning of the year	Imposed	71	45	1·5	×2·1
7	Class at the time of the research	Imposed	55	45	1·2	×1·7
8	Marital status group	Given	71	72	1·0	×1·4

* If we take the discussion group as an example for calculation of percentage and total mutual choices per person, the analysis was done in two stages: it was found that 30 per cent of the mutual choices of the participants were among members of the same group. These 30 per cent were divided by 7 (the number of members in each group) which gives the 4·3 per cent of mutual choices per person.

† The random being— $\dfrac{100\%}{143 \text{ students in } 1965\text{–}66} = 0.7\%$

For the exact method of calculating these figures see Weinshall and de Bettignies 1971.

belonging to class at end of year, almost twice more than random.

Personal factors: originating from the same national group, 3 times more than random.

having obtained the same first university degree, almost 3 times more than random.

belonging to the same marital status group, 1·4 times more than random.

MIXING WITH PARTICIPANTS FROM OTHER COUNTRIES

Table 8.8 presents the mutual relationships inside and between seven country groups. In order to arrive at larger groups, the participants were grouped by countries: three single countries (Switzerland, Britain and France), two double country groups (United States and Canada, Austria and Germany), one four country group (Scandinavia) and one three country group (Mediterranean).

Table 8.8 The social structure: mutual relationships inside and between country groups*

| Country groups | No. of participants | | Mutual relationships per participant | | | | | |
| | Total in study | Appearing on sociograms† | Total | | Inside country group | | Out of country group | |
			No.	%	No.	%	No.	%
1. US and Canada	6	6 (100%)	4·33	100	0·33	8	4·00	92
2. Switzerland	10	7 (70%)	4·60	100	0·80	17	3·80	83
3. Scandinavian countries (3)	6	5 (83%)	4·00	100	0·67	17	3·33	83
4. Mediterranean countries (4)	10	7 (70%)	4·09	100	0·82	20	3·27	80
5. Britain	16	9 (56%)	3·56	100	1·13	31	2·44	69
6. German-speaking countries (6)	18	13 (72%)	4·39	100	1·67	38	2·72	62
7. France	34	23 (68%)	3·47	100	1·82	53	1·65	47
Total	100	70 (70%)						

* Only country groups with at least six participants in the study. These include 100 of the 115 who participated in the study.
† The numbers of participants appearing on the sociograms (Figs. 8.2 and 8.3) are smaller than the total number of participants in the study because the sociograms, including only participants with mutual relationships on two, three and all four indicators (i.e. do not include mutual choices for one indicator only).
(3) Scandinavian countries including participants from Denmark, Norway, Sweden and Finland.
(4) Mediterranean countries—including participants from Israel (5 part.), Italy (3 part.) and Lebanon (2 part.).
(6) German-speaking countries—include participants from Austria (4 part.) and Germany (14 part.).

The chance of having more mutual relationships within a group increases, of course, the larger and more monolithic the group is. This is why the comparison should be made separately for the four first country groups and for the larger groups of Britain, German-speaking and France. The United States and the Canadian participants appear at the top of the list in their out of group relationships (92 per cent). Next come the Scandinavian and Swiss participants who should be considered to some extent as a country group (83 per cent each). Very close to them come the participants from the Mediterranean countries (80 per cent). This bringing together of Israel and the Lebanon may seem artificial to outsiders; in reality, however, the Israeli students had, for different reasons, close links with both the Italian and the Lebanese students. As for the larger groups, Britain is the biggest (69 per cent), closely followed by the German-speaking countries (62 per cent), with France lagging behind (47 per cent), which could be explained to some extent by the size of this group (34 participants). Such figures indicate that an institution like INSEAD has to limit the participants from single countries, as indeed it does.[16]

SUMMARY

It has been demonstrated how during a period of only about six months, from September 1970 to March 1971, the attitudes of INSEAD students towards the anti-mobility value have significantly changed. It has been pointed out that those ready to ignore the anti-mobility value had reached 33 per cent towards the end of 1968–69. It seems that the organisation of the curriculum and its contents have a major effect on the way that an institution like INSEAD can affect the attitudes and values of its students.

The findings as to the social structure of the students were at least as impressive as those regarding the attitudes. It has been found that the social structure has been mainly affected by the factors imposed on the students by INSEAD and in the following order—their discussion group, the participants with whom they live on the same floor and in the same building, and the class in which they study. Personal characteristics have less effect and operate in the following order—their national origin, their first degree and their marital status. In other words personal characteristics, which could be expected to affect the social structuring of the same people had they met without the formal intervention of the factors imposed by INSEAD, were pushed aside into secondary importance by imposed factors which had been in existence for only six months.

All these phenomena have been observed and studied under the conditions of the protected environment of INSEAD. The big question mark is whether the observed behaviour lasts after the students graduate from INSEAD and for how long and with what intensity? We have some indications that at least some of these manifestations of internationalisation and integration among the students have been perpetuated among the INSEAD alumni.

Can multinational corporations and management education change cultural values, norms and manifest behaviour?

This chapter has presented first the problem facing those responsible for the development of multinational managers, and then one educational solution to some aspects of the problem as practised by one institution.

First were described differences between countries in the behavioural and social indicators which are generally attributed to cultural differences. These include communication patterns, educational system, social and organisation structures and language. Then the attitudes of INSEAD students were explored and it was demonstrated that the intensity of the anti-mobility value is related to national origin. It was likewise shown that internationalist attitudes were correlated with factors like the family's national complexity and the length of time spent in foreign countries. Some changes which occurred in the attitudes and relationships of INSEAD participants, as a result of the education undergone, were then demonstrated. The findings themselves constitute a positive answer to one part of the question posed, namely that management education *can* change cultural values, norms and manifest behaviour.

This, however, is not enough. In the last resort we are interested in the behaviour of managers in multinational companies and not just during their studies in school. For this reason further examination of the interrelationships between the various findings and their significance is necessary. The role of multinational firms in changing cultural values, norms and manifest behaviour is discussed in the following section and finally some of the aspects requiring further research are considered.

CROSS NATIONAL EFFECTS ON VALUES, NORMS AND MANIFEST BEHAVIOUR

There is sound reason to believe that the sociocultural environment in different countries is affecting organisation behaviour in these countries. Table 8.9 presents a comparison between the degrees of the anti-mobility value, measured by the percentages of students 'firing' Jim Fairfax, and the degrees of social stratification, measured by the inequality of opportunities.

Although the ranking correlation ($\S = 0\cdot3$) is quite low, Table 8.9 indicates some relationship between social mobility and attitudes towards interorganisational mobility.

Table 8.10, on the other hand, presents some comparisons between the attitudes, values and relationships of students after having been subjected to INSEAD'S education. This table is divided into 'large homogeneous country groups' and 'other country groups'.

Observing the first three groups we see that the measured parameters all progress in the same direction. Thus, while the British students are perceived to be the best international mixers of the three country groups, they themselves express more favourable attitudes to interorganisational mobility, and are the highest of the three in their mutually perceived relationships with students out of their own group. French students, on the other hand, score the lowest of the three country groups and are perceived the worst mixers, with the highest anti-mobility attitudes, and are the lowest in their mutually perceived relationships out of their own group.

In the smaller and less homogeneous groups the trends change somewhat. The anti-mobility value and the social structure are related to each other as in the case of the large country groups. The United States and Canada are the highest both as to their low anti-mobility attitudes and their high mutually perceived relationships with other students out of their own groups. However, the trend as to the degree of mixing is in the opposite direction to the other two trends and unlike that in the large homogeneous country groups. The Dutch and Belgian students were perceived to be very high international mixers, yet expressed the highest anti-mobility attitudes.

The main reason for this reversal of the trends in the smaller and less homogeneous country groups is probably that the studies supplying the data for each of the three parameters were carried out among different classes of students. Those from the large country groups are more or less representative of the culture of their countries and their values, norms and manifest behaviour do not drastically change from one year to another. The students from

Table 8.9 Cross-national summary analysis: comparison of attitudes towards management anti-mobility and inequality of opportunities in eleven countries

Country	Rank orders		Difference in order ranked (2) −(3)	Square of difference
	From low to high anti-mobility value	From low to high inequality of opportunities		
(1)	(2)	(3)	d	d²
US	1	5	−4	16
Israel	2	1	1	1
Italy	3	10	−7	49
Sweden	4	6	−2	4
Britain	5	2	3	9
France	6	4	2	4
Norway	7	8	−1	1
Germany	8	9	−1	1
Holland	9	7	2	4
Belgium	10	11	−1	1
Denmark	11	3	8	64
			Total	154

$$\rho = 1 - \frac{6 \, \Sigma d^2}{N(N^2 - 1)} \qquad \rho = 1 - \frac{6(154)}{11(121 - 1)} = 1 - \frac{924}{1320} = 0\cdot3$$

the smaller country groups sometimes vary considerably from one class to the next. Any comparisons with regard to the attitudes and relationships of students from smaller and less homogeneous country groups should therefore be related to the same students of the same class; while in the larger, homogeneous country groups comparisons between different groups of students in different classes are relevant.

IMPLICATIONS FOR MULTINATIONAL MANAGEMENT EDUCATION

Let us now consider some of the implications for multinational management education, drawn from the findings of this chapter. On the whole it has been shown that INSEAD'S educational process achieves favourable results in developing multinational managers. There are, however, some aspects of this education which, the findings suggest, could influence further development:

- Small groups studying and living together.
- Larger groups also studying and living together.
- Not reshuffling the classes in the middle of the academic year.
- The size of the larger national groups should be limited to a lower percentage of the total student body, and the size of very small national groups increased.
- Increasing the parts of the curriculum in which participative learning methods are used and sociocultural differences are exposed and discussed.

CAN MULTINATIONAL CORPORATIONS INTRODUCE CHANGES?

There is very strong evidence that multinational corporations are affecting the national environments in which they operate. Indeed it may be that changes in the values, norms and behaviour of people in nation states are gradually occurring mainly through the penetration into them and operation within them of organisations with different cultures than their own. Multinational corporations may be producing bigger changes in this respect than individuals learning from other cultures through reading, visiting and the like. Organisations with different cultures from those of the countries in which they operate are able to maintain a bridgehead for the introduction of new values, norms and behaviour. This depends, of course, on such organisations being strong enough to resist the efforts of the host nations to prevent the penetration and continued operation of a culture within a culture. There are signs that multinational corporations are penetrating even the most resistant countries with comparative ease.

The managerial personnel of multinational corporations is essentially composed of three types of people: those who have few internationalist tendencies and abilities, those who do have them but without having been exposed to formal multinational management education, and those who have

Table 8.10 Cross-national summary analysis: different effects of management education on behaviour of students from various countries

I. Large homogeneous country groups

Country group	Attitude to mixing		Anti-mobility value ('firing' Jim Fairfax)			Rate of change from beginning of year	Social structure		Extra-mural relation-ships %
	Rank order	Level	Rank order	%	Level		Rank order	Level	
Britain	3	High	3	39	High	×2·3	5	Low	69
Germany and Austria	12 8	Low	8 10	21 17	Low	×4·0	6	Low	62
France	11	Very low	11	12	Very low	×1·3	7	Very low	47
From figure/table	Fig. 8·1a		Table 8·6b				Table 8.8		
No. of countries studied	12		14				7		

II. Other country groups

Country group	Attitude to mixing		Anti-mobility value ('firing' Jim Fairfax)			Rate of change from beginning of year	Social structure		
	Rank order	Level	Rank order	%	Level		Rank order	Level	Extra-mural relationships %
USA	Not available	Not available	1÷2	50	Very high	×1	1	Very high	92
Canada			n.a.	n.a.		n.a.			
Israel +	10	Low	1÷2	50	Very high	×1·5	4	High	80
+Italy	5–6	Medium	6	29	Medium	×1·3		High	
+Lebanon	5–6	Medium	n.a.	n.a.	n.a.	n.a.			
Sweden +	7	Medium	5	33	Medium	×3·5	2–3	High	83
+Norway	2	High	7	29	Medium				
+Denmark	9	Low	14	0	None				
Holland	4	High	12	8	Very low	×*			
Belgium	1	High	13		None				

* Increase from 0 to 6 per cent

gone through an educational system similar to INSEAD. The last two have been nourished on the consequences of the enormous technological developments in communication and transportation.

FUTURE RESEARCH IN MULTINATIONAL MANAGEMENT EDUCATION

The subject area to which this paper is the closest is that of anthropology. Comparatively little has been done in the anthropological study of organisation behaviour in the countries mainly covered by this chapter. The books describing behavioural factors pertaining and akin to management and organisation are few. The most urgent task for future research is therefore to compare organisation behaviour across national frontiers in the industrialised countries. One such research project which started in the Anglo-Saxon countries is now being extended to other Western European countries, Japan, Israel and elsewhere. This is a specific study on managerial behaviour within business.[17]

Matters more directly and specifically related to multinational management education have also been little researched. This chapter has been concerned only with the management education aspects of the three parts of the INSEAD research project. The project, however, has much wider implications in that it could help us explore the personal characteristics of 'internationalists', and discover ways by which to train people for a better understanding between the nations of the world. In order to arrive at more conclusive findings both as to the effects of multinational business education and as to such things as furthering understanding between the nations and the chances of peace, a lot of additional research will have to be carried out.

First of all it would be necessary to process all the data collected from several classes of students analysing it systematically, in addition to the few and scattered analyses described in this chapter. It would be of great interest to try to substantiate some of the findings reported here. Thus, for example, with regard to the personal characteristics conducive to internationalist traits, the substantiation of the correlation between length of stay out of his country and a man's subsequent tendencies is of special importance. Unlike factors such as family, national complexity, age, marital status, nationality, social class and even previous education, the length of stay outside one's own country is a factor which could be influenced by outside intervention. Indeed, if this finding is verified in further research, institutions interested in understanding between nations and world peace could concentrate their efforts and funds on encouraging young people to spend their time in foreign countries. Multinational corporations, too, could encourage and support travel and study in foreign countries. They could also emphasise time spent abroad in their management development programmes.

A study of the values, norms and behaviour of the alumni of formal international management education by exploring their attitudes and relationships after, say, three, five, and ten years would also be of value. This would enable us to discover the impact of such an education on people returning to their own or different sociocultural environments, as time goes on. The values, norms and behaviour in these real life situations should be compared with both the sociocultural environment of the alumni at the time of the study and with their original attitudes and relationships while still within the educational institution.

9

Problems of resource allocation in an international corporation

Different species

The term international firm covers a wide variety of species. This is so not only because firms in different lines of business differ in important organisational and functional respects, but also because international operations have tended to evolve gradually, and often a trifle haphazardly. They have seldom, if ever, been set up within the framework of a single master plan, though the recent trend has been towards determining the future development of international operations by reference to long-term corporate plans. The picture currently presented by international business organisation is remarkably diverse and, despite dramatic but scarcely realistic visions of some 300 giant global firms controlling around two-thirds of the world's industrial production towards the end of this century, it is likely to remain so.

Most manufacturing firms with international interests have first moved outside their home markets through direct exporting.[1] As export markets are increasingly penetrated, selling subsidiaries are often established abroad. A not uncommon first step in the direction of foreign manufacture consists of making licensing agreements with foreign firms whereby the latter undertake manufacture in stipulated territories. Such arrangements may be of relatively declining importance; at any rate, many firms tend to move directly to a subsequent stage at which it becomes apparent that some markets are better penetrated and developed by way of local assembly or full production operations. Many possible reasons can underlie decisions to make this most significant step towards the internationalisation of operations. Among these reasons may be high exporting costs and the presence of tariff and other barriers to direct trade, as well as political pressures. Longer-term strategic factors include the existence of substantial growth opportunities and the need to take anticipatory measures against domination of the market by competitors. Moves into foreign manufacture may be implemented through joint ventures with, or a minority interest in, a local firm, through the acquisition of a local company, or through the establishment of operations from scratch; use of either of the last two methods may well follow experience gained in shared ventures.

As a foreign operating unit becomes more deeply involved in and acquainted with the market in which it is engaged, it may well begin to supply variants on the firm's basic product range in order to satisfy a different balance of needs. It may also begin to diversify on its own account. Additionally, or alternatively, operating units may become part of a corporate global or regional logistic system. It is at or around these stages of development that foreign operations increasingly take on the role of profit and decision-making centres within the firm as a whole, and that problems of global co-ordination start to arise. As the number of operations and the range and scale of activities abroad expand, the parent company headquarters tends to take on a new role in the planning, integration and control of operations on a world-wide basis. Global planning systems and reporting lines become established.

When such stages are reached it becomes difficult to distinguish degrees of global thinking and integration. It is tempting to regard firms with a rela-tively high degree of logistic integration of production and marketing on a worldwide, or regional, scale as the most sophisticated international operators. But such logistic systems are simply not appropriate to many industries; firms operating in such industries may nevertheless be just as global in their approach to their international operations as those with complex logistic systems. A more generally applicable measure of a firm's worldwide outlook and integration is to be found in the extent to which strategic planning and the control of the rate and direction of its growth are carried out on a global basis. But, by its very nature, this unit of measurement is imprecise, and the categories of firms it attempts to delineate are inevitably blurred. A distinc-tion that has gained some currency is based on the use of the terms 'trans-national' or 'polycentric' to refer to firms operating largely compartmentalised facilities in several countries; and of 'multinational' or 'geocentric' to refer to those whose planning and control systems are of the type in which the strategic plans of each operating unit are specifically traded off against those of all the other operating components of the group and an integrated global plan produced. While conceptually useful, distinctions of this sort remain of limited value because it is so difficult to draw lines between the different categories in practice. The appropriate placing of each firm into these cate-gories can be determined only after a close examination of its organisation, planning and decision-making systems; and it may then be that as many cate-gories can be distinguished as there are firms. Moreover, structures and systems are constantly changing in growing international firms.[2]

Resource allocation: What is special about the international firm?

The parameters and problems of resource allocation clearly differ substan-tially as between firms at different stages of their development; but there is no sharp demarcation line between the processes of resource allocation appropriate to each category of firm. The emphasis here is on firms that have the scope for conceiving and planning their objectives and resources allocation on a global scale, even if all of them do not yet do so. However, it should not be forgotten that a decision by a purely 'national' firm on the commitment of resources to export rather than to expansion or diversification at home is, in its way, as much a part of the process of international resource allocation by the firm as is a decision on the relative rates of expansion of several foreign subsidiary companies. In fact, provided their overall objectives are broadly similar, much the same general principles apply to resource allocation in a company operating in a purely national setting as apply in an international firm. In their application, however, important differences are very evident, and it is these differences that constitute the main subject matter of this chapter.

Systematic resource allocation is neither meaningful nor possible without the focus of a central objective. In line with the argument in the preceding paragraph, there is no obvious or particular reason why the main corporate objectives of international firms on the one hand and purely national firms on the other should differ markedly. The ground rules within which the two groups of firms decide to pursue their objectives will, however, tend to be different in their scope and nature. For the purposes of this discussion it is implicitly assumed that the central corporate objective is couched in terms of a specified rate of earnings per share, or degree of coverage for a given dividend rate, combined with a specified rate of growth over the long term. At any given time there may have to be an element of 'trade-off' between the shorter and the longer term components of these profit oriented corporate aims.

Apart from the obvious questions raised by such a bald assumption in relation to the objectives of either international or national firms, at least three points need to be made about the special considerations arising in connection with international corporations. First the existence of local ownership in subsidiary or associated companies abroad, statutorily imposed in some cases, means that objectives at odds with corporate goals have to be pursued from time to time in some parts of the organisation. Secondly, it can be difficult to match the objectives of individual operating units with those of the firm as a whole. The various forms of control and surveillance exercised by different national governments over profits, retentions and remittances can mean that profit optimisation for the firm as a whole does not involve profit optimisation at each operating location. Transfer pricing policies initiated by the firm itself can have similar effects. Factors of this sort, of course, can and should be built into the operating strategies and tactics of the international corporation. But changes in the relevant circumstances can produce conflicts in objectives in the short term at least. A large unit operating abroad cannot be told to change its objectives overnight without creating some potentially severe strains. Thirdly, the very fact that a firm has 'gone international' itself suggests a special importance for the longer-term element in its objectives. The achievement or maintenance of long-term growth in earnings, and the smoothing out of year-to-year fluctuations, frequently figure among the basic reasons for going fully international. Once a complex global organisation has become established, objectives might have to be conceived in terms of a time scale extending beyond the normal medium term planning periods of around five years; even ten-year projections may not be adequate for this purpose. Political factors and competitive strategic factors, for instance, might dictate the retention of elements in a firm's global strategy that should, strictly, be discarded on the basis of five or even ten year targets.

In both national and international firms allocations of management, labour, knowledge, material and capital resources need to be made to products and to market areas in the light of perceived profit and growth opportunities and competitive threats, and in accordance with their overall objectives. More specifically decisions on the geographical allocation of resources can be, and often are, required of firms operating on a purely national level. An example of this is the penetration of new geographical areas by firms in industries, like brewing, whose production processes are localised. The same is true at the first base of the internationalisation of operations, with decisions to export. Decisions in both these categories can be seen, in terms of product and market strategy, as decisions to expand by means of market extension; and they should imply the prior consideration of possible alternative strategies such as product development or diversification. Further, even within a national market, a firm with several plants can have important and sometimes difficult logistic decisions to make on issues like sourcing.

Viewed in this light, some of the mystique is taken out of the idea of strategic planning in international firms. Nevertheless, it would be ostrichlike to attempt to ignore the considerable differences that do exist between purely national and international firms in terms of the parameters and problems of resource allocation.

There can be no doubt that the number and complexity of the relevant variables in resource allocation are much greater in an international than in a national firm. In addition, special factors enter into the resource allocation problems and procedures of international firms which scarcely impinge on the planning of resource allocations in a purely national firm. Several of these special factors (see Table 9.1) are of a broadly cultural and political nature, and are therefore essentially unquantifiable, often unpredictable, and even indefinable. While these have sometimes been overstressed as problems in operating international businesses, they certainly cannot be ignored.

Table 9.1. Some factors which make for special complexity in international business planning.[3]

CULTURAL
  Language
  Custom
  Labour—relations, attitudes and organisations
  Management—ethics, outlooks, style and competence
  Sophistication—technological and commercial
  Life style and expectations

POLITICAL
  Systems unfamiliar to the foreign businessman
  Governments hostile or restrictive towards foreign business
  Home government restrictions on investment abroad

ECONOMIC
  Different growth rates
  Different economic policies
  Diverse markets (this should not be overemphasised)

FINANCIAL
  Exchange rates, and their movements
  Capital market facilities
  Different interest rates
  Restrictions on the movement of money
  Problems of transfer pricing

FISCAL
  Different tax systems, and their special features relating to foreign ownership
  Tax treatment of international remittances and other ways of moving funds
  Tax concessions
  Trade barriers

LEGAL
  Differences in company law, especially concerning foreign firms and their relations
    with domestic firms
  Differences in general commercial law
  Monopoly and restrictive practices legislation

ORGANISATIONAL
  Implications of widespread foreign operations
  Problems of control, especially in the light of other factors listed
  Problems connected with information and communications

Some apparent contradictions in resource allocation in an international firm

Factors such as those noted above help to create several apparent contradictions in the planning systems of large international firms. Three broad issues may serve to illustrate this point.

FLEXIBILITY

Operating on a global basis, a large multinational firm can juggle with the size and nature of its various activities on a vast scale so as to optimise the use of its resources in the light of differential economic, fiscal, legal and geographical conditions. An inner flexibility to its efforts to achieve overall corporate objectives is thus provided. In practice, however, there are formidable problems of reacting quickly to localised changes in such conditions. As in most businesses, plants cannot be run down lightly or new ones built quickly; and, in the case of the multinational firm, the special emotive and political factors that may surround major decisions cannot be disregarded. Arrangements involving a commitment shared with other firms or shareholders in a particular country can reduce the financial repercussions of failure there. Equally, the rewards of success are reduced by such arrangements, and flexibility may not be increased. Joint ventures with national firms cannot be undone overnight; trading agreements and licensing arrangements cannot usually be unwound at short notice. Minority interests in national firms may be more quickly disposed of, though this procedure may often be hedged about with legal restrictions and political constraints. Almost all forms of partial involvement tend, however, to mean some reduction in the degree of control that can be exercised by corporate headquarters. The latter's ability to react quickly to changes in economic and other conditions throughout the world by shifting the balance of its total resource allocations may be impaired by such arrangements. The long-term horizon, to which multinational concerns normally have regard in the formulation of their strategies, also militates against quick reactions to shifts in business conditions in particular countries. The flexibility of the international firm should not therefore be overemphasised.

RISK

To spread risks is one of the basic reasons for going international, even though this may not be made explicit. Yet, typically, a good deal of the business a firm conducts abroad comes into the relatively high risk category. This is an anomaly that demands careful treatment in the planning of international resource allocation. The dangers of a faulty assessment of risk do not, however, arise only from underestimation. Risk assessments made, for example, in the light of essentially short-term considerations, such as a wave of labour unrest that has special and specific causes, can have unfortunate long-term effects in terms of opportunities foregone. The subject of risk is taken up again in a later section.

INTERNATIONAL SYNERGY, MOTIVATION AND CONTROL

Operating on a global scale should give firms enhanced scope for obtaining synergistic benefits. In this context 'synergistic benefits' may be understood to connote the profits derived from a firm's global operations over and above the sum of the profits from each individual operation if it were independent of the others. The scope the multinational firm has for realising these benefits depends, among other things, on:

- the complexity of the firm's product mix
- the universality of the factors affecting demand for its products
- the volume of demand and the degree of competition in different countries
- the nature (flowline, assembly, batch, one-off) and minimum optimum scale of the productive processes involved
- the degree of vertical integration and the scope for developing beneficial transfer pricing policies
- the ease and costs of shipping materials, components and finished products between countries
- the relevant tariff and other fiscal barriers to international trade in the product or its components
- the technical sophistication of the products
- the amount of research and development required
- political and legal factors affecting foreign controlled operations in different countries
- the current international structure of the firm and the means by which this has evolved.

In some cases complicated logistic systems involving the international movement of materials, components, knowledge and finished goods may be developed on a global or regional scale. These can take into account relative tariff rates and other barriers to the international flow of goods, the optimum scale at which various operations and functions may be performed, the scope for transfer price manipulation, and many other factors. In other cases the potential synergistic benefits may not extend beyond, say, some regionalisation of marketing arrangements, the availability of alternative sources of supply when production in particular countries is disrupted, and the centralisation of certain research and development and management services functions.

On the other side of this particular coin are the organisation structures and administrative procedures that are often required to support the realisation of synergistic benefits. One of the key difficulties of making international resource allocation planning work to the full is that the more synergistic potential is tapped the greater is the danger that its benefits will be offset by corresponding organisational and procedural problems. The greater the complexity and sophistication of the international operations, the greater are the chances of error in the detailed plans underlying them. In addition, a full realisation of synergistic potential often leaves little operational margin for mistakes; failure in one part of a logistic system, for instance, can have repercussions on the system as a whole. More important, where international operations are designed to release maximum synergy, the potential advantages to be derived from national managers developing their own objectives and plans can be lost. Their own operations' performance and potential can be adversely affected when their plans have to be formulated in terms of a predetermined international framework. More generally the entrepreneurial drives of national management can be inhibited to a dangerous degree. In addition the control mechanisms for highly synergistic international operations can themselves become overcomplex, self-indulgent and costly.

Resource allocation planning and organisation structure

Past allocations of resources, and the means by which the international firm has evolved, have a fundamental effect on the organisation structure and the balance of power within the firm. Equally, in the short term at least, current organisation structures and the current balance of power themselves profoundly affect the processes of resource allocation planning and control, and help to determine the key strategic decisions. The basic precepts and attitudes of top management at corporate headquarters are also, of course, a crucial ingredient in shaping the organisation. It is difficult to believe that, even in the largest multinational firms, managers at corporate headquarters never allow themselves to think in terms of national loyalties rather than on a truly global basis. Against this, however, in many large firms a relatively mobile corps of senior managers is being developed on a multinational basis. This means that, increasingly, senior managers at corporate headquarters may be conversant with the operational details of foreign units, while their colleagues abroad may have had managerial experience at corporate headquarters or elsewhere in the group. Close formal or informal relationships may thus be established between headquarters and operating units, which can make a real contribution to the success of planning processes.

The reporting lines specified for the foreign subsidiaries form one of the main structural factors which influence resource allocation planning. Do the subsidiaries, for instance, report direct to corporate headquarters, to an international division, to a regional office, to a national headquarters, to a product division, or to some combination of these? Are there also functional reporting lines to divisional or headquarters level? These matters affect the efficiency of the planning process itself. In addition, to the extent that each layer of organisation almost inevitably becomes something of a pressure group within the firm as a whole, the organisational form can affect specific strategic decisions.

Another structural issue concerns the need to involve foreign operating units closely in coordinated strategic and profit planning systems which they accept as useful and necessary, allowing them at the same time to retain some measure of planning autonomy and operational independence. Also relevant is the competence of operating units and the office to which they report in assessing the prospects for profits and growth in particular countries and product markets.

Some guidelines for resource allocation planning in an international firm

The diversity of scope, organisation and outlook of international firms has already been emphasised. It is therefore difficult to take a prescriptive line on resource allocation planning, especially as it is important that planning systems are tailored to the unique needs of each organisation. It is also difficult to form a clear view of the state of the art of international strategic planning. The general impression is that, like the matter of international organisation, it is in a state of flux. Case histories can be instructive; but they are each unique and reflect responses to specific past situations. In some cases there is also doubt about the extent to which the planning system actually influences business decisions. Moreover, the success of different systems and methods of resource allocation is difficult to assess because it is not possible to tell what would have happened with different systems and methods and with different sets of circumstances outside the firm's control.

In a relatively large international firm there exists the potential for planning resource allocation within the framework of a global cash flow and profit model designed in the light of overall objectives. It is tempting to refer to a profit 'optimisation' model. The development and use of such a model is a desirable aspiration. But it is doubtful whether an optimisation model in any mathematical sense is applicable to the problem of resource allocation in the currently typical international firm. The reasons for this include sheer complexity, difficult political considerations, the margins of error to which most long-term forecasts are prone, the changing restrictions affecting the investment and flow of funds in and between different countries, and the presence of power groups inside the firm representing product and geographical interests. Above all, resource allocation is essentially a long-term matter. The relevant time scale for the major investments that form the pattern of a firm's international allocation of resources often extends well beyond normal planning periods of five or even ten years;[4] and there are often unavoidably long lags between decisions to build new plants, or to run down existing ones, and their implementation. Nevertheless, allowing for varying degrees of sophistication, which may correspond with varying organisation structures, some use can usually be made of the general principles involved in a profit optimisation model. At least, these principles might be harnessed to form a coherent framework within which proposals for major projects may be appraised and decisions on them taken.

In the present state of the art of strategic planning, and at the present stage of development of the majority of international firms, there are good reasons why the process of international strategic planning should be structured not from the top down but from the bottom up. The operating units would then be involved with the development of objectives, through strategy formulation, to the implementation stages. In this way, intimate knowledge of local political and economic conditions and business opportunities and threats may be better used. A greater personal commitment and greater speed of action and reaction in the implementation phases should be generated, and the development of management resources throughout the firm facilitated. This proposal does not, however, run counter to the powerful argument that the synthesis, review, approval and control of plans and their implementation should be centralised. Corporate headquarters must retain final responsibility and authority in relation to international strategic planning, and the final power of endorsement and veto. Without centralised co-ordination and control the greater opportunities often open to multinational firms for realising synergistic benefits may be dissipated.

There is no particular problem peculiar to an international firm in putting together the 'unit' plans, either short term or longer term, to form a group plan. If the group's structure is particularly complex, computer programmes are available which can be used to do the synthesising and draw out the financial implications. Included at this stage could be a cash flow projection which suggests the desirability of holding or transferring liquid funds in and between different countries in accordance with investment opportunities, likely exchange rates movements, national regulations on fund transfers, differential tax rates, and other such considerations.

The summation of annually submitted 'unit' plans ought to indicate the need for action to close any gap between likely global performance and overall objectives, or to anticipate any severe cash flow problems. In order to use the synthesised group plan as a framework for decisions on the form such action should take, it is desirable that the plans and the planning system should exhibit certain basic characteristics.

The assumptions underlying the unit plans need spelling out in detail and need to cover the same ground in the case of each planning unit so as to facilitate comparisons of the basic factors affecting the future level and profitability of business in different countries. Assumptions should be made about future trends in qualitative as well as quantifiable factors, and should preferably be extended beyond the detailed planning period. Medium- or long-term forecasting of high quality is of vital importance in an international firm. Whether the political and macro-economic elements in this forecasting should be carried out at operating unit or headquarters levels is a difficult problem to resolve. A centralised or regionalised system in which specialised expertise can be brought to bear, but which actively gathers together the localised knowledge of the various operating units, would seem to be the most economic in operation and potentially the most effective.

Considerable emphasis must of necessity be put on the forecasts of qualitative factors, such as political and legal factors and labour attitudes, despite the scepticism such prognostications tend to arouse. Forecasts of this sort can help in the evaluation of business risks in different countries and in forming a view of long-term economic growth prospects. Simply because these factors cannot be precisely quantified is no reason for ignoring them or for making no real effort to get below the superficial impression. The development of alternative forecasts based on various political and other assumptions is a valuable discipline. It at least helps in the establishment of ranges of probability for the occurrence of relevant events and, above all, it helps to focus attention on the factors likely to prove critical for particular operations or projects, and on likely sources of risk. In fact, most long-term forecasts, quantitative as well as qualitative, can be usefully expressed in terms of ranges of probability.

The difficulties of quantifying some of the relevant factors when forecasting over the medium or long term recur in a more critical form at the decision stage in resource allocation planning. The practical nub of the problem of making such decisions lies in weighting against each other the many disparate factors usually involved. There is no obvious way, even in the context of a particular project, of assessing quantitatively the relative importance of the rate of economic growth, regulations concerning foreign ownership and the repatriation of funds, political stability, likely trends in tariff protection and so on. When, as is often the case, several countries need to be compared in these various respects, the problem is multiplied.

One device that has gained some support for the want of anything better is the 'rating scale' used in conjunction with a general 'premium for risk' approach to the problem of international resource allocation.[5] The premium for risk approach involves the screening of a global portfolio of possible projects through the use of different rate of return cut-off points for different countries, the higher cut-off rates applying to countries whose investment climates are regarded as relatively poor. The fundamental difficulty with this approach lies in determining the appropriate risk premium for each country, and each project.

So far as countries are concerned, the weighting problem has been tackled in some firms by assigning weights to each major factor affecting the investment climate, and rating different countries on a scale applying to each factor. An overall score is thus obtained for each country, the lower the score the higher being the premium for risk. However, while the use of a rating scale helps to discipline the application of judgment, it is no substitute for the latter. Judgment still has to be applied in the assignment of the weights. Moreover the weights used in the process of assessing risk premiums for countries might be inappropriate to different types of projects. Indicators of domestic economic activity and growth might, for example, deserve little if any weighting in the case of a plant established primarily to serve export markets. The threat of labour disputes might be even more serious, and therefore merit a heavier weighting, in the case of a plant performing a unique and vital role in a vertically integrated international operation than that of a relatively self-contained supplier of a finished product to the local market. The possibility of nationalisation or government insistence on a high proportion of local ownership may deserve a heavier weighting for large and basic operations such as mining than for operations in industries organised within the country concerned on a less concentrated basis and in smaller units. These difficulties constitute serious conceptual and practical flaws in the premium for risk approach, even when some rating scale is applied.

A possibly more promising approach to the whole problem of strategic planning in an international business context lies in sensitivity and risk analysis. This approach has two interrelated benefits: it focuses attention on the really critical variables affecting profitability and indicates the likely upper and lower limits on ultimate payoffs. In practice, the possible strategic moves required to underpin the long-term growth of profits must be crystallised into alternative major investment programmes whose effects on long-term profit plans have to be appraised. It is in these appraisals in particular that sensitivity testing and risk analysis are valuable tools.

Sensitivity analysis simply involves varying the assumptions underlying the appraisal of possible investment projects so as to gauge the impact of various combinations of assumptions, or each individual assumption, on over-all profitability. Once some experience has been gained with this approach, the really critical factors in operations of particular types in different countries soon become apparent, thus reducing the range of future sensitivity exercises required. This sort of approach can be used in connection with factors that apply across national frontiers, such as currency exchange rates and profit remittance regulations, as well as with essentially local factors affecting profitability in different countries.

A more sophisticated extension of sensitivity analysis involves estimating the probabilities attaching to events that would affect profitability. Thus probabilities may be attached to different values for each critical factor, such as market growth rates and price levels, or to the occurrence of specific events, such as the imposition of new taxes, the introduction of restrictions on the repatriation of profits, or the removal of import protection, for each year of the plan or project period. This is often best done in terms of asking questions in the form: 'What are the chances that the sales of product A in market B will reach £x in the first year, £y in the second year, and so on?' Computerised simulation models can then be used to obtain a distribution of the profits to be derived from a given course of action in terms of the chances that given rates of return will be achieved or bettered. The use of decision trees can help in structuring the problem-decision area at the outset. To perform these exercises for several types of strategic moves and several locations is a complex undertaking. Performed as part of a computerised global profit planning system, the whole process is, however, more sharply focused and also less time-consuming. It is a feasible proposition, provided that planning procedures have been formulated to facilitate its application.

This type of approach appears to inject a little rigour and discipline into the strategic investment decision-making process. If only because it does this, it commends itself for serious consideration in the particularly complex setting of the large multinational corporation. Yet once again this very complexity makes for considerable problems of application. The results obtained can only be as good as the forecasts, including those of the non-quantifiable factors, that lie behind them; and much judgment has to be applied at varying levels in the organisation in assigning probabilities.

It is also very doubtful whether approaches to strategic investment decision-making of the sort outlined can stand the weight of detailed analysis that would be placed upon them by taking fully into account the special logistic and financial factors that can influence decisions on the location, scale and nature of specific investment projects in a large international firm.[6] In practice factors of this sort tend to be dealt with more effectively in optimisation models designed to achieve the best results for a particular product group, function or region within the firm's global operations. The results are seldom as satisfactory when attempts are made to gear such models specifically to optimising the results of the firm as a whole.

There are partial exceptions to this view. These occur, for instance, in firms like the major oil companies whose processing operations are based on their own widely dispersed sources of raw materials, and in firms in industries like vehicles which are characterised by large-scale assembly processes, relatively homogeneous products and standardised international markets. For such firms the logistics of transnational raw material supply and processing, and of international component sourcing, assembly and marketing, may be central to their total operations and their overall profitability. In these circumstances logistic planning, in which operational research techniques play a large part, must form an integral part of resource allocation planning. The two forms of planning are interdependent. It would, however, be short-sighted, even in these cases, to attempt to frame strategies exclusively in terms of logistic factors.

Finally, none of the approaches discussed removes the need for a high degree of old-fashioned judgment in relation to the really fundamental strategic issues on which decisions are required in a large international corporation.

This is partly a consequence of the very long time scale on which such decisions have to be made. There appears to be no standardised way of reaching objective decisions in this area, although some of the techniques briefly mentioned above can obviously help in supporting analyses. In the end there is no substitute for disciplined and informed judgment on such matters as the extent to which basic and very long-term political factors at home and abroad should be allowed to weigh against finite, purely commercial considerations. The same goes for the basic questions of whether the firm's overall expansion should focus on diversification, more international extension of existing product lines, or some combination of the two. Strategic guidelines and precepts of relevance to such basic issues abound, but none is universally applicable. Judgment needs to be exercised in the specific circumstances of each case.

This is not intended to amount to a completely negative conclusion concerning global resource allocation planning. The point about the adoption of a global approach to the problem is that it provides a disciplined and consistent framework for decision-making; it allows tests to be made on the sensitivity of plans to alternative outcomes in the key variables; it helps to define the relative degrees of risk involved in alternative courses of action; and it points to the need for contingency plans and the form these might take.

The future

Strategic planning on a global basis is likely to become more efficient and more effective. The accumulation of experience and the development of more sophisticated computerised data processing and control systems will both assist this process. One implication of such trends is the greater centralisation of resource allocation and control at corporate headquarters. This is already becoming noticeable in several large international firms.

At the same time, the philosophy of decentralising to give foreign profit centres a large measure of autonomy remains strong. It could well be sustained by the greater interest of national governments and the authorities of regional groupings in the activities of multinational corporations. Their efforts to ensure beneficial effects for their respective territories from the operations of international firms are almost certain to result in some shift in the internal balance of power of the latter from central headquarters to national operating units. In addition, the development of logistic systems may help to boost the relative power of regional forces within the firm and to cement the resultant organisational, operational and control patterns.

Thus, despite the technical potential for the greater centralisation of planning and control and hence for the use of truly global resource allocation systems, there is likely to be little diminution of countervailing forces inhibiting the direct application of such systems. The strategic aspects of resource allocation in the international corporation are therefore likely to remain areas in which judgment and a regard for organisational implications are of vital importance.

10

Guidelines

This book has identified some of the problem areas in the management of an international business, in particular the related concerns of finance, planning, organising and staffing. The emphasis placed on each of these subjects is necessarily different and it would be easy to arrive at contradictory conclusions, especially when international opportunities have to be fitted into national constraints. Nevertheless, some clear points emerge. Political, economic and social considerations all point to the need for companies to adopt policies that are less dominated by the interests of the home country organisation. This is one theme which is picked up in these closing paragraphs. Another is a more precise identification of how to make the best use of the advantages of the international investment and the spread of facilities. Thus international borrowing may prove to be more profitable than international tax planning. Organisations are heavily influenced by products and market strategies. Education for international business is more relevant if it is conducted with an international faculty and student body. It has been observed that some companies assume that the options open to them are unlimited and others that the range of possible decision-making is more limited than in fact it is. The research developed by the authors of this book has attempted to show both the breadth and the limits of the choices available.

In view of the difficulties experienced in maintaining joint ventures, it may appear surprising that a strategy providing for a greater orientation towards the interests of the host country, including local participation in the investment, is advocated. In particular, corporate financial policy is affected by such a development, for it is here that some of the most obvious advantages of a multinational span of operations are obtained. The opportunities open to firms to minimise taxes, exchange risks and capital costs were pointed out in chapter 2. The limits to such practices were also indicated, and the pressures on companies to permit some local autonomy and participation in their affairs, and perhaps some control *over* their affairs. This latter aspect has reached a critical importance in the minds of some following the recurrent monetary crises in the latter part of the 1960s and early 1970s. How long will national governments or regional authorities tolerate a situation where a few dozen financial executives can, by uncoordinated yet simultaneous response to a perceived exchange risk, create chaos in the currency markets—even force revaluations or devaluations with concomitant and far-reaching economic and political consequences? It may be that governments can do little that is very effective; this does not mean that they will not try. Such attempts will be very likely to take the form of pressure for some local autonomy, more exposure to public view, less freedom of action in pursuing group objectives at the potential expense of a particular part of the group and its host country. Financial strategy will have to take more account of the various local interests in the future, and this is not without its inconveniences, as has been pointed out.

In the light of these probable developments, the recommendation is that companies involve the subsidiary in the planning system from the start, and that central planning services should assist the local managers to fit their strategies into a global scheme. We have tried to show throughout the book that overcentralised planning seems to be unprofitable and self-frustrating, though it is recognised that there are costs in the schemes here being proposed. For one thing, it is often difficult to stimulate an adequate and imaginative concern among subsidiary managers; for another, a company with many small units can hardly involve them all. Nevertheless the main point remains: centralised planning stultifies international management, and can easily bring the whole idea of future projections into disrepute. But the stimulation and guidance of the local subsidiary demands special skills and expertise. The development of these may well turn out to be critical for the future of any particular company.

The dangers inherent in existing organisation structures form another theme of this book. Closer attention to the problems of growth and diversification should enable corporate managers to prepare for shocks and surprises. These may come when joint venture partners want to go their own way just at the moment when other pressures are working towards rationalisation and centralisation. By understanding such pressures European firms considering partnerships with American counterparts may plan ahead and avoid the disillusionment and resentment felt by one executive on the day of the dissolution of such a venture. He accused the United States partner of 'not meeting obligations, high-handed management, and disregard of human values'. The findings contained here may also be useful to governments who are interested in the potential of such projects as joint ventures which combine the international transfer of technology with a measure of local autonomy.

On staffing issues, there is emphasis on the development of international outlooks and local entrepreneurial initiatives at the same time. The opposite tendencies—towards a home-country nationalism and overelaborate, bureaucratic controls on the local operations—have frequently been observed. The development of a new type of international manager has been noted, one who can work easily and naturally between different cultures. The general marketing skills of the company are expected to grow considerably with a more effective cross-fertilisation. It has also been pointed out that there are political dangers in a development which produces local national managers too much out of sympathy with their environment. Staffing policies need to produce a strong international management corps, with global promotion prospects, who can negotiate effectively with governments for the transfer of personnel in the face of restrictive immigration policies, but also ensure that the local company does not affront cultural standards. Such a policy implies some limits to local autonomy in the personnel function. Indeed the traditional degrees of centralisation which made this the most autonomous department may need to be reversed. International staffing and promotion schemes may be needed to run an otherwise decentralised system.

These pages consider more how companies can cope with existing rather than future tasks, but these are inseparable. The decisions involving financing, organising, planning and staffing are not being conducted independently of the environment. Some of the chapters, notably those on finance and education, demonstrate the interaction between influences internal to the company and a range of external pressures more clearly than the others. Nevertheless the whole book brings together studies which concern the manager and the policy-maker alike. Adaptation to the local environment is a subject about which more, much more, will be heard.

Notes

References to books and articles are made by author and date. Full particulars can be traced in the Bibliography.

CHAPTER I. GROWTH AND CHANGE IN THE INTERNATIONAL COMPANY

1. There is a strong body of opinion, supported by at least one of the present authors, that the word 'multinational' should be dropped altogether along with other terms which are supposed to identify different stages of the development of the global firm. These words do not identify precise and usable categories, but they do carry undertones which hinder clear thinking. Supporting this view, the managing director of one of Britain's largest international concerns has said: 'This expression "multinational" should never have been invented, it suggests that "national" is a dirty word. It reminds me of the time after the war when people disapproved of profits and this firm talked only about "operating surplus"!'
2. Principal of the Istituto Superiore per Imprenditori e Dirigenti d'Azienda, the business school in Palermo.
3. See p. 33.
4. An example of the elusiveness of cultural differences is shown by the description of the European executive on p. 86.
5. A project financed by the Social Science Research Council to develop such tools has been undertaken by the International Business Unit at the University of Manchester Institute of Science and Technology. The best current account of problems in the communication systems of international companies is Chorafas 1969. Research in Britain into organisation measurement has been pioneered by Professor D. S. Pugh of the London Business School; see Pym 1968, pp. 374–96.
6. See chapter 7, note 10.
7. See Vernon 1971, chapter 1. However, the sales of all foreign controlled subsidiaries are considerably larger in some European countries.
8. See Servan-Schreiber 1969, pp. 23–4.
9. American figures are drawn from various issues of the *Survey of Current Business*, British figures from the *Board of Trade Journal*, and its successor the *Journal of Trade and Industry*. Figures for other countries are given in the annual *Balance of Payments Statistics* of the IMF.
10. Another volume in this series will be looking at this issue in detail. A very clear statement of a national dilemma is contained in Cordell 1971. On adjacent pages (49–54) he shows the damage to the national research effort caused by a substantial foreign investment in high technology industry, *and* the ineffectiveness at research of local firms!
11. This possibility is suggested in chapter 9 of this book. It is spelt out in more detail in numerous writings including Macrae 1972 and Samuels 1972, chapter 13.

CHAPTER 2. DETERMINANTS OF FINANCIAL STRATEGY IN FOREIGN OPERATIONS

1. See, for example, the three 'orientations' identified in Perlmutter 1969, and the four 'archetypes' described in Rutenberg 1970a.
2. For more detailed evidence on this point, see Meister 1970, and Brooke and Remmers 1970.
3. This is unfortunately rather an imprecise concept. Here it implies that a price which reflects value received will be synonymous with the term *arm's length* price, that is, a price which is reasonable and commercially defensible.
4. There might be some argument over whether a loan from a bank in the host

country secured by a formal guarantee of the parent company is not in effect more in the nature of a loan from the parent company since at least in theory some fraction of its borrowing capacity is used up by such a contingent liability. In practice, it is doubtful whether this does happen except in the case of a very large loan in relation to the size of the group. Imperfections in the market tend to diminish the impact of foreign debt obligations on the group's consolidated accounts.

5. See *Report of the Committee of Enquiry into the Relationship of the Pharmaceutical Industry with the National Health Service 1965-1967*, London, HMSO, 1967.
6. It is our opinion, supported by others, that transfer prices are being used less and less for these ends. The advantages are not worth the extra cost and inconvenience in most circumstances. For some evidence see Greene and Duerr 1970.
7. Where the taxes on distributed earnings are lower than on retained earnings (the case of Germany in the past), this may be advantageous to the firm.
8. The advantages described are generally not applicable to US-owned companies since enactment of the US Revenue Act of 1962. Income received by the holding company would be termed 'subpart F income' and subject to US taxes whether or not it is held abroad.
9. This subject is discussed in chapter 5. See also Lietaer 1970, where a computer model is used.
10. Under certain conditions repayment of the loan may be considered by the tax authorities at home to be what is called a 'constructive dividend' and therefore taxed as ordinary foreign income.
11. This estimate finds support in the 'recoupment period' (that is, number of years to recover the initial investment) calculated by Hufbauer and Adler 1968, p. 12.
12. See Rutenberg 1970b, pp. B671-83.

CHAPTER 3. ACCOUNTING PRACTICES: TRANSLATION AND CONSOLIDATION

1. *Accountancy*, December 1969, p. 937.
2. See also *Consolidation of Company Accounts in Europe*, 1970 and *Survey of Published Accounts 1969-1970*, 1971.
3. Law of 12 July 1965, Article 22; Decree No. 67-774 of 11 September 1967.
4. Notes d'Information, see *Commission des Opérations de Bourse*, 1969, p. 101.
5. *Consolidation des Bilans et des Comptes* (1968); Corre 1969 follows this report closely.
6. *Consolidation des Bilans et des Comptes*, 1968, 26.
7. *Accounting Trends and Techniques*, 1970, 17-18.
8. *Accounting Research and Terminology Bulletins*, 1963; *Bulletin No. 51*, August 1959.
9. *Accounting Research and Terminology Bulletins*, 1963; *Bulletin No. 43*, 1953, chapter 12.
10. American Institute of Certified Public Accountants, 'Status of accounting research bulletins', *Opinion of the Accounting Principles Board*, No. 6.
11. The leading professional accounting bodies are now in the process of issuing 'Statements of standard accounting practice', departures from which must be disclosed and explained by the company or, failing that, by the auditor. The Institutes have, however, no sanctions, apart from a qualified audit report, against non-members.
12. As reported in *Accounting Problems in Foreign Operations*, 1960.
13. Hepworth 1956.
14. Assisted by the publication of Hepworth 1956 and the 1960 *Research Report of the National Association of Accountants*.
15. See Goudeket 1960.
16. See Parker and Harcourt 1969, Introduction.
17. 'Statement of the Accounting Principles Board No. 3: Financial statements restated for general price-level changes', *Journal of Accountancy*, September 1969, p. 67.
18. An account of how the closing rates should be calculated is contained in Breek 1967, pp. 195-9.

CHAPTER 4. THE ROLE OF THE NATIONAL MANAGER IN A MULTINATIONAL COMPANY
1. See chapter 6. See also Fouraker and Stopford 1968.
2. See chapter 5.
3. See Drucker 1969.
4. See Chorafas 1967; see also below, chapter 8.
5. See Lee 1966.
6. See, for example, Servan-Schreiber 1967, as well as chapters 6 and 8 of the present book. The question of synergy is further developed in chapter 9 below.
7. See chapter 6.
8. See Sloan 1964.
9. Fayerweather 1969, p. 148.
10. Lord Kearton at the Annual Meeting of the company, July 1970.
11. See Drucker 1969, p. 3.
12. Official French policy towards foreign investment, although not hostile, has been tempered by a concern to prevent undue foreign domination of key sectors of industry. This led to the requirement that a significant proportion of the equity of General Electric-Bull, the French computer firm, should remain in French hands. A further concern of the French authorities in this case was that defence projects undertaken by General Electric-Bull would remain under French control. General Electric was only allowed to invest after such conditions were assured. For more details see, for example, Dickie 1970.
13. See Learned and others 1963. For the following passage the author draws on the teaching at Barcelona of Professor Antonio Valero.

CHAPTER 5. THE ART OF CHOOSING AN AMERICAN JOINT VENTURE PARTNER
1. This chapter is based on the results of two research projects. The author wishes to acknowledge his indebtedness to the sponsors of both. The material concerning United States companies' joint ventures in Europe is based primarily on Franko 1971a. This study drew heavily on the data bank of the project 'Multinational Enterprise and the Nation State' sponsored by the Ford Foundation and the Harvard Business School and directed by Professor Raymond Vernon. A portion of this work was done jointly with Assistant Professor Louis T. Wells, Jr, co-author of Stopford and Wells 1972. Data and conclusions concerning European companies' joint ventures in the USA are based on a forthcoming book resulting from a joint research project between Business International S.A. and the Centre d'Etudes Industrielles on European strategies for US operations. This research project was directed by the author.
2. The figures concerning joint ventures entered in Europe relate to pre-1968 entries of the 170 American corporations on the *Fortune* '500' list that owned 25 per cent or more of not less than six overseas manufacturing operations in 1964; see Vaupel and Curhan 1969, p. 386. Figures concerning European companies' US joint ventures relate to the pre-1970 joint venture entries of forty-six European companies on the 1969 *Fortune* "200" list having a 25 per cent or greater interest in US manufacturing operations.
3. *Business International*, 5 March 1971, p. 75.
4. *Ibid.*
5. *The Economist*, 27 April 1968, p. 79.
6. Knoppers 1967.
7. See Cyert and March 1963.
8. Ansoff 1965, p. 25.
9. Chandler 1962.
10. Ansoff also notes this basic dichotomy in corporate strategy choice between strategy of product concentration—referred to by him as one of simple expansion of an old product line—versus product diversification. See his article, 'Towards a strategic theory of the firm', in Ansoff 1969.

11. See Franko 1971a.
12. For examples of this kind of very loose relationship in the early days of United States corporate foreign involvement see the history of the Ford Motor Company Overseas, Wilkins and Hill 1964 and Aharoni 1966.
13. See Stopford and Wells 1972.
14. See Chandler 1962. Wickam Skinner has also noted the relationship between the foreign product diversification of American multinational companies and the degree to which subsidiaries are allowed wide latitude in formulating their own plans and policies. See Skinner 1968. The fact that diversified, so-called 'world-wide' product division firms allow a high degree of decentralisation to local manufacturing subsidiaries is documented at length in Franko 1971a and Stopford and Wells. See above, note 1.
15. See C. R. Williams 1967, p. 88.
16. For an exposition of the role of the international product life cycle in this process see Franko 1971a and b.
17. Indeed, a phenomenon of 'peaking' of multiple joint venture divorces during the year of changeover to regional organisations is noticeable in the United States multinational corporate system. See Franko 1971a, chapter 3. The 'survival odds' indicated here were calculated by taking the reciprocal of the joint venture instability rates presented in that chapter. The rates presented therein were defined as the number of a company's joint venture divorces divided by its years spent in joint ventures. These rates are conceptually similar to the 'disease arrest rates' used in biomedical research (see chapter 1 of Franko 1971a for a complete explanation of the methodology involved). Such rates were calculated for firms across all countries where the option of 100 per cent ownership was legally available. No significant difference between 'global' and 'European' rates was found; largely, of course, because European manufacturing operations loom very large in most United States companies' total overseas manufacturing operations.
18. See Behrman 1970, p. 121.
19. Which is documented in Franko 1971a.

CHAPTER 6. ORGANISING THE MULTINATIONAL FIRM

1. Chandler 1962 provides a comprehensive discussion of this necessary correspondence between strategy and structure.
2. See Chandler 1962, p. 479.
3. See Stopford and Wells 1972.
4. Such as Lovell 1966.
5. See, for example, Kolde 1968, chapter 15; Aharoni 1966 gives an excellent description of the initial foreign manufacturing decisions.
6. See Chandler 1962 for a graphic description of such problems.
7. See Vernon 1968a for an economic assessment of this relationship.
8. See Lovell 1966.
9. See Newman 1970.
10. See, for example, Haire, Ghiselli and Porter 1966; the quotation is from p. 9.
11. 'Nestlé's multinational mode', *Management Today*, October 1968.
12. See McCreary 1964.
13. US Department of Commerce, *Survey of Current Business* (Washington, DC: Government Printing Office, October 1969), Chart 15.
14. See Lovell 1966, p. 84.
15. Contrast, for example, Haire, Ghiselli and Porter 1966 with Harbison and Myers 1959 on the question of European attitudes to trust, authoritarianism, and participative management.
16. 'Leyland: spending £25 to make a manager', *The Sunday Times*, 22 March 1970.
17. See Nowotny 1964.
18. Crozier 1964, p. 288.

19. Haas 1967, p. 103.
20. Chandler 1962, p. 50 describes the same phenomenon occurring in American firms with similar functional structures. In the United States, however, functional structures have largely been replaced by divisional structures. For example, only 8 of the 170 firms in the US sample described earlier retained their functional structure in 1968.
21. Haas 1967, p. 135.
22. This analogy is developed in an illuminating way in Fayerweather 1960.
23. Parks 1966.
24. Normally considered to be 25 per cent or less of the equity of a firm, or preference shares, or bonds.
25. 'Nestlé's multinational mode', *Management Today*, October 1968.
26. Lombard 1969, p. 43. Data on many other similar cases are contained in *Organizing for European Operations*, New York; Business International, 1968.

CHAPTER 7. PROBLEMS IN THE DECISION-MAKING PROCESS
1. Under questioning about motives for foreign operations, most managers can be shown to express these objectives defensively. They refer to maintaining their return on investment, growth and market share and not increasing them as in the text. See Brooke and Remmers 1970, chapter 9.
2. The phrase 'rational and natural' as used here is discussed by Gouldner, in Merton, ed., 1965.
3. See Blau 1955, and Gouldner 1954.
4. See Brooke and Remmers 1970, p. 28.
5. See *Trades Union Congress Economic Review 1970*. London, TUC 1970.
6. 'Arm's length' is used of dealings between companies within a group when, for instance, goods are transferred at the market prices that would obtain if separate and independent firms were involved.
7. See Brooke and Remmers 1970, pp. 42–3.
8. See Blau and Scott 1963, and Dalton 1959.
9. See *Management Japan*, vol. 3, no. 2, 1969.
10. See pp. 130 ff. Servan-Schreiber (1969, pp. 201–2) states that the ability to decentralise decisions is one advantage that the American corporation has over the European. It is not clear what evidence he has for this. Some successful American companies are highly centralised. The contrary view has been pointed out by a writer in the *Financial Times* for 12 November 1971; see p. 17, 'The Americanisation of Rank-Xerox'.
11. See above, note 4.
12. The following are the figures, as percentages of the total working day.

Activity	Work sample foremen	Interview foremen	Work sample asst. foremen	Interview asst. foremen
Observing and inspecting	7·2	8·7	26·6	28·1
Verbal comm.	27·6	28·2	11·4	17·1
Direct work	12·8	13·7	16·7	19·5
Paperwork	11·0	10·6	12·3	10·3
Walking	7·2	5·8	8·2	5·3
Relaxing	9·5	7·4	11·6	7·6

13. These facts come from researches by M. G. Dorrell at the University of Manchester Institute of Science and Technology. The results of researches covering communications over many years are expected to be available shortly.
14. Another example is to be found in *The Times* for 8 December 1971: 'The trail of commercial wreckage left by the combined efforts of high pressure computer

salesmen and incompetent managers is providing a lush pasture for management consultants, who are finding themselves a rich market in advising companies how to put their computers to better use. The arrival of Walter J. Schroeder in London to head up the British arm of A. T. Kearney, international management consultants, is a sure sign that the mistakes of the recent past in computerdom are to be capitalized upon.'

CHAPTER 8. COMMUNICATION, CULTURE AND THE EDUCATION OF MULTINATIONAL MANAGERS

1. This paper is based exclusively on the author's own research. For other publications see under 'Weinshall' in the Bibliography.

The *communications study* was first conceived in 1959 during an examination of the managerial relationships and attitudes in a United States company. The analysis concentrates on the different degrees of the use of oral communication in different countries. This in itself is one of the most important differences affecting national management, and therefore an appropriate focus.

The *comparative organisation behaviour study*, started more recently, drew upon the work of many others. Differences and similarities in the social and organisational behaviour of four countries—France, Britain, Israel and the United States were discussed.

The *multinational management education study* is based on a longitudinal cross-national research project begun at the European Institute of Business Administration (INSEAD) in 1965. This was carried out in three stages:

Research focus	Started in	The three stages*			Publications
		1 Before INSEAD	2 While at INSEAD	3 After INSEAD	
Attitudes	1965–66	+	+	(+)	Weinshall 1971
Relationships	1966–67		+	(+)	Weinshall and De Bettignies 1971
Values	1968–69	+	+		Weinshall 1973

★ These marked stages are discussed in this paper. (+) Planned future research.

As background, the following is an official description of the school: INSEAD was founded in 1958. Its purpose is to prepare future directors and managers for the careers in industry, commerce and banking with a particular emphasis on international business. It provides a practical management education designed to bridge the gap between university and business life. Stress is laid on the cultivation of an international approach to business problems and on the effect of European integration on management decisions. Unique of its kind because of its truly international character, INSEAD provides an exceptional meeting place for students from many countries and teachers of different nationalities. Teaching is in three languages: English, French and German. The programme lasts for one academic year and deals with the most up-to-date techniques of business management. Teaching is primarily done by the case method of instruction. Each student first analyses the case by himself, then discusses it within a discussion group composed of ± 7 students and, finally, participates in class discussion with ± 50 other students, led by a professor.

When the present author first came to INSEAD he discovered that the wives of a large number of the married students were of a different nationality from their husbands. Likewise, when interviewing non-directively about twenty students from a variety of national origins, it was discovered that all of them considered the German students to be less mixed with students from other nationalities than the other students. However, all the interviewees mentioned specifically four or five German students who behaved differently from the majority of Germans. All of those specifically mentioned as internationally mixing received their first university degree out of Germany, while none of the other German students had done so.

This suggested that:

(*a*) Some aspects of the INSEAD are 'internationalist', that studying at INSEAD is important not only for students who are only interested in a business administration career, but likewise to students who need such things as mixing with other nationalities and desiring to work in the future in an international setting, in a multinational organisation.

(*b*) Were the 'internationalist' students to be segregated from the purely career motivated students and the characteristic personal differences between the two discovered, such characteristics would indicate the background required not only for multinational managers, but for people who wish to promote and maintain better understanding between nations. In other words, such things as the length of time one stays out of one's country and being married to a wife of a different nationality could well be characteristics which are conducive to becoming an 'internationalist'.

This further suggested the three stages of the research, the findings and preliminary conclusions of which are summarised in this chapter.

2. The *informalogram* is a technique for establishing the managerial structure based on a comparison between the formal and the informal relationships. It is carried out through the measurement of actual relationships among the managers, as they are perceived by themselves. The data are collected by way of one single sociometric question: 'Name the persons with whom you generally work most closely, regardless of their position in the organisation.' The matching of the responses of the various managers provide the mutually perceived working relationships (MPWRs), i.e. the relationships between managers who mention each other in response to the above mentioned question. On the basis of the comparison between these MPWRs and the formal positions of the managers, the managerial structure is established by way of the informalogram.

3. Especially by Michael Crozier, in Crozier 1964. See also above, chapter 6, p. 86.

4. See Sutton 1956, p. 2.

5. See Yoshino 1968.

6. See Servan-Schreiber 1967, p. 66.

7. For an account of the position in Israel, see Weinshall 1968a.

8. See also Weinshall 1971.

9. For evidence of this statement see Yoshino 1968.

10. The rejection of big business is a theme also in the United States. See, for example, Glover 1954.

11. Quoted from the Book of Genesis, 11:1–9, *The New English Bible*, Oxford University Press 1969.

12. 'In the U.S.A. a large enterprise finds itself on the verge of bankruptcy. Its charming, debonair General Manager is liked by all, but no longer has full control over the business. Discipline is non-existent. The personnel take an easy-going attitude towards their work. Morale is good, but turnover is going down fast.

'The Board of Directors is becoming concerned. It quickly takes the decision to appoint a new General Manager to put things right. A strong, energetic man is chosen: Jim Fairfax.

'Fairfax is of an extremely sharp intelligence, has a striking personality, is extraordinarily dynamic and ambitious. Discipline is re-established in a short time. The place buzzes with activity. The new manager is indefatigable, leaves nothing to chance, supervises everything, decides everything and makes his personnel work hard.

'Some of the personnel live in continual fear of having misunderstood Fairfax's orders, others complain bitterly of having no real responsibility or of having no powers to use their own initiative. The psychological climate starts to deteriorate. In fact, it becomes very bad. At the end of a trial period of several months, the Board meets again. Fairfax's successes are noted. Business has improved and become profitable again. The Board also notes the worsening atmosphere within the company which is taking on such proportions that it could in the long run cause the complete breakdown of morale amongst the managers.

'In these circumstances, the Board was confronted with the problem of what to do about Jim Fairfax. The possibilities open to the members of the Board were:
  a. Fire him.
  b. Appoint him as Chairman of the Board of Directors.
  c. Leave him in his present position, but appoint one or more deputy managers to help him.
  d. Remove him from his post and appoint him as a consultant to the company.
  e. Other solutions.
You are a member of the Board of Directors and you have to vote for one of the alternatives. Please explain your choice.'

13. 'National complexity' was a category which included both those who had wives of another nationality and those whose parents were from different countries. It is regrettable that it was not possible to examine those of mixed parentage separately. Recent observations suggest that there may be significant differences among these latter, depending on the political relations between the countries of origin of the parents.

14. For further discussion of this point, see Weinshall 1968a.

15. For the exact method of calculating the figures in Table 8.7 see Weinshall and De Bettignies 1971.

16. In 1971 the limit was 25 per cent of the student body for any particular country. In recent years France and Germany have usually had more than 20 per cent each. This might seem a high figure for purposes of integration.

17. See Heller 1971.

CHAPTER 9. PROBLEMS OF RESOURCE ALLOCATION IN AN INTERNATIONAL CORPORATION

1. The process outlined in this and the following paragraphs applies primarily to manufacturing firms; those in extractive and many service industries tend to follow rather different courses of international development. There are numerous interpretations of the process described. See, for example, Hovell 1969 and *The Growth and Spread of Multinational Companies*, Economist Intelligence Unit Q.E.R. Special no. 5, London, 1969; revised 1971. The present author was a contributor to the latter.

2. Broad classifications of company structure are discussed in chapters 7 and 8 above. For more detailed examinations see, for example, Brooke and Remmers 1970, Stopford 1972, Robinson 1967, Fayerweather 1962.

3. This list is by no means exhaustive. For a more thorough discussion see Farmer and Richman 1966.

4. See above, p. 154.

5. For a more thorough discussion of the approaches and techniques outlined in this and the following paragraphs see Stobaugh 1969.

6. Some of the specific issues involved in logistic and financial planning in multi-national companies are outlined in Rutenberg 1969. More general and extensive works which cover these among other aspects of international business planning include Salera 1969, Steiner and Cannon 1966, and Zenoff and Zwick 1969.

Bibliography

This Bibliography is in no sense comprehensive. Books and articles listed below are either quoted in the text or notes, or have been selected by one of the authors on the grounds that they make an important contribution to the subject.

ABEGGLEN, JAMES C. (1958) *The Japanese Factory*, Free Press of Glencoe.

Accounting Research and Terminology Bulletins Final Edition (1961) New York, American Institute of Certified Public Accountants.

Accounting Treatment of Major Changes in the Sterling Parity of Overseas Currencies (1968) Institute of Chartered Accountants in England and Wales.

Accounting Trends and Techniques (1968) 21st edition. New York, American Institute of Certified Public Accountants.

ÁDÁM, GYÖRGY (1970) *Amerika Europában Vállalatbirodalmak a Világgazdaságban*, Budapest, Közgazdasági és Jogi Könyvkiadó.

AHARONI, Y. (1966) *The Foreign Investment Decision Process*, Harvard Business School.

ANSOFF, H. I. (1965) *Corporate Strategy*, McGraw-Hill.

ANSOFF, H. I. (1969) *Business Strategy: Selected Readings*, Penguin.

Applying Financial Controls in Foreign Operations (1957) New York, International Management Association.

BAKER, R. L. (1962) *Business Leadership in a Changing World*, McGraw-Hill.

BARBER, P. J. (1966) 'Les entreprises internationales', *Analyse et Prévision*, **2**, no. 3, Paris, SÉDÉIS.

BARKIN, SOLOMON (1968) *International Labour*, Harper & Row.

BARLOW, E. R. (1953) *Management of Foreign Manufacturing Subsidiaries*, Harvard University Press.

BARZINI, LUIGI (1964) *The Italians*, New York, Athenaeum.

BERHMAN, J. N. (1970) *National Interests and the Multinational Enterprise*, Prentice-Hall.

BENDIX, R. and LIPSET P. M. (1966) *Class, Status and Power*, New York, Free Press.

BERG, K. B. and others (1969) *Readings in International Accounting*, Houghton Mifflin.

BERLE, A. A. (1960) *Power Without Property*, Sidgwick & Jackson.

BLAU, P. M. (1955) *The Dynamics of Bureaucracy*, University of Chicago Press.

BLAU, P. M. and SCOTT, W. P. *Formal Organisations*, Routledge 1963.

BLOUGH, ROY M. (1966) *International Business in its Environment*, McGraw-Hill.

BODDEWYN, J., ed. (1970) *Comparative Management*, New York University Press.

BRANNEN, T. R. and HODGSON, F. X. (1965) *Overseas Management*, McGraw-Hill.

BREEK, P. C. (1967) 'Accounting problems peculiar to international enterprises', *The New Horizons of Accounting*, Paris, Proceedings of the Ninth International Congress of Accountants.

BREWSTER, KINGMAN (1958) *Anti-Trust and American Business Abroad*, McGraw-Hill.

BROOKE, M. Z. (1969) 'The multinational company: change factors in a complex organisation', *Acts of the Institut International de Sociologie*, Rome.

BROOKE, M. Z. and REMMERS H. L. (1970) *The Strategy of Multinational Enterprise: Organisation and Finance*, Longman.

CARLSON, SUNE (1969) *International Financial Decisions*, Scandinavian University Books.

CHANDLER, A. D. (1962) *Strategy and Structure*, Massachusetts Institute of Technology.

CHORAFAS, D. N. (1967) *Developing the International Executive*, New York, American Management Association.

CHORAFAS, D. N. (1969) *The Communication Barrier in International Management*, American Management Association.

CLEE, G. H. (1966) 'Guidelines for global enterprise', *Columbia Journal of World Business*, Winter no.

CLEE, G. H. and DI SCIPIO, A. (1959) 'Creating a world enterprise', *Harvard Business Review*. **37,** no. 6.

CLEE, G. H. and SACHTJEN, W. M. (1964) 'Organising a worldwide business', *Harvard Business Review*. **42,** no. 6, 55–67.

Commission des Opérations de Bourse (1969) Le Rapport Annuel, Paris.

Consolidation des Bilans et des Comptes (1968) Conseil National de la Comptabilité, Paris, Imprimerie nationale.

Consolidation of Company Accounts in Europe (1970) Paper presented to the European Federation of Financial Analysts' Societies, 6th Congress, Montreux, October.

CORDELL, ARTHUR J. (1971) *Sociétés multinationales Investissement direct de l'étranger et politique des Sciences du Canada*, Ottawa, Science Council of Canada.

CORRE, J. (1969) *La Consolidation des Bilans* Paris, Dunod.

CROZIER, M. (1964) *The Bureaucratic Phenomenon*, Tavistock.

CYERT, R. M. and MARCH, J. G. (1963) *A Behavioural Theory of the Firm*, Prentice-Hall.

DALTON, MELVILLE (1959) *Men Who Manage*, Wiley.

DE BETTIGNIES, H. C. (1969) 'L'observation de la société Américaine incite-t-elle à l'inquiétude?' *Le Figaro*, 26 April 1969, pp. 13–14.

DICKIE, R. B. (1970) *Foreign Investment: France, a case study*, New York, Dobbs Ferry, Oceana Publications.

DONNER, F. G. (1967) *The World-Wide Industrial Enterprise*, McGraw-Hill.

DRUCKER, P. F. (1969) *The Age of Discontinuity*, Heinemann.

DRUCKER, P. F. (1971) 'What we can learn from Japanese management', *Harvard Business Review*, March–April, Vol. 49. pp. 110–22.

DUNNING, JOHN H., ed. (1971) *The Multinational Enterprise*, Allen & Unwin.

FALCON, W. D. (1965) *Financing Foreign Operations*, New York, American Management Association.

FARMER, R. N. and RICHMAN B. M. (1966) *International Business: an operational theory*, Homewood, Ill, Irwin.

FAYERWEATHER, J. (1960) *Management of International Operations: texts and cases*, McGraw-Hill.

FAYERWEATHER, J. (1962) *Facts and Fallacies of International Business*, Holt, Rinehart & Winston.

FAYERWEATHER, J. (1969) *International Business Management*, McGraw-Hill.

FENN, D. H. (1957) *Management Guide to Overseas Operations*, McGraw-Hill.

FOURAKER, L. E. and STOPFORD, J. M. (1968) 'Organisational structure and the multinational strategy', *Administrative Science Quarterly*, June.

FRANKO, L. G. (1969) 'Strategy choice and multinational corporate tolerance for joint ventures with foreign partners', unpublished doctoral dissertation, Harvard Business School 1969.

FRANKO, L. G. (1971a) *Joint Venture Survival in Multinational Corporations*, Praeger.

FRANKO, L. G. (1971b) 'Joint venture divorce in the multinational company', *Columbia Journal of World Business*, May–June 1971.

FRIEDMANN, W. G. and KALMANOFF, G., eds (1961) *Joint International Business Ventures*, Columbia University Press.

FURLONG, W. L. (1966) 'Minimising foreign exchange losses', *Accounting Review* (Chicago), **41**, no. 2, April.

GLOVER, J. D. (1954) *The Attack on Big Business*, Harvard Business School.

GOODE, W. J. (1966) 'Family and mobility', in R. Bendix and S. M. Lipset, *Class, Status and Power*, 2nd edn, New York. Free Press, pp. 582–601.

GORDON, R. A. (1966), *Business Leadership in the Large Corporation*, new edn, University of California Press.

GOUDEKET, A. (1960) 'An application of replacement value theory', *Journal of Accountancy*, July (reprinted in Berg 1969 and Breek 1967)

GOULDNER, A. (1954) *Patterns of Industrial Bureaucracy*, New York, Free Press.

GRANICK, D. (1962) *The European Executive*, Doubleday.

GREENE, J. and DUERR, M. G. (1970) *Intercompany Transactions in the Multinational Firm*, New York, N.I.C.B.

Growth and Spread of Multinational Companies (1969) London, Economist Intelligence Unit, October.

HAAS, H. VAN DER (1967) *The Enterprise in Transition* London, Tavistock.

HAIRE, MASON, GHISELLI, E. E. and PORTER, L. W. (1966) *Managerial Thinking: An International Study*, Wiley.

HALL, D. J., DE BETTIGNIES, H. C. and AMADO-FISCHGRUND, G. (1969) 'The European business elite', *European Business*, October, no. 23.

HALL, E. T. (1959) *The Silent Language*, Doubleday.

HALL, E. T. (1960) 'The Silent Language in Overseas Business', *Harvard Business Review*, **38**, no. 3, 87–96.

HARBISON, F. H. and MYERS, C. A. (1959) *Management in the Industrial World: An International Analysis*, McGraw-Hill.

HELLER, F. (1971) *Managerial Decision-Making*, Tavistock.

HELLER, R. (1968) 'The march of the multinationals', *Management Today*, April.

HEPWORTH, S. E. (1956) *Reporting Foreign Operations*, University of Michigan Press.

HODGSON, R. W. and UYTERHOEVEN, H. E. R. (1962) 'Analysing foreign opportunities', *Harvard Business Review*, **40**, no. 2, 60–79.

HOVELL, P. J. (1969) 'International operations and corporate planning', *Journal of Management Studies*, **6**, October.

HUFBAUER, G. C. and ADLER, F. M. (1968) *Overseas Manufacturing Investments and the Balance of Payments*, US Treasury Department.

International Operation Conference Papers (1966) London, British Institute of Management.

INSTITUTE OF CHARTERED ACCOUNTANTS in England and Wales, General Educational Trust (1971) *Survey of Public Accounts 1969–1970*.

JOHNSTONE, ALLEN (1965) *United States Direct Investment in France: an Investigation of the French Charges*, Massachusetts Institute of Technology.

JUDGE, A. J. N. (1969) 'Multinational business enterprises', *International Associations*, no. 1, pp. 3–11.

KAHN, H. and WIENER, A. J. (1967) *The Year 2000*, Macmillan.

KNOPPERS, A. (1967) *The Role of Science and Technology in Atlantic Economic Relationships*, New York, International Publications Service.

KOLDE, E. J. (1968) *International Business Enterprise*, Prentice-Hall.

LEARNED, E. P. and others (1963) *European Problems in General Management*, Irwin.

LEDERER, W. J. and BURDICK, E. S. (1958) *The Ugly American*, New York, Norton.

LEE, J. A. (1966) 'Cultural analysis in overseas operations', *Harvard Business Review*, **44**, no. 2, 22–30.

LEVINSON, CHARLES (1971) *Capital, Inflation and the Multinationals*, Allen & Unwin.

LIETAER, B. A. (1970) 'Managing risks in foreign exchange', *Harvard Business Review*, **48** (March–April), 127–38.

LOMBARD, A. J. JR (1969) 'How European companies organise their international operations', *European Business* **22**, (July), 37.

LOVELL, E. B. (1961) *Organizing Foreign-Base Corporations*, New York, National Industrial Conference Board.

LOVELL, E. B. (1963) *Managing Foreign-Base Corporations*, New York, National Industrial Conference Board.

LOVELL, E. B. (1966) *The Changing Role of the International Executive*, New York, National Industrial Conference Board.

MCCREARY, E. A. (1964) 'Those American managers don't impress Europe', *Fortune*, December.

MAGE, M. L. (1966) 'The President and International Operations', *Harvard Business Review*, 44, no. 6, 72–84.

MCMILLAN, JAMES and HARRIS, BERNARD (1968) *The American Take-Over of Britain*, Frewin.

MACRAE, N. (1972) 'The multinationals', *The Economist* 29 January.

Management Accounting Problems in Foreign Operations (1960) New York, National Association of Accountants.

MARTYN, HOWE (1964) *International Business: principles and problems*, New York, Free Press.

MARTYN, HOWE (1967) 'Effects of multinational business affiliation on local management', *Michigan Business Review*, March.

MEISTER, I. W. (1970) *Managing the International Financial Function*, New York, National Industrial Conference Board.

MERTON, R. K. and others, ed. (1965) *Sociology Today*, Harper.

MILLER, E. J. and RICE, A. K. (1967) *Systems of Organisation*, London, Tavistock.

MILLER, S. S. (1963) 'Management by Omikoshi', *Management International*, 3, no. 1, 59–69.

MORELLO, GABRIELE (1969) 'Dall'esportazione all'Azienda Multinazionale: il ruolo del Mercato estero nella dinamica dell'Impresa', *Quaderni dell' Associazione Italiano per gli Studi di Mercato* n.16, Roma.

NEWMAN, WILLIAM H. (1970) 'Is management exportable?' *Columbia Journal of World Business*, (Jan.–Feb.), 5, 7–18.

NOWOTNY, OTTO H. (1964) 'American versus European management philosophy', *Harvard Business Review*, (March–April) Vol. 42.

PARKER, R. H. and HARCOURT, G. C. (1969) *Readings in the Concept and Measurement of Income*, Cambridge University Press.

PARKS, F. NEWTON (1966) 'Group management, European style', *Business Horizons*, 9, no. 3, 83.

PERLMUTTER, H. V. (1965) 'L'entreprise internationale—trois conceptions', *Revue Economique et Sociale* (Lausanne), May, no. 2.

PERLMUTTER, H. V. (1969) 'The tortuous evolution of the multinational corporation', *Columbia Journal of World Business*, 4, (Jan–Feb.), 9–18.

POLK, J., MEISTER, I. W. and VEIT, L. A. (1966) *Production Abroad and the Balance of Payments*, New York, National Industrial Conference Board.

PRINS, D. J. (1968) 'International business: a challenge to management and to education', *Management International* (Wiesbaden) 8, no. 1, 123–7.

PYM, DENIS (1968) *Industrial Society: Social Sciences in Management*, Penguin.

REDDAWAY, W. B. (1968) *Effects of U.K. Direct Investments Overseas*, Final Report, Cambridge University Press 1968.

ROBINSON, H. J. (1961) *The Motivation and Flow of Private Foreign Investment*, Stanford Research Institute.

ROBINSON, R. D. (1964) *International Business Policy*, Holt, Rinehart & Winston.

ROBINSON, R. D. (1967) *International Management*, Holt, Rinehart & Winston.

ROIG, BARTO (1970) *La Empressa Multinacional*, Ediciones Universidad de Navarra.

RUTENBERG, D. P. (1969) 'Planning for a multinational synergy', *Long Range Planning*, 2, no. 2.

RUTENBERG, DAVID P. (1970b) 'Maneuvering liquid assets in a multinational company: formulation and deterministic solution procedures', *Management Science*, 15, no. 10, (June), B-671–83.

RUTENBERG, DAVID P. (1970a) 'Organisational archetypes of a multinational company', *Management Science*, 16, no. 6, February.

SALERA, VIRGIL (1969) *Multinational Business*, Houghton Mifflin.

SAMPSON, A. (1968) *The New Europeans*, Hodder & Stoughton.

SAMUELS, J. M. (1972) *Readings on Mergers and Takeovers*, Elek Books.

SCOTT, B. R. (1968) 'Stages of corporate development: a descriptive model', Unpublished thesis, Harvard Business School.

Selected Aspects of International Business Operations: Problems and Opportunities (1966) Summary Report I.U.C. 13th Annual Conference, Rotterdam, 15–17 September.

SERVAN-SCHREIBER, J. J. (1967) and (1969) *Le Défi américain*, Paris, Editions Denöel; English edition, Penguin 1969 (the references in the text are to this edition).

SKINNER, C. W. (1968) *American Industry in Developing Economies*, Wiley.

SLOAN, A. P. (1964) *My Years with General Motors*, Doubleday.

SMITH, G. A., JR (1958) *Managing Geographically Decentralized Companies*, Harvard Business School.

SMITH, R. A. (1964) *Corporation in Crisis*, Anchor Books.

STEINER, C. A. and CANNON, W. M. (1966) *Multinational Corporate Planning*, New York, Macmillan.

STOBAUGH, R. B., JR (1969) 'How to analyse foreign investment climates', *Harvard Business Review*, 47, (Sept.–Oct.), no. 5.

STONEHILL A. and NATHANSON, L. (1968) 'Capital budgeting and the multinational corporation', *California Management Review*, Summer no.

STOPFORD, J. M. (1968) 'Growth and organizational change in the multinational firm', unpublished doctoral dissertation, Harvard Business School.

STOPFORD, J. M. and WELLS, L. T., JR (1972) *Managing the Multinational Enterprise*, Basic Books.

SUMMERS, CLYDE W. (1965) 'Labour Relations in the Common Market— differences between European and US policies, practices and attitudes in

184   *Bibliography*

industrial relations and American management's failure to recognize it', *Harvard Business Review*, **43**, no. 2.

SUTTON, F. X. (1956) *The American Business Creed*, Harvard University Press.

TANNENBAUM, A. S. (1968) *Control in Organisations*, McGraw-Hill.

TANNENBAUM, F. (1968) 'The survival of the fittest',*Columbia Journal of World Business*, **3**, no. 2, March–April.

'Towards the European company' (1968) *The Economist*, **227** (15th June), 60–1.

'The trade union response to multinational enterprise' (1967) *Monthly Labor Review*, 90–III–IV (December).

'The treatment in company accounts of changes in the exchange rates of international currencies' (1970) *Accountants' Magazine*, September, pp. 415–23.

TURNER, LOUIS (1968) *Politics and the Multinational Company*, London, Fabian Research Pamphlet.

TZIRULNITSKY, D. (1969) 'Quantitative and qualitative measurement of the elements affecting the organisational structure of the MATSLAH military unit' (in Hebrew), unpublished M.B.A. Dissertation, Graduate School of Business Administration Tel Aviv University.

VANSINA, L. S. (1968) 'Cultural issues within multinational organisations', Paper presented to the International Congress of Psychology, Amsterdam.

VAUPEL, JAMES W. and CURHAN, JOAN P. (1969) *The Making of Multinational Enterprise*, Boston: Harvard Business School.

VERNON, R. (1967) 'Multinational Enterprise and National Sovereignty', *Harvard Business Review*, **45**, no 2.

VERNON, R. (1968a) *Manager in the International Economy*, Prentice-Hall.

VERNON, R. (1968b) 'Economic sovereignty at bay', *Foreign Affairs*, July.

VERNON, R. (1971) *Sovereignty at Bay*, New York, Basic Books.

WATKINS, M. H. and others (1968) *Foreign Ownership and the Structure of Canadian Industry*, Ottawa, Queen's Printer.

WEBBER, R. A. (1969) *Culture and Management*, Homewood, Ill, Irwin-Dorsey.

WEINSHALL, T. D. (1960) 'Effects of management changes on organisation relationships and attitudes', unpublished Ph.D. thesis, Harvard.

WEINSHALL, T. D. (1966) 'The communicogram', in J. R. Lawrence ed., *Operational Research and the Social Sciences*, London, Tavistock.

WEINSHALL, T. D. (1968a) 'Organisational behaviour in Israel and the West', unpublished MS, Tel Aviv.

WEINSHALL, T. D. (1968b) 'The reciprocal perception of communication', in R. Dubin, *Human Relations in Administration*.

WEINSHALL, T. D. (1970) 'Some Uses of Communications Pattern Research', in *La Empresa Multinacional*, edited by Barto Rio-Amat, Colection IESE, Serie AC-3, Ediciones Universidad de Navarra pp. 301–26.

WEINSHALL, T. D. (1971) Beal and Silver, M. 'Patterns of Communication and Organisation Structure in a Management Training College', a research report, Ashbridge Management College.

WEINSHALL, T. D. (1971) 'Multinational business education—research methodology and attitudes study', *Management International Review*, 11, no. 2–3.

WEINSHALL, T. D. (1972) 'Changing the effects of culture on problemsolving in management education', *Management International Review*, 13, no. 4–5.

WEINSHALL, T. D. and DE BETTIGNIES, H. C. (1971) 'Multinational business education—the social structure study', *Management International Review*, 11, no. 4–5.

WILKINS, M. and HILL, F. E. (1964) *American Business Abroad: Ford on six continents*, Detroit, Wayne State University.

WILLIAMS, C. R. (1967) 'Regional management overseas', *Harvard Business Review*, 45, no. 1, 87.

WILLIAMS, J. R. L. (1968) 'L'entreprise multinationale dans le cadre de l'économie nationale', *Humanisme et Entreprise* (Paris), no. 52.

YOSHINO, M. Y. (1968) *Japan's Managerial System: Tradition and innovation*, Massachusetts Institute of Technology Press.

ZENOFF, D. B. and ZWICK, J. (1969) *International Financial Management*, Prentice-Hall.

Index